W.H. Strobridge

# Catalogue of the Stenz collection of modern coins, medals, and tokens

W.H. Strobridge

**Catalogue of the Stenz collection of modern coins, medals, and tokens**

ISBN/EAN: 9783741139659

Manufactured in Europe, USA, Canada, Australia, Japa

Cover: Foto ©ninafisch / pixelio.de

Manufactured and distributed by brebook publishing software (www.brebook.com)

W.H. Strobridge

# Catalogue of the Stenz collection of modern coins, medals, and tokens

# CATALOGUE

OF THE

## STENZ COLLECTION

OF

**Modern Coins, Medals, and Tokens,**

THE MOST EXTENSIVE EVER PUBLISHED IN AMERICA.

*The Whole to be Sold by Auction*

AT THE

## ROOMS OF GEO. A. LEAVITT & CO.,

Clinton Hall, Astor Place, New York,

ON

## Monday, the 17th of May,

*and following days, commencing each day at 2 o'clock P.M.*

**THE MESSRS. LEAVITT, AUCTIONEERS.**

CATALOGUE BY WILLIAM H. STROBRIDGE.

MAY, 1875.

## Names of Purchasers.    F K

| | | | |
|---|---|---|---|
| Anderson | Darley | Mathews | G R. |
| Anthon | Elliott | Maxwell | Rice |
| Appleton | Ely | Miller | Ross |
| Balmanno | Emory | Mitchell | Kissam |
| Baker | Enro | Moore | Sampson |
| Banks | Europe | ~~Mitchel~~ | Slack |
| Barnes | Evandsh | Mott | Snow |
| Baron | Farrest | Murray | Spear |
| Barnck | Fisher | Nelson | |
| Birch | Fontain | Nichols | Stables |
| Brewer | Fireward | North | Steig |
| Brown | Gilbert | Oliver | Sheward |
| Brown | Gorton | Oram | Slusser |
| | Graham | Oegen | Painter |
| Bucks | Haines | Paine | Thurston |
| Campbell | Hail | Pamela | Trumbull |
| Cash | Ias Henry | Parish | Wall |
| Chadiourne | Holland | Payer | Walas |
| Chud | Henway | Pearson | Waiter |
| Chuders | Jackson | Phipps | Waisn |
| | Jones | Picot | Ward |

# INTRODUCTION.

The extensive and varied collection of coins and medals introduced to the notice of the American public in the following pages, has been well known in Europe for many years, a large part of it having been formed by Dr. F. Vieweg, of Berlin, Prussia.

Its foundation was laid from the collections of Baron Welzl von Wellenheim, of Vienna; Prince of Pless, Berlin; Baron of Schultheiss Rechberg; and Mr. K. Vander Chijs, Amsterdam.

But although thus distinguished in its origin, this rare cabinet is under great obligations to its present owner, Mr. George Stenz, of Hanover, Germany, for large and costly additions to the original stock. This gentleman's plan comprehended the coins of all modern nations, beginning with their earliest history. A glance at the various divisions of the catalogue will show how fully his scheme was carried out, but it will appear to have been more nearly completed in the German than in any other department.

The number, quality, and rank of the coins of German cities, principalities, and minor governments, many of them long since, and others but recently sequestrated, will strike the American numismatist as very large. No opportunity has before occurred to purchase coins of the same importance at an American sale, and it may be safely predicted that in future years, coins from this cabinet will be pointed out with pride as the ornaments of many a famous collection.

Yet, if we admit the superiority of this particular class, we do not forget the long list of English coins, both before and after the conquest, with the almost unique set of the XX shilling pieces of the first Charles—those of French kings, barons, and dignitaries of the Church, extending back to the time of Charlemagne—the rare collection brought together from the various Italian States, a long line of Doges and Popes recalling the extinct glories of Venice, and we had almost said, Rome, but Rome is the *Eternal* city—or the array of single, double, and triple crowns that adorn the ranks of almost every prince of Northern Europe for the last 400 years.

Never before has a representative collection of such coins as we have been enumerating, of anything like the magnitude of this, been offered for sale in this country, and we may further add that the Western continent has a larger representation than would be expected in such a cabinet; every South American State presenting a pretty full series, with large numbers from the Mexican and Central American Republics. An occasional gem from our own mint comes back to us in surprising preservation, and, although few in numbers, these will undoubtedly attract a degree of attention quite out of proportion to their numismatic importance.

It is not our purpose here, neither is it necessary, to go at any length into an analysis of the catalogue, but we may be pardoned for further referring, as among the many attractions which it offers, to a number of CLUSTERS of favorite coins, as well as to many others of kindred subject and character that might with advantage have been gathered together in groups. Of the former, a good example is the splendid series of the Teutonic Knights; as instances of the latter may be selected, those that relate to Luther and the Protestant Reformation, coins and tokens issued by monastic institutions and orders, and such as bear heads of great military leaders, like Charles V. of Germany, Henry IV. of France, and Gustavus Adolphus of Sweden: Fine examples of all these will be found under their appropriate heads, or dispersed throughout the catalogue wherever their destinies cast their lot.

The arrangement of the catalogue is so simple that an index of the headings only has been thought sufficient. It might have been better to have given more titles, but as the classification was as thorough as it could conveniently be made, and an attention to dates and alphabetical order pretty generally observed, it is hoped no serious difficulty will be found.

While a careful examination of the catalogue is respectfully invited, the author is free to confess that the labor of preparing it has left him in no frame of mind to exult over his performance: He is convinced that a perfect catalogue of German coins can be made only by one " to the manor born." Yet, so far as regards truth of statement and propriety of attribution, he feels it due to himself and the interests of his friend to whom alone the entire collection belongs, to declare that he has not followed blind guides.

WM. H. STROBRIDGE.

NEW YORK, *March* 15, 1875.

# INDEX.

| | |
|---|---|
| BRITISH COINS, | 1 |
|     Saxon Heptarchy, | 1 |
|     Sole Monarchy, | 2 |
|     Earliest Coins of Ireland, | 2 |
|     Coins of Church Dignitaries, | 3 |
|     Anglo-Norman, | 3 |
|     Coins of Scotland to James VI., | 6 |
|     English Coins, | 7 |
|     Gold Coins of England, | 16 |
|     Copper Coins of English Sovereigns, | 16 |
|     English Medals, copper, | 20 |
|     English Silver Medals, | 22 |
| COINS OF FRANCE, | 25 |
|     Kings from Charlemagne, silver, | 25 |
|     Kings of Navarre, silver, | 30 |
|     Baronial and Ecclesiastical, silver, | 31 |
|     French Baronial, copper, | 37 |
|     French Kings, copper, | 37 |
|     Republic and Empire, copper, | 38 |
|     Meraux and Jetons, copper, | 39 |
|     Speil Markes and Tokens, copper, | 39 |
|     Medalets, copper and brass, | 40 |
|     War Medals, | 40 |
|     Bronze Medals, | 41 |
|     Silver Medalets and Jetons, | 42 |
| COINS OF PORTUGAL, | 44 |
| COINS OF SPAIN, | 44 |
| COINS OF SWITZERLAND, | 49 |
| COINS OF ITALY, | 54 |

[*The States alphabetically arranged.*]

| | |
|---|---|
| CARRARA and other Rare Medals, | 62 |
| ANTIQUE COINS | 63 |
|     Family Denarii | 63 |
|     Imperial Denarii | 64 |
|     Greek Silver | 64 |
|     Roman and Greek Copper | 65 |
| MODERN GREECE | 66 |
| SILVER COINS AND MEDALS OF RUSSIA | 66 |
|     Bronze Medals | 69 |
|     Copper Coins | 71 |
| COINS OF POLAND | 72 |
| UNITED STATES COINS | 74 |
|     Gold | 74 |

## Index.

| | |
|---|---|
| Silver Dollars | 75 |
| Half Dollars | 76 |
| Quarter Dollars | 77 |
| Dimes, Half Dimes, and 3-cents | 78 |
| Cents | 79 |
| Half Cents and Colonials | 80 |
| Medals and Tokens | 81 |
| COINS OF MEXICO | 84 |
| CENTRAL AMERICA | 86 |
| SOUTH AMERICA | 87 |

[*The States alphabetically arranged.*]

| | |
|---|---|
| WEST INDIES | 91 |
| AFRICA | 92 |
| PROVINCES UNDER THE BRITISH CROWN | 93 |
| ORIENTAL COINS | 95 |
| DENMARK | 99 |
| SWEDEN | 102 |
| NETHERLANDS | 107 |

[*The Principalities, Duchies, etc., in alphabetical order.*]

| | |
|---|---|
| BAVARIA | 115 |
| ANHALT | 117 |
| BADEN | 118 |
| HESSE | 119 |
| LIPPE | 121 |
| LIPPE—SCHAUMBERG and DETMOLD | 123 |
| MECKLENBERG | 124 |
| OLDENBERG | 125 |
| BRUNSWICK AND LUNEBERG | 126 |
| HANOVER | 133 |
| SAXONY | 135 |
| NASSAU | 141 |
| HOLSTEIN | 142 |
| REUSS | 143 |
| PRUSSIA | 144 |
| SCHWARZBURG | 150 |
| WALDECK | 150 |
| WURTEMBERG | 151 |
| AUSTRIA | 152 |
| AUSTRIA, BOHEMIA, ETC., COPPER | 159 |
| SILVER MEDALS | 161 |
| MISCELLANEOUS GOLD COINS | 166 |
| SILVER COINS of the Duchies, Principalities, and Sequestrated Cities of Germany | 170 |

[*Catalogued in alphabetical order.*]

| | |
|---|---|
| MISCELLANEOUS SILVER COINS | 228 |
| COPPER COINS and TOKENS of the Sequestrated German Cities, etc. | 229 |
| SUNDRIES | 235 |
| NUMISMATIC BOOKS, CATALOGUES, and Paper Money | 236 |
| IRON FIRE-PROOF CABINET | 236 |

# CATALOGUE.

## BRITISH COINS.

1 TIN Coin, copied from the Stater of Philip II. of Macedon; rude head, and more rude biga; in perfect preservation. Very rare. Size 15
2 SKEATTA, rude head; rev. square. Fine.
3 —— Obv. VOT. in crescent; rev. like last. Fine.
4 STYCA. Cross on both sides and ins. Fine.

### *Saxon Heptarchy.*

All are silver pennies to No. 46 inclusive.

5 CUTHRED (King of Kent), A. D. 794, helmeted head to r.; sceptre; rev. cross voided with crescents at the ends. Ex. fine and rare.
6 OFFA? (Mercia), A. D. 757, rude head, short cross. Fine, ex. rare.
7 BURGRED (Mercia), the last King of; obv., head rudely executed within a small circle; the shoulders extending to the edge of the coin. BVRGRED REX; rev. the moneyer's name, etc., in three parallel lines. Splendid, rare.
8 EADMUND (East Angles), A. D. 855, commonly called St. Edmund; obv. his name, with title, Rex. and large A in the centre; rev. the moneyer's name and a short cross. Very fine and rare.

## British Coins.

### Sole Monarchy.

9 Æthebred, A. D. 866, EDELRED REX. AN., head crowned; rev. long double cross with square in centre, at the corners three pellets. Fine and ex. rare.

10 Eadred, A. D. 953, EDRED R. Extremely rude head to r. sceptre; rev. voided cross terminating in crescents. Penny of large size. Fine and extra rare.

11 Edward the Elder, (son of Alfred the Great), A. D. 901. Full face; rev. short cross and anulet. Extremely fine and rare.

12 Aethelred (son of Elfrida), A. D. 978. EDELRED · REX.. ANGLO. Bust to l.; rev. short cross. Splendid, rare.

13 —— Another—head with sceptre; rev. long voided cross; letters in angles. Fine, rare.

14 Canute. A. D. 1017. Crowned head, l. CNVT REX. ANG; rev. long cross. In splendid preservation. Scarce.

15 Hardi Canute, or Harthcnut. A. D. 1040. Head with sceptre; rev. voided cross. Equally as fine as last, very rare.

16 Edward the Confessor. A. D. 1042; obv. full length figure; rev. in the angles of a cross, four martlets. Very fine, large size, rare.

17 —— Head and sceptre (profile); rev. cross.

18 —— Standing saint; rev. cross in a lozenge. Fine, very rare.

### Earliest Coins of Ireland.

19 Imars or Ifars (King of Limerick); obv. head dotted, full face; rev. long cross, hand and other crosses in angles. Very fine and extremely rare.

20 Ifars II. (King of Dublin), A. D. 993. Similar to the last, but head in profile, with rays. Very fine and rare.

21 Sithric. Similar to last. Very fine and rare.

22 Anlaf. A. D. 1059. Head and script. Very fine and rare.

## Anglo-Norman.

23 ASKEL. A. D. 1158. Head and script, the head nothing but rays; very rude and remarkable. See Humphrey's Coinage of the Br. Emp., pl. 18, No. 6.

24 DONALD. Head with rays; large fine penny, cracked. *Very rare.*

### Church Dignitaries.

25 WIGMUND (Archbishop of York). Cross with crosslet on one side; on the other short cross and script. Splendid, very rare.

26 CUNHET (York). Similar. Equally fine.

27 CITY OF YORK, CIVITA EBRAICI. Extremely fine and rare.

### Anglo-Norman.

28 WILLIAM I. (Conqueror). A. D. 1066. Head, full face, PAXS. Fine, scarce.

29 HENRY II. A. D. 1154. Full face; rev. cross. Fine.

30 RICHARD I., (Cœur de Lion). A. D. 1189. Denier, PIC-TAVIE-NSIS, (Poiteau). Fine, rare.

31 JOHN. A. D. 1199. Obv. King's head in a tringle, JO-HANNES REX.; rev. crescent in a triangle. Good, rare.

The triangle on this coin, and on the Irish Coins of Henry III. and Edward I., is supposed to be symbolic of the Trinity.

32 HENRY III. A. D. 1216. Head; rev. short cross. Fine.

33 —— Head; rev. long cross. Fine.

34 —— do. do. do.

35 —— do. do. do.

36 —— do. do. do.

37 EDWARD I. A. D. Obv. head, full face, crowned, ED-WRANGLDN; rev. cross extending through the legend. London. *Extremely* fine, scarce.

38 —— Another slight variety. Scarce.

39 —— do. do. do.

40 —— EDWRE* ANGLDNSHVB. Scarce.

41 —— Head in a triangle, (for Ireland). Very fine and rare.

## British Coins.

42 EDWARD II. A. D. 1307. For Canterbury; rev. CIVITAS CANTOR. Ex. fine.
43 —— do. Very fine.
44 —— do do.
45 —— Canterbury and London Mints. 3 pieces
46 —— EDWARD III. A. D. 1327. London. Fine.
   After this the denomination will be given. See note before No. 5.
47 —— Full face London Groat. Fair, rare.
48 EDWARD THE BLACK PRINCE, son of Edward III., for the Principality of Aquitaine. Obv. half-length figure of the Prince to r.; rev. cross and script in two circles. Half groat. Very fine and rare.
49 —— Another Half-groat, struck at Bordeaux. Fair, very rare.
50 HENRY IV., A.D. 1399, and Henry V., A.D. 1413. Crowned head, full face. HENRIC, DGRA REX, etc. "Villa Calisie." Very fine and rare.
51 —— Light Groat. Very fine, rare.
52 —— Half-groats. Fair (Calais). 3 pieces
53 HENRY VI. A.D. 1422. Grand-blanc (Groat), struck in France. Obv. two shields, bearing the arms of France and England, HERICVS; rev. lily and lion separated by a cross, the King's name as before; around the edge, the motto of France. Very fine and rare.
   No *English* silver coin bore the royal arms until a hundred years after the date of this "grand-blanc."
54 HENRY VII. A.D. 1485. Fine full face London Groat. Very scarce.
55 —— Groat, with the head in profile to r., with the numerals "VII." Fair.
56 HENRY VIII. A.D. 1509. Light Groat. Fine.
57 —— Half-groat. Fine.
58 —— Penny, with A. W. (Arch. Wolsey) on rev. Rare.
59 —— For Ireland. Harp. H. crowned and J. crowned to r. and l. Fine Groat.

*Anglo-Norman.* 5

60 EDWARD VI. A.D. 1547. Shilling. Obv. crowned bust facing to l., rose to r., XII; rev. arms on a shield, quartered. No date. Fine, scarce.
This is the first English coin that has its value on it, and the last with a full face.

61 —— Crown. Obv. the King on horseback, with a sword in his hand; his horse caparisoned, the date under him 1551; rev. arms quartered by a cross. This is a fine example of the first English crown. Rare.

62 MARY. 1553. Groat. Head to l. Poor, rare.

63 —— Half Shilling, 1554, after her marriage, with heads of Philip and Mary looking at each other; rev. oval shield of arms crowned, the denomination VI between crown and shield; spots worn, occasioned by bending; generally sharp and fine. *Very rare.*

64 —— Groat, coined for Ireland, and base. Obv. heads of Philip and Mary, 1557; rev. harp. Very good, rare.

65 —— Another. Not as good.

66 ELIZABETH. 1558. Penny. Fine, but pierced.

67 —— Half-groat (two dots). Fine, rare.

68 —— Threepence (rose). Fine, rare.

69 —— Sixpence    do.    do.

70 —— Shilling. Fine.

71 —— Crown. *Very fine and rare.*
Here the sceptre reappears for the first time since Henry III.

72 —— Milled Sixpence, without inner circle; the edges grained (1566). M. M. star. Fine.

73 —— Another. 1572 (cross fleurie). Fine.

74 —— Hammered and milled Sixpences. Good.
                                                                              2 pieces

75 —— Hammered alone. Different M. M. Good.
                                                                              3 pieces

76 —— Similar to last. Different M. M.    3 pieces

There seems to be good reason for taking up the coins of Scotland at this point, as the next King of England was the son of Mary Stuart. Therefore, we shall bring that series down to the present time, and afterwards continue the coins of England, Ireland, and Scotland under one head.

## Coins of Scotland to James VI.

77 ALEXANDER II. 1214. Penny. Crowned head and sceptre to l.; rev. cross and stars of 6 points. Fine.

78 JOHN BALIOL. A good Penny. *Extremely rare.*

79 ALEXANDER III. 1249. Penny. Like those of Alexander II. Fine.

80 —— Others. Equally fine. 2 pieces

81 —— Smaller. Rude execution. 2 pieces

82 DAVID II. 1329. Groat. Head and sceptre, l.; rev. inscription in two circles, divided by a cross; in the innermost VILL–AED–INBV–RGH.; stars with 5 points. Ex. fine and rare.

83 ROBERT II. 1371. Groat. Quite similar in type to last. Also Edinburgh. Fine, rare.

84 JAMES III. 1461. Groat. Full face. Rev. inscription in two circles; in the angles of the cross, 3 pellets and five-pointed star. Very fine and rare.

85 JAMES V. 1514. Groat. Head crowned to r.; rev. arm on a shield; cross (so placed for the first time). A fine groat, and rare.

86 MARY. 1542. Billon coin. Obv. thistle crowned, M–R at the sides; rev. St. Andrew's cross, with a crown in the centre. Fine.

87 —— Testoon. 1558. Arms crowned; rev. large cross, with 4 small do. in the corner; "Maria Dei G. Scotor. Regina." Very fine, rare.

88 —— Silver Royal, Mary and Henry Darnley. 1565. Obv. arms crowned; on each side of shield a thistle; rev. a tree, on the tree a label, with "Dat gloria vires." Very fine full royal or crown, counterstamped with a thistle. Fine and rare.

89 —— Same. Without countermark. Also fine and rare, but not equal to last.

90 JAMES VI. 1587. XXX Shilling piece of 1569, issued by authority of the Lord Regent. Obv. arms of Scotland crowned, JACOBVS 6. DEI. GRATIA. REX.

SCOTORVM +; rev. a crown on the point of a sword.·.· PRO-ME. SI-MEREORIN. ME.·.· Full royal, countermarked with a thistle. Very fine and rare.

91 JAMES VI. Royal of XXX Shillings, 1570, without countermarks. Equally fine and rare.

92 —— Balance Mark, 1591. Obv. arms crowned; rev. a sword and scales, HIS DIFFERT REGE TYRANNVS. Fine and very rare.

> This coin is as large as the English shilling of the same period, and of the same quality.

93 —— Thistle Mark, so named from the thistle on reverse. Obv. like last. Fine, rare.

94 —— Mark, 1598. Obv. his bust to the waist; rev. like last. Ex. fine and rare.

95 —— Quarter Thistle Mark. Only fair.

96 —— Penny. Obv. thistle; rev. rose. Fine.

97 —— Half-penny. Rare. Fine.

98 —— Billon coin. St. Andrew's cross. Fine.

## English Coins.

*(Continued from No. 66.)*

After the coins of James I. of England and VIth of Scotland the Anglo-Scottish coins will be included in each reign.

99 JAMES I. 1602. Penny. Ex. fine.

100 —— Sixpence, 1603. Good.

101 —— Sixpence, 1607. Good.

102 —— Shilling, without date. Fine, scarce.

103 —— Shilling and Sixpence. Fair. 2 pieces

104 —— Crown. Obv. the King on horseback, carrying in in his hand a sword; rev. arms on a garnished shield, with a motto, used for the first time, allusive to the union of the two crowns, " Que Deus Conjunxit memo separat." Extremely fine. Nearly uncirculated. Very rare.

105 —— Irish Shilling. Rev. harp. Fair.

106 —— Another Irish Shilling.

## British Coins.

107 CHARLES I. 1625. Penny. M. M., rose. Ex. fine.
108 —— Pennies. Two varieties. 2 pieces
109 —— Penny. Very fine.
110 —— Twopence. Good.
111 —— Groat. Very fine.
112 —— Sixpence. Fair.
113 —— Shilling. M. M., fleur-de-lis (coined before 1626). Fine and very rare.
114 —— Shilling. Different type. Very good, rare.
115 —— 1628. Arms on a shield within the garter; rev. sceptre and trident crossed "Regit. VNUS VIROQVE." Of excellent workmanship, and in fine preservation. Pattern shilling (by Briot.) Rare.
116 —— Half-crown. York mint. *M. M. lion passant gardant*, EBOR under the horse. Very rare, but considerably rubbed.
117 —— Crown. Coined at the Tower. The King on horseback, with a raised sword in his hand, Welch plume behind. The silver stained or tarnished, but uncommonly well preserved. Really *fine*, *rare*.
118 —— Pound piece. 1642. A small figure of the King on horseback, very little ground under the horse, the plume higher in the area than the King's head; rev. in two straight lines RELIG. PROT. LEG. ANG. LIBER. PAR; date below; usual motto around, XX and three Welch plumes above the legend. Very fine.
119 —— Pound piece of 1642; obv. the King on a larger and finer horse, his dress and the caparisons more rich, the plume on a line with his sash; heaps of armor beneath the horse; rev. nearly same as last. Still finer than before.
120 —— Pound piece of 1643. In all but date like one last described; it also differs slightly in the division of the legend. Fully equal to last.
121 —— Pound piece of 1644. Obv. similar to last; rev. the legend in three curving lines on a sheet; below, date and OX. Fine and rare to excess.

It is hardly necessary to refer to the rarity of these XX. shilling pieces, but that the four varieties, as described and engraved by

Snelling, should be found in the same collection is certainly remarkable. The old German labels or tickets, by one hand, show that the set has been together a long time.

122 CHARLES I. Scotch XL. d. piece. Obv. crowned bust; rev. crowned thistle. Very good, rare.

123 —— Duplicate. Not as good.

124 —— Obsidional Crown; struck in Ireland under a commission dated at Oxford, May 25, 1643; obv. C. R. (for Carolus Rex), a crown above the letters; rev. a large V, filling the area of the coin. Fine example, but not strictly a fine impression. Rare.

125 —— Duplicate. Not as fine.

126 —— St. Patrick's Half-penny; struck at the same time as the crowns above described (1643), also a piece of necessity; obv. a king kneeling, playing on a harp; a crown of brass above; FLOREAT REX.; rev. St. Patrick with crozier and trefoil, a group of figures to l., and arms of the City of Dublin to r., with the legend ECCE GREX. Very fine and rare. Copper.

127 —— Farthing of the same issue; obv. like half-penny; rev. St. Patrick with a cross staff. A church behind him.

[Simon says these Irish coins were struck by the Rebels during Charles' troubles.]

128 COMMONWEALTH. 1648. Half-penny. On one side Cross of St. George, on the reverse a harp. Extremely fine, rare.

129 —— Penny. Obv. Cross of St. George within a palm and olive branch; rev. two joined shields, one bearing cross; the other, harp. Uncirculated and brilliant. Very rare.

130 —— Twopence. Same as last in all but size. Uncirculated. Rare.

131 —— Sixpence. Same type, with the addition of inscription and legend. On the obv. around the device THE COMMONWEALTH OF ENGLAND; on the rev. motto GOD WITH VS. 1654. *Fine.*

132 —— Shilling. 1656. Same in all respects except size. Rubbed.

133 COMMONWEALTH. Half-crown. Same type 1654. Extremely fine; very nearly uncirculated. Rare.
134 —— Crown. 1653. Fine, but weak impression; somewhat rubbed. Rare.
135 —— Half-penny, Penny, and Twopence—the latter very fine; the others pierced. 3 pieces.
136 CROMWELL, 1648 to 1660. Shilling, 1658. Obv. laureated head; rev. shield bearing his escutcheon in the centre of the Arms of England, Scotland, and Ireland, with the legend, PAX QVÆRITUR BELLO. Fair.
137 —— Half-crown. Same series. Uncirculated; in this condition, *very rare*.
138 —— Crown. Struck before the dies were cracked, *without the least trace of the well-known flaw*. Edge plain, minted without the collar, fine and sharp. Nearly uncirculated. Excessively rare.
139 —— Crown, cracked die, lettered edge. As fine as last. Rare.
140 —— Same in tin; edge plain. Very fine and rare.
141 —— Same. Lettered edge, equally fine and rare.
[These tin crowns are as valuable and more rare than the silver from the same dies. They were struck in 1658—guaranteed genuine from the Protector's dies, under the supervision of Blondin. The next piece is equally remarkable.]
141* CROMWELL. "For necessary change" a piece of tin money, having the Cross of St. George on one side, and a harp on the other. "½ ounce of fine pewter." See Reeding Pl., xxxi., No. 15. Very interesting and valuable, fine.
142 —— Small oval medallion, without reverse. Cromwell's bust, with inscription commemorating the Battle of Dunbar, THE LORD OF HOSTS, etc., with "Simon" on the edge of the arms; size about 13 x 18. Unique and very fine. Silver.
143 CHARLES II. 1660. Penny. Crowned bust to l. By *Simon*. Very fine, rare.
144 —— Twopence. Same type. Rubbed.
145 —— Threepence. do do.

*Coins of England.* 11

146 CHARLES II. Penny, Twopence, Threepence, and Groat; laureated bust to r. Fine and rare. Set Maundy money nearly uncirculated.
147 —— Another Maundy set of 4 pieces. Very fine.
148 —— Shilling. 1663. Very good.
149 —— Half-crown. 1671. do.
150 —— Crown. 1662. Rose under bust. *Extremely* fine, rare.
151 —— One and Twopence. 2 pieces.
152 —— Pattern farthing, 1665. Proof impression from the dies in silver. Obv. laureated bust to " Carolus A Carolo "; rev. Britannia seated, QVATVOR MARIA VINDICO. Very beautiful and rare.
153 —— Same in copper. Proof and red. Rare.
154 JAMES II. 1685. Penny, twopence, threepence, and groat. Fine Maundy set. Three of the pieces uncirculated. Rare.
155 —— Penny, twopence, and threepence. Fine. 4 pieces.
156 —— Crown (1687). Unusually fine. Rare.
157 —— Brass and copper coins struck in Dublin; A.D. 1690, called gun money, which had a forced circulation among the Protestants, VI., XII., and XXX. d. pieces with one which they had to take for a crown on pain of death; this last has the King on horseback, with 4 shields arranged as a cross—a crown in the centre on the reverse. An *extremely fine* set. 4 pieces
158 —— Another set of this provisional money. Nearly all fine. 4 pieces
159 —— Plantation tin piece. The King on horseback; rev. 4 shields. Fine.
160 —— " Hibernia " Half-penny. Obv. " Voce Populi ;" rev. " Hibernia " over a harp. Struck in Limerick in 1700. A good example; scarce.
161 WILLIAM AND MARY. 1688. Penny, Twopence, Threepence, and Groat. A fine set of Maundy money. All nearly, and some quite uncirculated. Rare.
162 —— Pennies. Uncirculated. 2 pieces
163 —— Twopence. Fine.
164 —— Groat. Uncirculated.

165 WILLIAM AND MARY Shilling. The cypher of their names in angles of the cross. Poor.
166 —— Half-crown. Same type; their portaits to r. Very fair, rare.
167 —— Half-crown, 1689. Portraits to r.; rev. arms on a plain shield under a crown. *Fine.*
168 —— Half-crown, 1690. Same type. *Uncirculated*, rare.
169 —— Half-crown, 1691. Their busts to l. Very fine, rare.
170 —— Crown, 1691. Their busts to r.; their cypher in the angles of the cross on reverse. Uncirculated, *very rare.*
171 WILLIAM alone. Penny. Uncirculated.
172 —— Penny, Threepence, and Groat. Fine. 3 pieces
173 —— Sixpence and Shilling. Fair. 2 pieces
174 —— Half-crown, 1698. Very fine.
175 —— Duplicate. Equally fine.
176 —— Crown, 1696. Very fine, rare.
177 —— Half-crown. With the date of the birth of "Sarah Dunkerly" (1779) on reverse. Neatly engraved.
178 ANNE. 1702. Penny, Twopence, Threepence, and Groat. A fine set of Maundy money. *Nearly* uncirculated, rare.
179 —— Penny. Very fine.
180 —— Twopence. Equally fine.
181 —— Threepence. do do
182 —— Two and Threepences. 3 pieces
183 —— Sixpence. Plain. Rubbed.
184 —— Shilling. Plumes. Good.
185 —— Shilling. E. under bust. Good.
186 —— Shilling. VIGO under bust. Uncirculated, rare.
187 —— Crown. VIGO under bust. Uncirculated, splendid, rare.
188 —— Crown. E. (for Edinburgh) under bust. Nearly uncirculated.
189 —— Pattern Farthing, 1714. Proof impression in silver. Very slightly rubbed, still *splendid*. On rev. Britannia, seated.

*Coins of England.* 13

190 ANNE Shilling Token. Obv. bust of Anne; rev. arms within the garter, the supporters lying down, the escutcheon crowned and resting on a pedestal, with the Queen's monogram. Uncirculated, rare.
191 —— Shilling Token. Obv. same as last; rev. arms supported by Cupid. Uncirculated, rare.
192 GEORGE I. 1714. Penny. Uncirculated.
193 —— Penny and Threepence. Fine. 2 pieces
194 —— Penny and Sixpence (S.S.C.). Fine. 2 pieces
195 —— Penny and Shilling (S.S.C.). Very fine. 2 pieces
196 —— Two-third Crown, 1724. Obv. laureated bust in the Roman habit; rev., arms in cross, the spaces plain, edge milled. Very fine, rare.
197 —— Crown. Obv. like last, II, C, B, under bust; rev. arms in the garter, lion and unicorn supporting. Date, 1718. Extremely fine, rare.
198 —— Crown. Rev. arms in cross, the cross of St. George in centre, S. S. C. (for South Sea Co.) in the angles. Very fine, scarce.
199 GEORGE II. 1729. Penny. Uncirculated.
200 —— Penny and Twopence. do. 2 pieces
201 —— Pennies and Twopences. Very fine. 7 pieces
202 —— Sixpence. Uncirculated.
203 —— Shilling. do.
204 —— Sixpence and Shilling. Fine. 2 pieces
205 —— Shilling. Rose in angles of cross. Fine.
206 —— Half-crown, 1746. Extremely fine.
207 —— Half-crown, 1750. Equally fine.
208 —— Crown, 1746. LIMA, under bust. Uncirculated, rare.
209 —— Crown. Rose in angles of cross; S. B. engraved on obverse. Very fine.
210 GEORGE III. 1760. Penny. Young head. Brilliant.
211 —— Penny. Old head. Brilliant.
212 —— Penny, Threepence, and Fourpence. Fine. 3 pieces
213 —— Sixpence, 1787. Very fine.
214 —— Shilling, 1787. Uncirculated.

## British Coins.

215 GEORGE III. Sixpence and Shilling; shield within the garter, old head. Ordinary. 2 pieces
216 —— Half-crown, 1817. Uncirculated. Rare.
<small>From the new dies by Wyon, from design by Pistrucci.</small>
217 —— Half-crown, 1819. Nearly uncirculated.
218 —— Crown, 1791; obv. laureated bust in Roman habit to r.; rev. handsome coat-of-arms, crowned legend BRUNS. & LUN. DUX. S. R. I. A. T. A. & ELECT. Uncirculated.
219 —— Crown, 1818. From new dies, by Pistrucci; obv. laureated head; rev. St. George and Dragon; on edge "Decees et Tutamen. Anno Regni Six." Splendid proof impression. Very rare.
220 —— Crown, 1819; same type. Uncirculated.
221 —— Crown, 1820; same type. do.
222 —— Dollar of Bank of England, 1804. Nearly uncirculated.
223 —— Bank of England Token. Fine Shilling and Sixpence, 1811; obv. laureated bust in Roman habit; rev. Britannia seated. Brilliant proof. Extremely rare.
224 —— Bank of England Dollar, 1804; proof impression in copper. Edge plain, rare.
225 —— Half-Dollar, Carolus III. Spain, with counterstamp at mint; small head of the King. Ex. fine, rare.
226 —— Carolus Dollar; counterstamped in the same way. Ex. fine, rare.
227 —— Dollar of Carolus III., 1776, counterstamped as before. Very fine.
228 —— Dollar of Carolus V., bearing stamp, "Thistle Bank, 4-9." Very fine, rare.
229 —— Fivepence, Irish Bank Token. Fair.
230 —— Tenpence, do. do. do.
231 —— Thirtypence, do. do. 1808. Fine.
232 —— One Shilling, Sixpence, Bank Token; young head 1811. Uncirculated.
233 —— One Shilling, Sixpence, Bank Token; old head 1814 and 1815. Very fine. 2 pieces

*Coins of England.* 15

234 —— Three-Shilling Bank Tokens, 1811 and 1813; old and young head. Very fine. 2 pieces

235 —— Peterborough Bank Token for 18 Pence, "Cole & Co." View of the Cathedral. Uncirculated.

236 —— Shilling Tokens, Bristol, Devonshire, Norfolk, New Castle, Worcester, Yarmouth, and York. All very fine. 7 pieces

237 —— Sixpenny Tokens and Colonial. 5 pieces

238 GEORGE IV. 1820. Penny proof.

239 —— Penny and Fourpence. Proof. 2 pieces

240 —— Sixpence, 1825. Uncirculated.

241 —— Shilling; rev. Lion on Crown. Uncirculated.

242 —— Shilling; rev. Armes Crowned; rose, thistle and shamrock. Proof.

243 —— Half-crown, 1826. Ordinary.

244 —— Half-crown, 1820; rev. Arms crowned, rose, thistle and shamrock. Splendid uncirculated impression. Rare.

245 —— Crown; rev. St. George and Dragon. By Pistrucci. Fine proof.

246 —— Crown, 1826; obv. bare head, after design by Chantry; rev. superb Coat-of-arms and Crest by Merlin. Splendid proof impression. Rare.

247 WILLIAM IV. 1830. One Penny-and-a-half, Fourpence, and 1-8 Gilders for British Guiana and Demarara, etc. 10 pieces

248 VICTORIA. 1837. Penny, Penny-half-penny, Twopence, Threepence, Fourpence and Sixpence, all but 4d uncirculated. 6 pieces

249 —— Model Coins and small silver. Extra fine. 10 pcs

250 —— Florin, "Victoria Regina." Owing to the omission of D. G., recalled. Very fine, rare.

251 —— Florin, "Victoria D. G., Bret., Reg. F. D.," 1859 Uncirculated.

252 —— Florin, brilliant.

253 —— Florin, ordinary.

254 —— Crown, nearly uncirculated.

## Gold Coins of England.

255 EDWARD III. 1327. Noble of the first coinage; obv. the King in the midst of a Ship; rev. cross fleurie, with lions under crown in the angles. IHS. AVTEM-TRANSIENS, P. MEDIVM. ILLORVM IBAT. As fine as when coined. Extremely rare in this condition.

256 EDWARD IV. 1461. Rial; obv. like last; rev. instead of cross, a sun, surrounded by lions and crowns. Very broad, and extremely fine. Very rare.

257 ELIZABETH. Angel; obv. St. Michael subduing a dragon; rev. a ship. In fine preservation. Very rare.

258 JAMES VI. (Scotch); obv. sword and sceptre, crossed with thistles and crown above, and date 1601 below; rev. Arms of Scotland. Well preserved and rare.

>I do not find this coin described. It contains the value of a half Angel, or nearly so.

259 —— Gold Crown of James, after he became King of England. Extremely fine, rare.

260 CHARLES I. Five-shilling, or Gold Crown. Very fine and rare.

261 COMMONWEALTH XX. Shilling-piece or Pound; obv. Cross of St. George; rev. two shields (Arms of England and Ireland), as it came from the die. Rare.

262 JAMES II. Gold Crown (Five-shillings). Extremely fine.

263 GEORGE II. Crown. Proof.

264 GEORGE III. One-third Guinea; rev. crown.

265 —— Half-guinea. Proof.

266 GEORGE IV. Five Guinea-piece; obv. Chantrey's bust; rev. arms on an ermine mantle. None were struck for general circulation. Splendid proof. Rare.

## Copper Coins of English Sovereigns.

267 IRISH Farthing of James I. Two sceptres crossed through a crown; rev. harp. Very fine.

268 —— Farthing of James I. Two sceptres crossed through a crown; rev. harp. Others equally fine.    2 pieces

269 —— Farthing of Charles I. Same type. Fine.

270 IRISH. St. Patrick's farthing. Royal harper kneeling. Ordinary.
271 —— Half-penny of Charles II. 1682. Rubbed. Scarce.
272 —— do James II. 1686. Rubbed. 2 pcs.
273 —— Gun money James II. 1690. Crown, half-crown (xxx d ), and shilling. Fine. 3 pieces.
274 —— Half-crown xxx. and xii. d. Good. 2 pieces.
275 —— Half-pennies and farthings of George I. under Wood's patent. Varieties. Fair. 6 pieces.
276 —— Pennies, half-pennies, and farthings, George II. and III. Ordinary. 9 pieces.
277 SCOTCH farthings of Charles II. Obv. C II. R under a crown ; rev. thistle. Fine. 2 pieces.
278 —— Farthings and bawbees. Thistle. Fair. 6 pieces.
279 —— Bawbees and half do. James II. and William and Mary, and several rare tokens. Miscellaneous. 10 pieces.
280 ISLE OF MAN. Penny of George III. 1786. Very fine. Scarce.
281 —— Athol penny. 1758. The legs in mail, and spurred. Extra fine, rare.
282 —— Penny, half-penny, and farthing. 4 pieces.
283 GUERNSEY. 8 doubles and 4 doubles. Very fine. 2 pieces.
284 —— 8 doubles, 4 doubles, and 1 double. 3 pieces.
285 JERSEY and Guernsey. 6 pieces.
286 ENGLISH. Charles II. "Carolus a Carolo" farthings. Rare. 2 pieces.
287 —— Pattern farthing of Charles II. "Carolus a Carolo." Struck with two rings in centre. Extra fine and rare.
288 —— Half-penny and farthing of William and Mary. Good, rare. 2 pieces.
289 —— Half-penny and farthing of William alone. Good, rare. 2 pieces.
290 —— Half-penny of William alone. Good, rare. 3 pcs.
291 —— Half-penny of George I. Good, dark. Scarce.
292 —— do do Poor.
293 —— Farthing do Very fine, rare.
294 —— Farthing of George II. Very fair.

295 ENGLISH Half-penny of George II. Very fine, rare.
296 —— Half-pennies and farthings George II.
297 —— Twopence George III. Rim raised, letters incuse. Very fine.
298 —— Penny. George III. Equally fine, same type.
299 —— do Duplicate, same in all respects.
300 —— Pennies, three varieties, 1799 and 1800. Ordinary. 3 pieces.
301 —— Pattern penny of 1788. On edge, "Render to Cæsar the things that are Cæsar's." Gilt. Very fine, rare.
302 —— Penny, half-penny, and farthing George III. Good. 3 pieces.
303 —— Others of this reign. Ordinary. 10 pieces.
304 —— Pattern half-penny and farthing of George IV. (1826.) Gilt. Beautiful. 2 pieces.
305 —— Penny, two varieties, and farthing George IV. Extra fine. 3 pieces.
306 —— Penny, half do., farthing, half do. 7 pieces.
307 —— William IV. penny and farthing. Fine. 2 pieces.
308 —— do farthing, and half do. 2 pieces.
309 —— Victoria. Set from penny to quarter farthing. 1853. Uncirculated. 5 pieces.
310 —— Victoria penny, and half do. 1860. Bright. 2 pieces.
311 —— do and other English. 14 pieces.
312 VICTORIA. Medals to keep her subjects informed of the names and number of her children. Very small. 9 plated. 11 pieces.
313 —— Jetons, on which her subjects are requested to "keep their temper" under very trying circumstances, with a ride "To Hanover," variously mounted. A curious collection, without duplicates, and generally very fine. Brass. 18 pieces.
314 RARE FARTHING TOKENS. Solyman coffee-house in Ivy Lane. 1663. With the turbanned head of the proprietor. Extremely fine and rare.
315 —— Abraham Ogden "On Wapping Walle." Fine.

*English Copper Coins.* 19

316 RARE FARTHING TOKENS. John Watson " in Gravesend heart pierced 1653;" by an arrow. Very fine and rare.
317 —— "At the S. John's head tavern in Ludgate." Head in oval. Very fine, rare.
318 —— "Bleeding and Tooth-Drawing." Rev. "Harrison, hair-dresser, No. 64 Long Lane, West Smithfield." Two busts vis a vis. 1797. Rare.
319 —— Andrew Melrose & Co. "Teas direct from India house." Ex. fine and rare.
320 —— Sparrow, Nail Merchant, London. "His Leather Sauce." A balloon flying. Three varieties. Very fine and rare. 3 pieces.
321 —— R. Orchard's and other rare old tokens for necessary change. 6 pieces.
322 —— Chevalier and others. 10 pieces.
323 TRADE half-penny tokens of about A.D. 1795. White Negress: J. Kilvington. "Success to the Coal Trade;" Tribute to Palmer for Mail Coaches—Picture of a Stage Team: Edinburgh half-penny, etc., etc. A very fine lot, some proofs. 10 pieces.
324 —— Fine. 10 pieces.
325 —— do 10 do
326 —— do 10 do
327 —— Good. 10 do
328 —— Ordinary. 10 do
329 —— do 10 do
330 —— do 10 do
331 —— do 17 do
332 PENNY TOKENS. British Copper Co—Obv. Lion. Stafford—obv. Gate: J. M. Fellows—rev. Castle: etc. Good lot. 5 pieces.
333 —— Fair. 4 do
334 —— Arms of Gloucester. Rev. St. Nicholas' Church. Fine proof.
335 —— "Patriæ et Decus et Tutamen." Three-towered gate—below—a lion; rev. soldier on guard. Proof.
336 RARE Tokens and Medalets of a political character. Charles I., his bust; rev. "Viret," Anna, Marquis of Granby, Wellington, etc. 6 pieces.

337 RARE Tokens and Medalets of a political character. "Iac, Princeps Walliæ (Pretender). 1697. The devil conducting Napoleon to Elba, riding reversed on a donkey. Fine and rare. 2 pieces.

337*CAROLINE REGINA. Rev. "Bill withdrawn," etc., Marriage of George and Charlotte; Punch's Medalet, and two of the Pretender, 1702. All extremely fine. Rare lot. 5 pieces

338 ADMIRAL KEMPENFELT. His ship going down; obv. view of Gibraltar. Splendid, rare.

339 —— Duplicate. Rubbed.

340 CRYSTAL Palace Exhibition, 1851. Silver-plated; rev. a wheel. Fine proof.

341 ROBERT PEEL Medalet, and other miscellaneous. Fine. 4 pieces

342 MISCELLANEOUS pieces; some religious. 10 pieces

343 PROF. HOLLOWAY. Rev. Health personified (advertising his pills). Rare. Size 22

344 ANTI-SLAVERY. "We are all brethren." Size 22

### English Medals—Copper.

There are a few tin and brass under this head, but they are fully described as such.

345 SOVEREIGNS of England. A series by *Dassier*, from William II. to George II., viz.: William Rufus, died 1100; Henry I., 1135; Henry II., 1189; Richard I., 1199; John, 1216; Henry III., 1227; Edward I., 1307; Edward II., 1327; Richard II., 1399; Henry IV., 1413; Henry V., 1422; Henry VI., 1461; Edward IV., 1483; Edward V., 1483; Richard III., 1485; Henry VII., 1509; Henry VIII., 1547; Edward VI., 1553; Mary, 1558; Elizabeth, 1602; James I., 1625; Charles I., 1649; Charles II., 1684; James II., 1688; Mary II., 1694; William III., 1702; George I., 1727; George II., 1760. With a single exception, in proof condition. Size 26. 28 pieces

346 —— Charles II., Edward VI., and Caroline, of the same series.

347 —— William III., by Rogat. Splendid bust. Size 27

*English Medals.—Copper.*

SOVEREIGNS OF ENGLAND. George II. Rev. Neptune in his car; FOEDVS VIENNENSE, 1731. Extremely fine. Size 30
—— William and Mary. Rev. an illustration of the golden age, "Securitas Britanniæ," 1689. Very beautiful medal, by P. R. M. (?); has been gilt. Size 36
—— George III. (by Kuchler). Obv. rich bust; rev. Peace. Fine proof. Size 32
—— George III. Another by same hand. Rev. Masonic signs. Fine proof. Size 32
—— George III. Splendid medal by Milton. Obv. laureated head; rev. Hygeia standing, SALUS POPU-LI, 15th Nov., 1798. Fine proof. Size 32
ADMIRALS Vernon and Blakney. The taking of Carthagena and selling of Minorca for "French gold." Brass. Uncirculated. 2 pieces
MEDAL in same style and material. Man hanging. Brass of Queen Anne; one of George II. in brass, and one of George III. rev. Proclaimed Oct. 2, 1760. The latter very fine. 4 pieces
—— William III. in lead; Edward VI., by Dassier. 2 pieces
ADMIRAL Nelson for victory of the Nile. Copper, gilt. Rare. Size 30
—— Obv. his bust; rev. Neptune and Hippocampus, Aug. 1, 1798. Lead. Rare. Size 22
GEORGE II. Rev. in a circle names of six military campaigns and their successful officers, the uppermost being Quebec and Wolf; in the centre arms of France upside down; 1759. Fine brass medal, and rare. Size 28
NAVAL Medal. Same year (1759). "Britain triumphed; Hawke commannded." Rev. "France relinquishes the sea." Proof. Size 28
CONQUEST of Canada Completed. Obv. Neptune with oar; rev. "Montreal taken;" the province weeping under a pine tree (compare with "Judea Capta"). Tarnished proof, rare. Size 28
WELLINGTON Medal in Iron. VOTA PUBLICA; another for the Peninsular campaign; both with his bust; struck in iron. Fine, and said to be very rare.
Size 28 and 32. 2 pieces

## British Coins.

362 WILLIAM III. Rev. Queen Mary. Two fine busts. Copper, gilt. Size 26

363 —— For the glories of his reign. VOTA ORBIS; Fame and Victory supporting a grand tablet, History and Time making the record; both sides covered with work; edge lettered. Uncirculated. Size 28

364 WILLIAM, Duke of Cumberland. Obv. bust; rev. man kneeling to a crowned lion; 1746. Extremely fine, brass. Size 20

365 WILLIAM MURRAY, "Comte de Mansfield." Rev. Justice, 1777. By Kirk. Proof. Size 24

366 CARDINAL WOLSEY. Obv. his bust; rev. Wolsey's gate. Splendid proof. Size 20

367 THO. HOWARD, "Comte de Effingham." Rev. Pro Patria; Britannia seated. Fine proof. Size 22

368 BRITISH Genius personified. Rev. Britannia standing before ships in port; Sept. 23, 1752. Splendid proof. Size 28

369 ROBERT WALPOLE, William Pultney, and Philip Stanhope (Counts of Oxford, Bath, and Chesterfield). Fine. Size 36. 3 pieces

370 SALISBURY Cathedral. Temperance Medal; To commemorate the passing of Robert Peel's Free Trade measures; Crystal Palace; Prince Albert, etc. All very fine, tin. 6 pieces

### English Silver Medals.

371 EDWARD VI. Young bust to the middle at three-quarters face, cap and plume and gold chain in oval within broad olive wreath; rev. coat-of-arms on garnished shield, also within wreath; with loop. Splendid medal. Old and extra rare. Size 30x36

372 PHILIP AND MARY. Marriage Medal (1625). Obv. busts face to face; rev. Cupid with roses and lilies. Original. *Fine* and *rare*. Size 15

373 —— Repetition of last.

JAMES I. and Charles I. Obv. James with hat: "Give thy judgments, O God, unto the king!" rev. young Charles bare-headed; "And thy righteousness unto the king's sonn." Engraved; original of the time of James I. Very fine and rare. Size 17

CHARLES II. Coronation Medal. Obv. crowned bust royally dressed; rev. the King seated with sceptre, an angel crowning him. By T. Simon (?). The area burnished; the medal but little worn. Very rare. Size 18

MEDAL struck to commemorate the institution of the Order of the Garter. Obv. St. George and Dragon, horse in mail; rev. inscription in nine parallel lines, 1678. Extremely fine, hardly circulated. Very rare. Size 32

CHARLES II. Crown, 1670. Very good, scarce.

JAMES III. 1701. Pretender. Obv. ship;. rev. St. George and dragon, "Soli Deo Gloria." Extra fine, rare. Size 13

WILLIAM AND MARY. Laureated bust of the former on the latter to r.; rev. inauguration, 1689. Very fine. Size 23

WILLIAM III. Splendid bust, laureated and draped; rev. Fame, with angels carrying shields; on them, WATER-FORT, ATHLONE, LIMRICH, GALOWAY, KINSAL, LONON-DERY; below, the battle-field of Drogheda; in ex. RESTITUTORE HIBERNIA; edge lettered. Extremely fine, rare. Sixe 26

MARY, Consort of William III. Bust laureated; rev. female seated on a barren rock, O DEA CERTE. Size 22

ANNA. Inauguration Medal, Obv. fine bust; rev. Minerva hurling a thunderbolt at a three-headed monster, 1702. Fine proof. Size 23

—— Obv. Mars down, Minerva standing over him, LUDOVICUS MAGNUS. ANNA MAJOR; rev. 12 shields, each bearing the name of a city taken from the French army, XII VRBES CUM PROVINCIS INTRA XV D RÆCEPTA 1706. Splendid medal. Size 32

384 ANNA. Splendid bust, laureated; rev. trophy of arms, Inspectant, Gall. Cent. Mille, 1710. Proof.   Size 30
385 —— Bust crowned; rev. May 1, 1707; cypher on pedestal, supporting arms. Very fine.   Size 17
386 —— Obv. like last; rev. different. Same size.
387 GEORGE I. Coronation Medal. Uncirculated.   Size 22
388 —— Duplicate. Very fine.
389 —— Obv. bust, laureated; rev. record of his life, ending "Osnabru—1827." Fine.   Size 18
390 GEORGE III. Coronation Medal. Very fine.   Size 22
391 CHARLOTTE, wife of George III. Her coronation. Corresponding to last.
392 GEORGE III. AND CHARLOTTE. Their busts conjoined; rev. angel-flying over London, FELICITAS BRITANNIA—1761. Fine, pierced.   Size 18
393 WILLIAM IV. Rev. Adelaid; two heads, engraved by WYON. Proof.   Size 21
394 VICTORIA. British Army Medal. Splendid crowned bust by Wyon, 1848; rev. Victoria crowning Wellington, 1793–1814; 8 bars, with inscriptions. Fine proof.   Size 23
395 —— To the Army of the Punjab, 1849; two bars, MOOLTAM COOJERAT; original ribbon. Very fine. Same size.
396 —— BALTIC, 1854–1855. Proof. Same size.
397 —— La-Crimea, 1855; rev. Turkeshins. Splendid proof, with original ribbon, clasp, and pin.   Size 10
398 —— India. Her bust; rev. Britannia and a lion. Same size as last. Also with ribbon and pin. Proof.
399 ST. GEORGE AND DRAGON. A silver badge for the St. George Society. About 2½ inches.
400 MASONIC BADGE. Edinburgh, 1847. St. Clair Lodge. Dollar size, gilt; loop and pin. Very fine.
401 —— Dollar size. Very fine.
402 HORATIUS NELSON. His bust; rev. naval column, 1805. Very fine, rare.   Size 25
403 RELIGIOUS MEDALS. Very pretty, and fine silver.
   2 pieces

404 IVORY BOX, with silver coin of James II. inserted in cover. Made to hold small coins, to bestow as a marriage gift. Rare and fine.

405 SILVER BOX, with Hebrew inscription. A Jewish custom, very old, is connected with this box. It seems to be explained by an attribute of Jupiter *Serapes*, who was represented with a measure or *bushel* on his head. This box, which is about the size of a thimble, is for the purpose for which it is used, called a bushel, and is given to the bride full of small gold coins. She is, therefore, said to have received in dowry "a bushel of gold." Very curious and uncommon.

406 CRUCIFIX. St. Andrew on a silver cross, laid on a sun, with rays; on the reverse a monogram. Fine silver, solid, heavy, and beautifully enameled. Length, two inches.

407 —— of solid silver. Two Christs, one with roses. Of very old work. Length, 3 inches.

## COINS OF FRANCE.

*Gaulo-Romano.*

408 EARLY SILVER SOLIDUS. Obv. rude characters; rev. horse. Small, thick coin. Rare.

*Kings from Charlemagne. Silver.*

409 CHARLES THE GREAT (Charlemagne). 768. Solidus (large silver penny). Obv. monogram of his name in centre; on outer circle MET + VLLO +; rev. short cross and moneyer's name. *Extremely fine* and rare.

410 CHARLES II. (the Bald). 840. Solidus. KARLVS REX METVLLO. Very fine and rare.

411 CHARLES III. (the Fat). 884. Denier. Fine, rare.

412 EUDES (Limoges). 887. Solidus. Obv. name obscure in centre; AT+IA— around; rev. short cross and moneyer's name. Broad, well-preserved, and very rare.

413 CHARLES (the Simple). 898. His name well executed in monogram, DEI GRATIA REX; rev. CIVITAS AVR— solidus. Extremely fine, rare.

414 RAOUL. 923. Solidus. Name in centre, ALIE— around; rev. cross, etc. Fine and very rare.

415 LOTHAIRE. Poiteau. Castle and short cross. A.D. 954. Denier. Rare.

416 LOUIS VII. (the Young). 1137. Solidus, LVDOVICVS REX.; various letters in centre; rev. short cross and moneyer's name. Fine, rare.

417 PHILIP AUGUST. 1180. Half Tournois (from being first coined at Tours). Name, castle, and cross. Good and rare.

418 LOUIS VIII. (the Lion). 1223. Solidus. Same type as last. LVDOVICVS REX. Very fine, rare.

419 LOUIS IX. (called Saint). 1226. Denier. Similar to Louis VIII. Rare.

420 PHILIP (the Hardy). 1270. Half Tournois. Poor, but rare.  2 pieces

421 PHILIP IV. (Le Bel). 1285. Grand-blanc (size of English Groat). Short cross in centre, name in circle, motto in outer circle; rev. castle in centre, CIVIS + TVRONVS. Very fine piece, but slightly cracked. Rare.

422 PHILIP VI. (Valois). 1327. Grand-blanc. Same type. Fine.  2 pieces

423 CHARLES VI. (Well Beloved). 1380. Grand-blanc. Obv. KAROLVS FRANCORV. REX. Spade-shaped shield with fleur-de-lis; rev. new motto, "Sit nomen Domini Benedicti," cross, fleur-de-lis, and crowns in angles. Extremely fine, rare.

424 —— Another. Very fine.

425 CHARLES VII. 1422. CAROLVS FRANCORV. REX. Same as Charles VI. Grand-blanc. Very fine.

426 —— Another. Type varied. Pierced, ordinary.

427 LOUIS XI. 1461. Grand-blanc a-la-Couronne. Same type as last and same in all respects except name. Fair, very rare.

428 CHARLES VIII. (the Affable.) 1483. Grand-blanc. Large R crowned; rev. cross. Ordinary.

428* —— Testoon. CAROLVS VIII., etc., laureated bust to l.; rev. shield with 3 lilies under a crown; C and crown on both sides; motto of France around. Thick coin, size and weight of one-third crown. Well preserved, rare.

429 LOUIS XII. (Pere du Peuple). 1497. Grand-blanc. Obv. LVDOVICVS REX; short cross and motto; rev. castle, TVRONVS CIVITAS. Ex. fine, rare.

430 FRANCIS I. 1514. Testoon. Crowned bust to l.; rev. arms quartered on shield, motto around. Very good and rare.

431 HENRY II. 1546. Testoon. Obv. bust; rev. shield with 3 lilies crowned, H crowned on both sides. Very fine, struck the last year of his reign, 1559. Rare.

432 —— Douzaine. (About groat size.) Obv. H. crowned and lilies; rev. cross with lilies.

433 —— Douzaine. Shield crowned and crescent crowned; rev. cross with H. + crown in alternate angles; counterstamped with a lily. Good, rare.

434 —— Same type, without counterstamp. Very fine. 2 pieces

435 —— Duplicates of Nos. 432 and 434. Good. 2 pieces

436 —— Douzaine and Turnoise. 2 pieces

437 CHARLES IX. 1560 to 1574. Testoon, with his bust laureated. Dated 1565. *Extremely* fine, rare.

438 —— Small silver coin.

439 HENRY III. 1574. Half-crown. Obv. laureated bust, H in the centre of a cross fleurie. Extremely fine, very rare.

440 —— Testoon. Bust laureated; rev. arms crowned and H crowned. 1575. Very fine.

441 Half-testoon. Large H between lilies, crowned; rev. cross terminating in lilies. Very fine.

442 —— Another, different. Very fine.

443 HENRY IV. 1589 to 1610. Testoon. Obv. "Henricus IIII. D. G. Franc E Nav, Rex. 1594." Large cross, rose in centre; rev. arms crowned and motto. (One-third crown in value.) Very fine, rare.
444 —— Testoon. With his bust laureated; rev. cross fleurie, II in centre. Ex. fine, rare.
445 —— Duplicate. Fine for so rare a piece.
446 —— Douzaine. Counterstamped with a lily.
447 —— Douzaines. Various types, all fine. 3 pieces
448 —— Douzaine. Nearly uncirculated, rare.
449 LOUIS XIII. (the Just). 1610 to 1643. Testoon. Obv. HENRICVS XIII. D. G. FRAN ET NAV REX: 1642; rev. arms (3 fleur de lis) on a shield under a crown. As it came from the die, rare.
450 —— Testoon. Different coat-of-arms. Very fine.
451 —— Small coin, with his bust laureated.
452 —— Half-crown. 1642. Entirely uncirculated, very rare.
453 LOUIS XIV. 1643 to 1715. Small silver coins, with his bust, young and old; one dated 1654, the other 1704. In fine preservation. 2 pieces
454 One-eighth crown. Old busts. Varieties, poor. 2 pieces
455 —— Quarter-crown. 1666. Young bust, laureated. Fair.
456 —— Quarter-crown. Old head; different reverse. Fair.
457 —— Quarter-crown. 1690. Bust, with long hair; rev. letter L's interlocked at right angles in such a way as to form a cross, a crown at each limb, and fleur de lis between the angles. Ex. fine.
458 —— Half-crown. Same type and date. Fair.
459 —— Half-crown of 1691. Nearly uncirculated, rare.
460 —— Crown of 1709. Obv. mailed bust; rev. three crowns. A rare type, in fair preservation.
461 —— Crown. 1711. Same type. Fine, rare.
462 LOUIS XV. 1715 to 1774. Francs and Half-francs. Laureated head to l.; different reverse. 3 pieces
463 —— Half-crown. 1728. Poor.

## Kings from Charlemagne. 29

464 LOUIS XVI. 1774 to 1792. One-eighth Crown. Very fine.
464* —— Quarter-crown. 1782. Very fine.
465 —— Half-crown. 1790. *Uncirculated*, rare.
466 —— Crown. 1775. Very fine on reverse; obv. rubbed. Rare.
467 —— Crown. 1791. Mint mark a swan. Fine, rare.
468 —— Crown. 1793. (After his death.) New type; "Regne De La Lois." Victory, fasces, and cock. Extremely fine, rare.
469 —— Crown of this type, struck in 1792. Edge milled as a vine, counter-stamped, "40 BZ." on one side and opposite, the Arms of Berne; but little circulated. Rare.
470 —— Half-crown, 1793. Fine.
471 —— Thirty Sols, and fifteen Sols. Same type. 2 pcs
472 FRENCH REPUBLIC. 1793. Six Livres. Fine, rare.
473 NAPOLEON. Premiere Consul. An. 12, Five Francs. Very good, rare.
474 NAPOLEON. Emperor, 1804 to 1815. Quarter Franc. By *Tiolier*. Uncirculated.
475 —— Others. Fine. 2 pieces
476 —— Quarter Franc, Half do. Franc, Two Francs, and Five Francs, making eight and three-quarters Francs value. A fine set, not uncirculated. 5 pieces
477 —— Quarter Franc. Brilliant.
478 —— Demi do. do.
479 —— Franc do. do.
480 —— Two Francs, do.
481 LOUIS XVIII. 1815 to 1824. Quarter Franc. 2 pieces
482 —— Five Francs. *Tiolier*. Fine.
483 —— Five Francs. *Michaet*. Fine.
484 CHARLES X. 1824–1830. Quarter Franc. Fine.
485 —— Five Francs. Nearly uncirculated. Rare.
486 LOUIS PHILLIPPE. 1830–1848. Quarter Franc. Fine.
487 —— Five Francs. Very fine. Rare.

488 REPUBLIC of 1848. Five Francs, by *Dupré*. REPUBLIC FRANCAISE, FIVE FRANCS, 1848; rev. three figures standing, LIBERTE EGALITE, FRATERNITE. Nearly uncirculated.
489 —— Duplicate, (1848). Very fine.
490 —— Another Five-Franc piece, 1848. Fine.
491 —— Five Francs of this type, 1849. Very fine.
492 —— Five Francs, 1849. Obv. Head of Ceres.; rev. like those of '48. Very fine.
493 —— Duplicate.   do.
494 —— Two Francs. Head of Ceres. Very fine.
495 —— Twenty Centimes of the years 1850 and 1851, uncirculated. 2 pieces
496 LOUIS NAPOLEON BONAPARTE as President of the Republic, 1852. Five Francs, by' *Barre*. Very fine scarce.
497 NAPOLEON III., EMPEROR. Obv. his head laureated; rev. ermine crowned, displaying two sceptres crossed with the Eagle of the Empire, Five Francs, 1867. Extremely fine, scarce.
498 —— Five Francs, 1870. Same type. Ex. fine.
499 —— Duplicate. Equally fine.
500 —— Franc and Half-franc. Empire. 2 pieces
501 FRENCH REPUBLIC of 1871. Five Francs; liberty, eqalité, fratornite, by *Dupré*. M. M., anchor and cross. Fine, scarce.
502 —— Five Francs, 1871. Mint mark, anchor and bee. Uncirculated. Scarce.
503 —— Two Francs, 1871. Head of Ceres. Uncirculated.
504 COMMUNE. Five Francs, 1871. Mint mark, anchor and trident. Extremely fine, and very rare.
   NOTE.—The silver pieces *actually coined* by the Commune are *rare*. They may be known by the mint mark, and by this only—the anchor to r, and the trident to l. of the letter A.

### Kings of Navarre—Silver.

505 HENRY II. 1577. Testoon, two busts facing; crown above, bull below; rev. "Gratia Dei sam Qd sum." Arms of France and Navarre, quartered on shield crowned. Very fine and rare.

## Baronial and Ecclesiastical. 31

JOANNA. 1567. Testoon. Bust "Joanna Dei Gra Reg. Navar, D. B." Below P. and bull; rev. similar to last. A fine coin, and most excessively rare.

FRANCIS I. Testoon, 1514 to 1546. A King of France and Navarre. A testoon with his bust crowned. Fine and rare.

*French Baronial and Ecclesiastical—Silver.*

In alphabetical order.

ALSACE. Ferdinand II., Austrian Count. Quarter-crown, with his bust to the waist. Very fine.

—— Ferd. Duke of Bur., etc. Small silver with arms of Alsace. Fine.

ANDUSE, (City). ANDVSIENSIS. Large B in centre; rev. cross. "Salviensés." Ex. fine, rare.

ANGERS, (City). Very fine and old Penny, or Denarius. In centre DO†; rev. cross and name of city. Rare.

ANGOULEME. Louis, Duke of Orleans, 1380, LVDOICVS; cross rev. EGOLISSIME. Four anulets. Denarius Fine and rare.

NOTE.—The term "denarius" is used instead of "penny" in the books out of which we get our knowledge concerning these coins. It seems to be proper enough, and the two terms will be found in this Catalogue in different departments, (and perhaps sometimes in the same), applied to coins of the same class. The writer has not been at all careful or discriminating in this regard, but hopes to be forgiven for such trifles in a work where graver faults will be found not particularly rare.

ANGOULEME. Similar to last; equally fine denarius.
—— Same. do.
—— do. 2 pieces

ANJOU. Geoffrey II., (Martel), 1040. GOSFRIDVS CO†; cross rev. ANDECAV. Solidus. Very fine and rare.

—— Folques IV., 1097. A fine denarius with FVLCO-COME* and cross; rev. A design which may have meant a castle or fortress. Very rare.

—— Charles I., Duke of France, 1246; obv. CAROLVS COMES; cross; rev. similar to last. Denarius. Very fine, rare.

519 ANJOU. Charles IV., 1480. King of Naples. Count. Small silver. Fine. 2 pieces
520 AQUITAINE. William X., Duke, 1127–1137. Denarius. EVILILMO†. Four small crosses; rev. † DVRDE-OHLA. Cross. Extremely fine, rare.
521 —— William X. Denarius. Same as last. Fine.
522 —— Another. Fine.
523 —— Edward I. England, 1272 to 1307. Denarius (Penny); figure nearly full length; rev. cross. Leopard and fleur de lis in the area. Very fine. Even uncirculated and excessively rare.
524 —— Edward I. ED. REX. ANGLIE; rev. plain cross. Not worn; impression faint. Rare denarius.
525 —— Edward I. Same as last. Fair.
526 —— Edward III. (England) 1327; fine and rare groat; has a French castle for principle type.
527 AUXONNE. Solidus. Rare.
528 BEARN. Centulus V. Count. 1130 to 1134, denárius, CENTVLIO COME, cross; rev. M. P and cross; fine. Very rare.
529 —— Same count. Obolus; a beautiful little coin, and very rare.
530 —— Duplicate. Equally fine.
531 BLOIS. Guido, Count; rev. BLESIS-CASTRO. Rude and remarkable denarius.
532 BRITTANY. John IV., Duke, 1364–1399; grand-blanc; rev. cross, motto of France. Fine.
533 BURGUNDY. John, Duke, 1404–1419, grand-blanc; obv. "Johnnes Dux Burgundie;" rev. cross with lilies and leopards. Fine, rare.
534 CAMBRAY. 1570. Two liards. Copper.
535 CHAMPAGNE. Theobald, or Thibaut, 1345, Count; denarius, TEBALT COMES, cross; rev. CASTRI PRVVNIS, curious crenated figure. Very rare.
536 CLERMONT. Denarius; obv. the Virgin Mary crowned, full face, STA—MARIA; rev. VRBS ARVERNA, cross fleurie, and St. Andrew's cross. Very fine and interesting. A D. 1361.
537 —— Duplicate. Nearly as fine.

538 DOMBES. Louis, Duc de Montpensier, 1576, L. crowned; rev. cross. Small silver. Rare.
539 —— Anna Maria Ludovica, 1673, Princess; half-crown. Bust draped, head bare; rev. arms of France. Fine and very rare.
540 —— Henri, Duc de Montpensier. Testoon, 1605; bust; rev. arms crowned, H. crowned. As it was coined. Splendid, rare.
541 —— Another of the Duke of Montpensier. Nearly equal to last. Very rare.
542 DREUX. Denier. "Robertus," (1331.) Rare.
543 GORZE. Denarius. Fine, rare.
544 LOTHRINGEN (Lorraine.) Charles de Kuhne, 1390, groat; obv. the Duke standing, armed and crowned, KAROLVS DVX LOTHOR Z M; rev. cross within two circles of inscription, "Grossus de Nancey" in inner. Very fine and rare.
545 —— Anton, Duke, 1508 to 1544; obv. coat-of-arms, ANTHON D G, &c.; rev. FECIT POTENCIAM, &c., arm holding sword. Groat. Entirely uncirculated. Rare.
546 —— The same. Testoon. Bust with coronet; rev. Arms, MONET NANCEI CVSA; in ex. 1533. Extremely fine and rare.
547 —— The same. Testoon. Similar to preceding. Good.
548 —— The same. Half-testoon, 1513; rev. arms and two double crosses. Fine, equally rare.
549 —— Charles II. (*Grosse*), 1545, Duke. Testoon. Bust in mail, and crowned; rev. coat-of-arms, "Moneta Nova Nancei Cusa." Extra fine, rare.
550 —— The same. Another testoon. Equally fine.
551 —— The same. Repetition of last.
552 —— Leopold I., 1697 to 1729; obv. eagle crowned; rev. large cross, crosses in angles, 1729. XXX deniers billon.
553 —— The same. Testoon (1712); obv. bust bare; rev. cross crowned. Fine and rare.
554 —— The same. Testoon, 1723; obv. same; rev. coat-of-arms crowned. Rubbed.

555 LYONS. Denarius; obv. "Prima Sedes;" rev. "Galliaru," cross. Fine, rare.
556 ——— The same. 2 pieces.
557 LE MANS. Denarius Erbertus I., 1036; obv. COMES CENOMAIIISI, monogram of Erbertus; rev. SIGNVM DEI VI VI, cross. *Extremely fine and rare penny.*
558 MEAUX. Stephen de la Chapelle, Bishop, 1162–1171. Denarius; obv. head front STEPHANVS EPE; rev. "Civitas Mele," cross, lilies and crescent. Hardly fine, but very rare.
559 MELQUEIL. Denarius, on one side cross; rev. 4 anulets. Very fine.
560 ——— Duplicate.
561 MONTBELLIARD, 1590; billon coin, F. crowned; rev. cross, M and lilies. 2 pieces.
562 MURBACH. Bracteate. Small, fine.
563 ——— Leopold, Emperor, 1614–1625, Crown; obv. Bishop seated, SANCTVS LEODGARIVS; rev. FERDINANDVS II DG ROM IMP, &c., double eagle crowned. Very fine, rare.
564 ——— Duplicate, but not as fine.

See Wellenheim, No. 1,047.

565 NANCY. Frederic III., the Fair, son of Albert of Austria, 1250 to 1303; obv. Frederic on horseback; rev. drawn sword MIRECORT. Small coin. Extra fine and rare.
566 ——— Duplicate.
567 ——— Solidus of Charles, Duke of Lothringen, 1390; coat-of-arms, CAR. D. G. LOT; rev. eagle crowned, "Moneta Cusa Nanccie." As fine as when struck. Rare.
568 NEUFCHATEL. Theobald, Count, 1345; obolus, the Count on horseback; rev. cross. Very fine.
569 POITEAU. Denarius. Alphonso, 1241. ALFVNSVS COMES, cross; rev. castle, PICTAVIENTSIS. Extra fine and rare.
570 ——— The same. Very fine.

## Baronial and Ecclesiastical. 35

PROVENCE. Alphonsus I., King of Aragon, 1166, denier; obv. REX ARAGON; rev. PRO-VI-NC-IA, long cross. As fine as when coined. Very rare.
—— Robert, Duke of Calabria, 1309; groat (Carlini); obv. crown; rev. cross, with crosslets and lilies. Fine and rare.
ST. QUINTIN. Department of Ain. Denarius.
RENNES. Brittany; obv. "Redonic CIVITAS," cross. Denarius.. Rare.
—— Similar; rev. cross united by crescents.
—— Another. Extra fine.
SANCERRE. Cross; in angles, star and lily.
SOUVIGNY. Denarius, full face, sceptre or crosier; SILVINIACO. Very fine and rare.
—— Same as last. Fine penny.
ST. MARTIN of Tours; castle and cross. Good penny. Rare.
STRASBURG. Three turnois of Charles, Cardinal of Lorraine under Rudolph of Austria. 1602. A R G is the abbreviation for Argentinensis. Strasburg. Very fine and rare.
TOULOUSE, Raimond V. 1143, denarius; obv. RICOIE-S-PALACI, Jesuit's cross; rev. DVX MARCH P V, crescent and star; brilliant. Valuable penny.
—— Raimond V. Another. Very fine.
—— Half-pennies; same duke. Varieties; fine. 2 pieces.
—— Raimond VI. RAMON COMES; cross; in one of the angles, S; rev. TOLOZI CIVI, short cross, A P. Extremely fine; valuable penny.
—— Raimond VI. Another; equally fine.
TOULS. John de Sierck, Archbishop, 1296; bust, front face, OHANNES, Denarius. Very fine and rare.
TURENNE. Raimond III., 1335. Denarius. Fine.
—— Repetition of last.
VALENCE. City; obv. VRBS VALENTIAL, rude figure (sense obscure); rev. S. APOLINARS, cross with balls on the ends. Very fine and rare Denarius.
—— Others precisely similar. Nearly as fine. 2 pieces.

## Coins of France.

592 VALENCIENNES. William III., 1349; groat size; four lions in a circle; rev. "Mone Nova Vale Ceis," long cross. Fine and rare.

593 —— Very fine denarius; lion and cross. Rare.

594 VENDOME. V and cross; rev. cross; denarius. Fine.

595 VERDUN. Theoderic, Bishop, 1047; obv. TE-ODERIC-EP below; rev. letters arranged in form of a cross, VIRGO MARIA.* Denarius.

    See "Wellenheim," 1875, where it is described as R.R.

596 VERMANDOIS. Eleonore. 1183. Denarius.

597 VIENNE. Bishopric. Obv. bust to left S. M. VIENNA ×; rev. MAXIMA GALL. Cross with dots. Superb penny, thirteenth century.

598 —— Similar. Very fine and rare.
599 —— Another. Equally fine.
600 ——    do         do

601 VIENNE (City). Charles VII. 1422. Dolphin and lily, CAROLVS, FRANCOR, REX; rev. cross, lilies, and crowns, motto of France. Fine and rare denarius.

602 CHARLES II., the bald; son of Louis the Debonaire. 840. Obv. in monogram, his name in centre; around, DEI GRATIA REX.; rev. cross, CVRTISASSIEN (coined at Court sessin). Extremely fine and rare penny.

603 TOULOUSE. Fine denarius.

604 VALENCIENNES. *Marguerite.* Cavalier galloping to left. A.D. 1324. (Struck for the wife of Louis V.) Well'n. 1862. Groat size. Splendid, very rare.

605 —— Cavalier to right; rev. cross and crescent. Similar to last.

606 PENNY and token to commemorate the union of Valois and Bourbon.     2 pieces.

### Gold.

607 NOBLE of Ludovicus, Count of Br., etc. Sun. In the style of English coin time of Edward IV. Uncirculated. Rare (not described).

### French Baronial. Copper.

608 ARRAS. "Ecclesis Atrebaten." Excessively rare. (Not in Well'n.)
609 BOUILLON and SEDAN. 1614. Henry de la Tour. Fine and bright. 2 pieces.
610 —— F. Maurice. 1633. Double Tournois. 3 pieces.
611 CUGNON. John Theodore. 1614. Double Tournois. Rare. 2 pieces.
612 DOMBES. Gaston and Henry de Bourbon. 1641. Good coins (double tournois). 6 pieces.
613 HENRICHEMONT. 1642. M.F. de Bethune. Double tournois. 2 pieces.
614 MONTBELIARD. "Liard." 1610. Bust. Ex. fine, rare.
615 MANTUA. 1636. Charles I. Duke. 3 pieces.
616 —— Same. 3 do
617 NANCY (Lorraine). Beautiful coin.
618 NEVERS. Charles Gonzales, Duke. 1610. Bust and handsome coat-of-arms. 3 pieces.
619 ORANIEN. 1641. Fred Henry. Double tournois. 3 pieces.
620 —— William Henry. 1653. Tournois. 2 do
621 PHALZBURG and Lixen. 1633. Henrietta D. Lor. Double tournois.
622 RENAUD (Chateau). Francis de Bourbon, Prince de Conté. Double tournois. 5 pieces.
623 —— Francoise de Bourbon. 1613. Double gro. tournois. Fine, rare. 4 pieces.
624 SEDAN. Godfrey, Duke de Bouillon. 1625. Double de Bouillon. Rare.
625 —— F. Maurice. 1639. 2 pieces.

### Kings of France. Copper.

626 HENRY III. 1589. Double tournois and deniers. 3 pcs.
627 HENRY IV. 1592. Do. Extra fine. 1606.
628 —— Same. 3 pieces.
629 LOUIS XIII. (died 1643). Double tournois and liards, with head to r. and l. One with head crowned. Fine. 6 pieces.
630 —— Double tournois. 12 pieces.

631 Louis XIV. 1643. Liards, 11 deniers, and Six deniers. Great variety. 10 pieces.
632 Louis XV. 1723. Liards, etc. Fine. 4 pieces.
633 Louis XVI. Liards and ½ sols. 1786–1791. 5 pieces.
634 —— 3 deniers, 6 deniers, 12 deniers. Rev. fasces and Cap of Liberty within wreath. Copper. Struck at Marseilles. Rare. 3 pieces.
635 —— 12 deniers, 2 Sols. L. au 4. Brass, by *Du Vivier*. Nearly uncirculated. Rare. 4 pieces.
636 —— Others. With counterfeit crown. 8 pieces.
637 Charles X. 10 cent., 5 cent. 3 pieces.
638 Louis Phillippe. 10 cent., 5 cent. Fine. 5 pieces.

### Republics and Empire. Copper.

639 Republic. 1791. L. au 5 and 8 de la Liberté. Un decime, cinq centimes, and 2 sols. Varieties. Very fine. 5 pieces.
640 —— Similar. Not as fine. 8 pieces.
641 Anvers. Obsidional. 1814.
642 Napoleon I. Un decime. 1815. N. under a crown. Varieties. Some very fine. 5 pieces.
643 Napoleon II. 1816. "10 centime Empire Francais." With head of young Napoleon bare. A pattern. Proof. Very rare.
644 Medail di Confiance-Monneron. 1791. For five and two sols. One splendid proof. 2 pieces.
645 —— Another pair. One fine proof. 2 pieces.
646 Republic. 1848. Pattern for 10 centimes; obv. head of Liberty. Bright. Rare.
647 —— Pattern for 3 centimes, by *Rogat*. Bright. Extremely rare.
648 —— 1791. Monneron. One proof. 2 pieces.
649 Napoleon III. Dix and cinq centimes. 4 pieces.
650 —— Two and one do. Bright. 2 pieces.
651 —— Liards, tournoises, centimes, etc. 24 pieces.

## Coins of France.

### Méreaux and Jetons.  Copper.

*Mereaux*, like Jetons, have a historical value, both bearing legends and armorial devices true to the time and place of their issue, but the former had originally a *monetary* value, and were hardly distinguished from coins.

652 MÉREAUX of the 15th and 16th centuries, with remarkable devices and mottoes, many portraits, the metal brass or copper, sometimes a mixture of both, from size 12 to 20. *All fine*, some patinated.   20 pieces.
653 —— Similar.   20 pieces.
654 —— Similar. Equally fine.   20 pieces.
655 —— Selected. Extra fine.   20 pieces.

The Abbe Barthelemy, in a history of the coins of Europe, from the time of Charles the Great, urges the importance of these tokens, and gives the only account of them that I have met with. They are entirely distinct from Jetons both in their nature and use. They have occasionally found their way into our collections, under the name of "Abbey pieces;" but many of the pieces, properly so-called, are legitimate COINS, examples of which are not wanting in this collection.

656 JETONS. Extremely fine. Thicker than the Méreaux. Many equal to the finest medals. From size 16 to 22.   10 pieces
657 —— Similar. Equally fine. Smaller.   10 "
658 —— Others. Good lot.   20 "
659 —— Another lot. Similar.   20 "
660 —— Large and small. Some fine.   50 "
661 —— Selected. Fine.   10 "
662 —— Similar lot.   10 "
663 —— do.   20 "
664 —— Miscellaneous. Some poor.   30 "

### Spiel Markes and Tokens.  Copper, Brass, and Iron.

665 SPIEL MARKES. No duplicates. All fine.   10 pieces
666 —— With busts. Very fine.   10 "
667 —— Miscellaneous.   23 "

668 TOKENS (nearly all French). Each deserving a separate description. Some satirical, *e.g.*, Maria Theresa; some with busts, *e.g.*, Jenny Lind; others relating to America, unknown to our collectors. An interesting lot. Without duplicates. 20 pieces
669 —— Almost as fine as last. Busts of Napoleon, Kossuth, Haydn, Handel, etc. 20 pieces

### Medalets. Copper and Brass.

670 RELIGIOUS. Small, with loops; brass-plated. 4 pieces
671 —— Very small. Fine silver. 3 "
672 PERSONAL. Prince and Princess Imp. Eugenie; Napoleon III. and young Pr. Imp. Duvivier, etc. All with loops. Brass. Fine. Size 15. 10 pieces
673 NAPOLEON I. Rev. his tomb, tin; with one in copper, representing him as "General Buonoparte." Fine and rare. Size 15 and 20. 2 pieces
674 —— Obv. bust, VIGILAT QVIESCANT; in exergue, "Bounaparte Prem. Consul;" rev. within laurel wreath, monogram; copper; with one in tin, representing him as the "Liberator of Egypt." Extremely fine and rare medals. Size 21. 2 pieces
675 "LA FIN DU DESPOTISME." Hercules breaking sceptre; rev. a pyramid. 1792. Copper. Fine proof. Size 21
676 LOUIS XV. and his Queen. Their busts vis a vis; rev. a bundle of arrows. Copper. Uncirculated. Size 20
677 DUC DE ORLEANS. His bust and tomb, by *Borrel*. Henry V., King of France, and Charles X., by *Montagny*. Extra fine medalets. Copper. 3 pieces
678 PERSONAL. Rubens, Cavignac, F. Phillipe, L. Napoleon, etc.; one representing the latter in a Prussian helmet (engraved by a profane hand on an imperial coin). A fine and rare lot. 7 pieces

### War Medals.

679 NAPOLEON, from St. Helena to his companion in glory, with original ribbon. Ex. fine. Copper.
680 —— The same, without ribbon. Ex. fine.
681 —— Triplicate. Very fine.

682 NAPOLEON III. Campaign of Italy, with loop. A fine silver medal, executed by *Burre.* 1859.
683 —— Expedition to China. 1860. Uniform with last. Silver.
684 —— Expedition to Mexico. 1862–1863. Same series. *Very rare.* Silver.
685 —— Obv. bust; rev. " Valeur et Discipline;" enamelled set in wreath and surmounted by an imperial eagle, the latter gilt. A fine medal of solid silver. Rare.
686 —— Duplicate of No. 682 (Italian Campaign).
687 —— Duplicate of No. 684 (Ex. to Mexico). *Very rare.*
688 —— Obv. female bust, " To Religion and Country," French; rev. Minerva, with an infant child, trampling on a dragon. Silver. Very fine. Size 15

*Bronze Medals.*

689 HENRY II. Bust laureated; rev. Victory driving four horses abreast, LAVRO ET FAMA, etc. Old medal, once gilt. Fine and rare. Size 32
690 LOUIS XVIII. Obv. a King, crowned and royally dressed, sitting in a chair, supported by lions; the area filled with lilies, a border of crowns and fleur-de-lis running round the circumference; rev. arms and crown of France. Brass-plated. Size 80 (or 5 inches). By *Beranger* and *Tiolier.* One of the most magnificent medals ever made. Rare and valuable.
691 CAROLUS. Decimus Francorum Rex; rev. crown. Old medal. Proof. Size 28
692 SERIES, uniform in style, bearing the busts of eminent Frenchmen. The dies executed by *CAQVE, VIVIER, PETIT, GATTEAVX, SALMSON, VEVRAT, DEPAVLIS, CAVNOIS,* and *BARRE.* All Proof. Size 25. 54 pieces
693 J. E. DUPONT, Gen. Foy, Garnier Pages, L. M. De Lescure, Alex. Bixio, F. Mazois. All strictly fine. Size 32. 6 pieces
694 NAPOLEON III. and the Emperor and Empress, with reverses of the Exhibition of Industry. Two very fine medals, by Caque. Size 32

## Coins of France.

695 J. B. Cant, C. M. Artus, and Car. Ferd. Ex. Atrebate, etc. All fine. Size 32. 3 pieces
696 "I. Vieux, Henri QVATRE SECOND;" rev. Henry IV. Two fine busts. Size 30
697 Lafayette. Deput. A. L'Ass. Nat., etc. 1775. Fine and rare medal, by *Dumarest*. Proof. Size 22
698 J. J. Rosseau. In same style.
699 Exhibition Prize Medals. Busts of Napoleon and Eugenie. Size 23. 3 pieces

*Medals, Medalets, and Jetons. Silver.*

700 Louis XIII. Obv. young bust in crown and royal robes; rev. the city of Rheims; a dove descending. Looks like the work of ·T. Simon. Extremely fine. Size 24
701 —— Obv. bust; rev. Rheims, hand holding a bottle above the city. Size 19
702 Louis XIV. Obv. bust; rev. view of water-works, "Payeurs des Rentes, 1709." Very fine. Size 20
703 Louis XVI. Obv. crowned bust, by *Du Vivier*; rev. a tomb, the King kneeling beside it, Religion pouring balm on his head. Ex. fine. Size 24
704 —— Bare bust, in royal dress; rev. the holy dove, "Ordre et Melice Du Saint Esprit." Octagon, proof. Size 22
705 —— Obv. bust by *Droz*; rev. two shields under a crown, cherub below. Ex. fine. Size 16
706 Louis, son of Louis XVI., born March 27, 1785. Bust of young Prince, by *Looz*; rev. Angel making a record on a tablet. Splendid proof. Size 20
707 Louis XVI. and Marie Antoinette. Their busts conjoined, crowned with palms. MÆRTYRER DURCH-UNGE HUER. IHRES VOLKS; rev. execution of the King of France by the guillotine. Upwards of 100 figures and heads wonderfully executed. In ex. D 20. JANUAR. D 16. Octob. 1793. A grand medal, and *very rare*. Size 22

## Medalets and Jetons. Silver.

708 ANNA. DG FR ET NAV REG. 1690. Fine. Size 18
709 —— ET. CAROLVS. 1744. Betrothal Medal. SPONSI. Extremely fine. Size 18
710 NAPOLEON. Obv. laureated bust by Droz; rev. the Emperor presenting a standard to the army. Splendid proof. Size 17
711 —— Obv. same; rev. the Emperor upheld by two men. " Le senat et le peuple." Size 17
712 —— Conquest of Egypt. Obv. Pyramid; rev. the Nile personified. Fair. Size 22
713 —— Medalets with his bust alone and with M. Thiers and Louis Philippe. Extra fine, small. 4 pieces
714 MEDALETS. Louis XVIII. on rev. of Henry IV., Duke and Duchess de Barry, Destruction of the Bastile, and Religious Token. All beautiful. 4 pieces
715 —— Henry IV., and Louis XVIII., and birth of the Count de Paris. Extra fine. 2 pieces
716 GREEK Medal. Obv. female bust. ΕΛΙΣΑ ΣΕΒΑΣΤΟΥ ΑΔΕΑΦΗ; rev. VIA DA LVCCA A PISA. Naked woman recumbent, supporting a wheel. Very fine. Size 15
717 PHILIPPE. Joseph Egalite Ci devant Duc D'Orleans. Bust; rev. ins. Fine, very rare. Size 15
718 JETON. " Maison Phil Anthropique de Paris;" rev. section of zodiac, Leo in the ascendant, a hand pouring water from the sky. 1781. Size 20
719 —— Louis XV. LAWFELT. 1747. Size 20
720 —— Louis XVI. A monster with seven heads holding balance and sword. SNITRACHT. 1793. Size 18
721 —— " Joanne Merlet Decane;" rev. 3 cranes under a meridian sun. 1646. Size 20
722 —— A hand applying a pruning knife to a garden of lilies. Size 20
723 —— A hand holding a wreath on the point of a naked sword. Size 20
724 —— A man supporting the pillars of Hercules? 1572. Size 20
725 —— Two towers united by a chain, the sea all around. 1629. Size 20
726 —— " Liberte Reconquese par les Francais. July, 1830. Fine proof. Size 20
727 —— Very pretty jetons. Old; size 16. 3 pieces

## COINS OF PORTUGAL.

### Silver.

728 JOHN. 1814. 400 Reis. Cross, motto, and arms. Very fine.
729 —— 1816. 400 Reis. Cross, motto, and arms. Very fine.
730 —— 1819. 960 Reis. Cross covered by globe, with arms of Portugal. Fair.
731 Two Macutas (one-eighth doll.) for Africa. 1733. Rare.
732 PETER V. 1854. 100 Reis (dime). Very fine.
733 —— 1857. 500 Reis (half-doll.)
734 —— 1861. 50 Reis (5 cts.) Very fine.
735 LOUIS I. 1862. 200 Reis. Fine.
736 —— 1867. 500 Reis. Uncirculated.
737 —— 1870. 500 Reis. Nearly uncirculated.
738 JOHN V. One Real.

### Copper.

739 SEBASTIAN I. 1557. Obv. arms; rev. large V. Fine.
740 PHILIP? 16—. Bust; rev. flaming cross, "In hoc," etc. Rare.
741 MARIA I. and Peter III. 1779. Their busts. Rare medal. Size 30
742 JOHN V., and Joseph I., and Maria II. 1748 to 1853. Copper of various denominations, with two weights (moidor and half do). Fine. 13 pieces

## COINS OF SPAIN.

### Silver.

743 ALFONSO I. 1166 to 1196. Obv. head crowned (profile); rev. long cross, annulets, and pellets. Very fine groat.
744 —— Penny. Same type, has been gilt. Rare.
745 JACOB I. 1213 to 1276. Aragon. Rude bust, in profile, crowned; rev. cross. Uncirculated, very rare.
746 —— Barcelona. Head; rev. cross. Rare penny, base. In good preservation.

## Coins of Spain. 45

747 PENNY of Aragon. Pillars of Hercules and golden fleece.
748 FERDINAND the Catholic, and Isabella. 1479 to 1516. FERDINANDVS ET HELISABET. Arms crowned; rev. REX ET REGIN CAST LEGIO ARAGO SI. Quarter-dollar size. Pierced, not rubbed. Very rare.
749 —— Same. Fine, but clipped.
750 —— Others. Badly clipped. 2 pieces
751 JOHN and CHARLES. 1555. (Charles I. of Spain, and 5th of Germany.) Quarter-dollar size. Fine, rare.
752 CHARLES and JOHN. 1555. Same as last (reversed on coin.) For Aragon. Pierced. Same size.
753 FERDINAND the Catholic. For Barcelona. Quarter-dollar size. Rare.
754 PHILIP and ISABEL (son of Charles V.) Their busts, face to face, a crown above; rev. peacock and caduceus. "Concera." Groat in style of Philip and Mary of England. Rare.
755 PHILIP II. Obv. bare bust of Philip (husband of Mary of England); 1573; rev. coat-of-arms and crown; ADIVTOR DOMINVS MIHI. Barely circulated and rare crown.
756 —— Crown without his bust; 1592. Rev. St. Andrew's cross with crown (for Brabant). Fine and rare.
757 —— Piece of two Reals. Same type; 1568. Fine.
758 —— Piece of two Reals *with* his bust. Very good.
759 —— Piece of four Reals with his bust. Fair.
760 PHILIP III. 1598 to 1621. With his bust (one in high ruff). Two pieces of about two Reals each. Nearly uncirculated. Rare.
760*—— For Barcelona. Bust, front face. Rev. arms; real.
761 —— Piece of one real. Rev. PAX ET LIBERTAS; a tree bearing a crown; one of Philip II. and others, a lot of rare Reals. 4 pieces
762 CHARLES II. (for Brabant). Extremely fine crown of 1694; two C's interlinked; edge ingrailed. Extremely rare.
763 —— Medalet. Real size. Obv. bust three-quarter face; rev. tower. Splendid, rare.

## Coins of Spain.

764 PHILIP V. (of Anjou). 1700 to 1746. Medal of two Reals. Obv. bust; 1702; rev. sun rising over landscape; RERVM HINC NASCITVR ORDO. Fine.

765 —— Pieces of two Reals. 2 pieces

766 CHARLES III. 1759 to 1788. Bust in long wig. Rev. a tree, a bird standing on the top; 1760. Piece of three Reals, pierced, but fine (has nearly the same obv. as the "Florida Piece.")

767 —— Pieces of 4, 2, and 1 Reals (scarce variety of 2 reals, one of Ferdinand VI. Rare). 5 pieces

768 —— Medal. Obv. ship; FELIX EXCITVS; rev. ins. in 12 lines. Two reals value. Extremely fine.

769 CHARLES III. 1788 to 1808. Dollar, counter-stamped with arms of Portugal. Fine.

770 —— Quarter and Sixteenth Dollar. Fine. 3 pieces

771 JOSEPH NAPOLEON. 1808 to 1814. Dollar of twenty Reals; 1809. Slightly rubbed, but seldom found strictly fine. Rare.

772 —— Piece of 4 Reals. Same type, and one do. counter-stamped. 2 pieces

773 FERDINAND VII. 1814 to 1833. Piece of two reals; young bust laureated; 1811. Rare.

774 —— One real. Rev. arms crowned between the pillars of Hercules. Very fine.

775 —— Piece of 10 Reals. Bare bust. Rev. "Reselado." Uncirculated. Rare.

776 —— Piece of 4 Reals. Plain shield under a crown; 1823. Nearly proof. Rare.

777 —— Peseta (1-20th Dollar) of Barcelona. 1813. Quarter Dollar, duplicate of last. 3 pieces

778 —— One-Sixteenth Dollar. 1811. Uncirculared.

NOTE.—The unit of Spanish money—the Real—is of three values. The first is one-eighth of a dollar, and is always used in Spanish-American countries. The second is one-tenth of a dollar; and the third and last, and the kind generally used in Spain proper, one-twentieth of a dollar; hence the pieces described above as 10 and 4 Reals, are of the value of half and quarter of a dollar.

FERDINAND VII. Gerona. Siege Dollar. FER VII. in punch-mark; rude milling, G N A—1808. UN-DURO; rude milling around edge, also milled. Very fine and rare.

—— Catalonia. Siege Dollar. At top 30 S.; at bottom 1808; rev. arms, edge and rim milled. Extremely fine and rare.

—— Same. Siege Dollar. At top 5 Ps. (5 Pesetas); at bottom 1809. Rev. arms; elaborate border on both sides, and milled edge. Extremely fine and rare.

—— Barcelona. Siege Dollar. 5 PESETAS; 1813. Rev. arms; fine oak wreath. Uncirculated. Rare.

—— Same. Siege Dollar. At top 1821; at bottom 30 SOVS. Rev. diamond-shaped shield; SALUS POPULI; border and edge reeded. Extremely fine and rare.

—— Duplicate of above, except that the shield is not, as before, in the centre of the coin. Equally fine and rare Dollar.

—— Valencia Siege Piece. Obv. bust, head bare; rev. diamond-shaped shield crowned, letter L, to r. and l.; 4 Reals. Struck in tin; proof. Excessively rare; 1809.

ISABELLA II. 1833 to ——. 1 Peseta of Catalonia, 1836, and Proclamation Quarter struck at Madrid, 1833. Both fine. Same size.     2 pieces

—— With her bust, each. "4 Reals," and "200 Reis." Extremely fine coins (Quarter-Dollar size).   2 pieces

—— Two and one Reals. Very fine and rare old Penny of Alfonso Rex.     3 pieces

—— War Medal of 1860. Beautiful proof of this rare piece. Small medal on a cross; has the original loop.

REPUBLIC Dollar of 1870. Obv. Spain seated; rev. arms; "5 Pesetas." Fine.

—— Two and one Pesetas. Fine.     2 pieces

AMADEUS I. 1871. Dollar. Obv. his bust bare; rev. arms; 5 Pesetas. Fine and rare.

—— Duplicate Dollar. Fine.

Two Pesetas of the Republic. 1869. Fair.

## Copper.

795 COINS prior to the time of Charles I. (5th). 1555. In good preservation; others of his time and some belonging to the Provinces of later date. All rare. Desirable. 12 pieces

796 PHILIP II. 1556 to 1598. 7 pieces

797 PHILIP III. 1598 to 1621. With the arms of Spain (Lion and castle). Beautiful. Uncirculated. Size 18

798 —— Various designs and sizes. 6 pieces

799 PHILIP IV. 1621 to 1665. Select and extremely fine lot (variety). 6 pieces

800 FERDINAND V. Coin 1710. Very rare.

801 CHARLES II. 1665 to 1700. On one side coat-of-arms; on rev. shields arranged in the form of a cross; 1693. Fine and rare.

802 —— Others. On rev. R. M. Rare. 2 pieces

803 CHARLES III. —— to 1788. Suite from size 7 to 16. Good coins. 4 pieces

804 CHARLES IV. 1788 to 1808. Dollar in brass (1792), and Copper coin. 2 pieces

805 FERDINAND VII. (1808). 1814 to 1833. 4 pieces.

806 ISABELLA. 1833. A variety of her coins for Spain proper and the provinces. Some very fine and rare. Eg "Medio Real, Cinco Decimas." No duplicates. 5 pieces.

807 —— With older coins. Rare lot. 11 pieces.

808 REPUBLIC. 1870. "Diez Granos," "Cinco," "Dos," and "Un Granos." Uncirculated. 5 pieces.

809 BARCELONA and Catalonia. Very fine. 6 pieces.

810 JETONS and money weights, with busts of old kings, and elaborate arms. An extremely interesting lot. 10 pieces.

811 —— Fine lot, 200 years old; in good and fine preservation. 9 pieces.

812 MEDAL of Philip II. Bust within two circles, with date (1567) below; rev. garnished coat-of-arms within circle of 18 shields, beaded border on both sides. Equal in

*Coins of Switzerland.—Silver.*

quality of work to any medal of the period that I remember to have seen. In splendid preservation.
Size 30

813 MEDAL OF CHARLES XI. 1716. Obv. bust in rich dress; rev. the world in a car, 3 crowns above. A gem.
Size 16

814 —— of the Emperor Charles V., from the series Numismatica, by Gayrard. Fine proof. Size 24

815 —— Charles III. (of Spain). 1705. Barcelona. Struck in tin. Size 26

816 —— Isabella (Bilboa). 1836. Proof. Size 26

*Gold. (Portugal and Spain.)*

817 JOHN V. 1706 to 1750. 400 Reis. 1-32 doubloon.
2 pieces.
818 —— Sixteenth doubloon. 1731-36-47. 4 pieces.
819 JOSEPH I. 1750 to 1777. Sixteenth doubloon.
820 PHILIP V. (Spain). Dollar. 1743.
821 CHARLES III. (Spain). Dollar. 1763.
822 —— do do 1786.
823 FERDINAND VII. (Spain). Dollar. 1817.
824 ISABELLA II. (Spain). Proclamation dollar. 1833.
825 —— do Uncirculated.
826 —— Dollar. 1861-64. 2 pieces.

## COINS OF SWITZERLAND.

*Silver.*

827 ARGAU. 20 Batzen. 1809. Tell seated. Half-dollar size. Very fine. Nearly proof.
828 —— 5 Batz. 1815. Extra fine.
829 —— 1 Batz, 5 rappen, and 5 batzen. Base. Not worn.
4 pieces.
830 APPENZELL. 1 rappen, 1 pfenning, 1 kreutzer, ½ batzen, 1 batzen, with the arms of the Canton—a bear erect.
8 pieces.

## Coins of Switzerland.—Silver.

831 BERNE. A collection of batzen and rappen, going back to the Bracteates of the 14th century. Generally fine. All legible. 18 pieces.

832 —— Varieties of one and five batzen. 3 pieces.

833 —— One franc. 1811. Tell standing, "XIX. Canton" on his shield; rev. arms of the Canton (a bear on a bend or, proper). Fine.

834 —— One franc. Artisan at work. Rare.

835 —— Quarter and half dollar. 1796. 2 pieces.

836 —— Five francs for shooting festival in 1857. Appropriate devices. Rich work, and in very fine condition. Rare.

837 BASEL. 1-6 thaler, 3 batzen, and 1 batzen. 5 pieces.

838 —— Episcopal, 20 kreutzers of John Conrad (1716), and 5 batzen of the Canton. 2 pieces.

839 —— Fine silver coin. 1633. Half-thaler.

840 —— Thaler. 1765. Rev. arms of Basel, supported by a cockatrice. "Domine Conserva nos in pace." Value, 84 cents.

841 —— Crown. The City of Basel; above are 8 small shields in an arch, and on a scroll "Basilea," in Ex., 1743, and cornucopia; rev. same as last—the edge lettered. Uncirculated.

842 —— Crown of the City. 1736. Nearly proof.

843 BEDA. 20 batz (half Ecu.); rev. "S. Gallus Abbas." Bear upright before the saint seated. 1774. Rare.

844 BRACTATES. A pretty lot. 4 pieces.

845 CHUR, both Episcopal and of the Canton. Fine and rare lot. No duplicates. From 1652. 10 pieces.

846 —— 10 batzen. 1634 (¼ Ecu), and 3 batzen of Charles VI.; rev. S. Lucius. Rare coins. 2 pieces.

847 FREIBURG. Varieties of the Canton. Base. 7 pieces.

848 GENEVA. A collection of base coins. Many varieties. 12 pieces.

849 —— Selection. Bright and uncirculated. From 1735. With the arms of the Canton. A demi-eagle and key on a divided shield. Beautiful. "Un Sol, Six D, 10 D, etc. No duplicates. 9 pieces.

850 —— Crown. 1723. Good.

851 GRAUBUNDEN (Grisons). 10 batzen (¼ Ecu). 1825. Pierced, but very rare.
852 —— Others of the Grisons. Rare. 7 pieces.
853 GLARUS. 1 schilling, 3 rappen. 1809. Rev. a shield draped with laurel. The device, a saint with staff and book. Others, 3 schillings, arms differently treated. Rare. 3 pieces.
854 HELVETIA. Varieties of the base coins of the Canton, from 1799. Two batzen, 1 rappen, and 5 centimes. Nickel. 8 pieces.
855 —— Republic of 1801. Obv. a plumed soldier carrying a banner; rev. "4 Franken." Dollar size. Very fine.
856 —— Under the Constitution of 1848. 5 francs. The Canton personified as a woman (Ceres) seated. Very fine.
857 —— 1863, July. "Tir federal a la Chaux-de-Fondes." 5 francs. Fine proof. Extremely rare.
858 —— Two and ½ franc. 1850. Fine. 2 pieces.
859 LUCERNE. Varieties of the base money of the Canton. One with "Sanctus Leodegario." Good coins. 10 pieces.
860 —— Half Ecu of Saint Leodegardus. 1623. His bust to the waist. Fair.
861 —— Square Medalet to Commemorate an Eccl. Council in 1633. Rare.
862 —— "5 Batzen," and "one-eighth" Ecu (same value). Fine. 2 pieces
863 —— 4 Francs. Soldier standing, supporting shield. "XIX Canton;" rev. arms of Lucerne under a crown. Oval shield, half plain, half in pales. 1814. Fine, rare.
864 NEUFCHATEL. Half-batzen. 1808. Arms of the Canton and of France crowned. "Alexandre Pr a Duc de Neufcha." With many other varieties. 13 pieces
865 —— Half-franc of the Duke de Longueville, with his bust. Pierced and poor. Rare.
866 NIDWALDEN. Schutzenfest, Crown of. 1861. Cross on a blazing sun; rev. "Arnold Winkelried," man with

## Coins of Switzerland.—Silver.

  club standing over two men prostrate, by Bovy. Uncirculated.
867 NIDWALDEN. Duplicate.
868 SCHUTZENFEST Crown by same hand. "Kanton Schwyz," lion guarding a shield with cross. Fine, rare.
869 SCHWYZ. From 16th Century. Rappen, batzen, etc., base coins; on the reverses half-length figure of Saint Martin. Rare.    8 pieces
870 SCHAFFHAUSEN, Crown of. 1621. A ram leaping out of an open door. In good preservation. Very rare.
871 —— Two small coins. Fine.    2 pieces
872 SITTEN. "Francis Joseph Supersaxo," 1701 to 1744, with two coats-of-arms. Rare. Base coins well preserved.    4 pieces
873 —— Francis Frederick. 1760 to 1780. Very remarkable devices. Base.    3 pieces
874 SOLOTHURN. Rev. "Sanctus Ursus," his bust. Without date. Old, very fine and rare. One-third crown.
875 —— Double denarius. Batzen and rappen. Fine.    10 pieces
876 TESSIN. "1 Quarto Franco." Very fine, rare.
877. —— Base coins. "Canton Ticino."    2 pieces
878 ST. GALLEN. Batzen and 5 Batzen. Fine.    4 pieces
879 SUITENSIS (?) X Schilling. 1786. Fine, rare.
880 THURGAU. 1 Batzen, half-Batzen, 1 Kreutzer, etc. Base. Well preserved.    5 pieces
881 TIGURINLÆ. Rare crown of 1647. "Domine Conservanos in pace." Two shields supported by lions. Fine.
882 —— "Pro Deo Et Patria." 811. 110 batzen, and 3 smaller base coins.    4 pieces
883 —— Obsidional. Square Coin 1717. "S P Q T Lehr Gibt E II R." Half-dollar size. Very fine, rare.
See Canton Zurich.
884 TURICENSIS. Crown of 1790; obv. Town and mole; rev. Arms. Extremely fine, rare.
885 TELL Medal. Dollar size. Obv. 3 Swiss patriots striking hands; rev. 20 Shields with arms of the Cantons. A.D. 1296. An original and very old medal. Silver gilt. Fine and rare.

*Coins of Switzerland.—Silver.* 53

886 UNTERWALDEN. Twenty kreutzers, half-batzen and rappen. 4 pieces
887 URI. Batzen and half-batzen, bull's head, front face. 2 pieces
888 VAUD. 5 batzen. Uncirculated.
889 —— 10 batzen, 1 batzen, two and a half rappen, 1 rappen. Base. 5 pieces
890 WALLIS. (Very rare). 3 coins.
891 ZUG. (Under the patronage of St. Wolfgang). 6 krs. (Arms Tugensis). Rappen and two-and-a-half rappen. Rare. 3 pieces
892 ZURICH. Bracteate. 14th Century, and small base coins. "3 Heller," "2 Rappen," and 5 Batzen of 1623. Rare. 4 pieces
893 —— Beautiful medal with loop, boy holding an apple pierced by an arrow. "Ub aug un hand, furs vaterland;" rev. Arms of the Canton. Proof. Size 16
894 —— Shooting Feast. 5 Francs of 1872. Fine.
895 —— Crown (40 Batz). 1813. Very fine piece.
  These pieces and the coins of Tigurinæ belong to the same Canton but I have catalogued them according to the inscriptions on the coins.

896 UNCLASSIFIED. Religious medal, baptismal scene, with loop. Large and extremely fine silver medal. Size 28
897 —— Medal with representation of St. Michael slaying the dragon; rev. Coat-of-arms with plumed helmet for crest. BERO COM DE LENZBVRG FVND ECCL BER. A medal of Bero Munster in the Canton Argau. Very fine. Size 24
898 —— Another fine proof. Size 22
  See Wellenheim, No. 5,711.

899 —— Dollar of the Canton Chur. 1689. Fine, rare.
900 —— "Moneta Nova Tugi." Half-crown, 1609. Half-length figure of St. Oswald. Another, same type, 1612. Same size. Varieties. Fine and rare. 2 pieces
901 —— Coins of the Canton Neufchatel. 1696 and 1713. Quarter-dollar size. 2 pieces
902 —— 21 Batzen (Thaler) of Fred. Will. III. of Prussia. 1799. Money of the same Canton. Rare.

## COINS OF ITALY.
### Silver.

903 PENNY. SENAVETVS, in centre letter S; rev. Cross. Extra fine.

904 —— Otho. Without date. OTTO IMPERATOR. St. Peter standing. SANTVS PETRVS. Fine and rare.

905 —— Francis Donatus. Without date. Crowned and bearded bust, front face S. DONATVS; rev. Cross. DEARITIO. Superb. Very rare.

<small>These Italian pennies are of Mediæval date, as shown by their workmanship, resembling those of the era of Charlemagne.</small>

906 PENNIES of later date, still very old. The latest one of Philip III. (Sicily). 1654. A double denarius. A rare lot.     6 pieces

907 ANCONA. Double denarius St. SO VIRIACVS full length; rev. Cross. Fine and rare.

908 GROAT. King seated with sceptre, globe and cross, two lions guarding; rev. Coat-of-arms. Without date. Fine.

909 PARMA. Similar. S. Hilarius standing. Otho Farnesi, 1556. Has been gilt. Fine and rare.

910 ARAGON (Sicily.) Groat, without date; Philip I. (1598); obv. arms; rev. eagle. Rare.

911 LOMBARDO Venetian K<sup>n</sup> *Azo Visconti*, Doge, 1328 to 1339; billon money; groat size. Well. 2,751. Rare.

912 —— Peter Gradonigo, Doge, 1290 to 1314; splendid double denarius; obv. Christ seated; rev. two figures standing, between them a cross. Well. 2,981. Rare.

913 —— Duplicate; clipped.

914 —— John Mocenigo, Doge, 1477 to 1485; extremely fine groat; Christ seated; rev. Virgin and another figure standing; inscription in the Byzantine manner. Rare.

915 —— Leonardus Lauredanus, Doge, 1501 to 1521; double denarius, pierced; similar to last. Rare.

## Coins of Italy.—Silver.

916 LOMBARDO. Laurent Priolus, Doge, 1556 to 1559; small coin. half denarius. Very fine. Well. 3,097.

917 —— Hieron Priolus, Doge, 1559 to 1567; extra fine denarius. Same style (with the Virgin.) Well. 3,100. Rare.

918 —— John Cornaro, Doge, 1709 to 1722; obv. figure seated; rev. winged lion. Well. 3,221; denarius; fine, and another in good preservation. 2 pieces

919 PADUA. Jacob von Carrara, 1350 to 1355; denarius; King standing; rev. cross and pellets. Extremely fine, rare. Well. 3,546.

920 VERONA. John Valerius Visconti, 1387 to 1402; uncirculated denarius; dragon; rev. cross. Well. 3,614,

921 —— Another penny; different.

922 MODENA. Louis XIV. (France); with his bust; base coin; groat size.

923 PISA. Cosmus III., 1670 to 1723; obv. Madonna; rev. "Aspice Pisis," a cross. Well. 3,975. Denarius, fine and rare.

924 SICILY. Charles I. of Anjou, 1266; obv. Virgin and angel; rev. arms, with lilies. Groat, in splendid preservation. Well. 4,968. Rare.

925 NAPLES. Ferdinand I., 1458. Extremely fine groat; bust crowned; rev. cross. Well. 5,037. Rare.

926 GENOA. Conrad II., 1577; ⅛ scudo. Well. 2,632. Rare.

927 —— Girolamo Defranchi, 1653, and Lorenzo Centavioni, 1713; Virgin seated, holding sceptre and infant Jesus; rev. cross, VIII Baiocchi. Extremely fine, little coins.
2 pieces.

928 —— Modern coins. 10 soldi and others. 4 pieces.

929 MAILAND (Milan), Republic, 1260; obv. cross with crescents in angles, MEDIOLNVM; rev. St. Ambrose seated. Very fine and rare coin; double denarius. Well. 2,749.

930 —— Maria Sforza, 1466-76; obv. bust; rev. winged dragon, and shield with dragon. A very remarkable, rare, and fine coin of the value of ½ crown. Madai 4,507.

## Coins of Italy.—Silver.

931 MAILAND. Duplicate. Also very fine.
932 —— Francis II., 1521; rev. St. Ambrose seated, &c. Fine and rare. 3 pieces.
933 MALTA. Emanuel Rohan. 1 tari, 1777. Fine.
934 MONTFERRAT. William VII., 1493 to 1518. Bust with cap: rev. coat-of-arms. ½ crown; fine and rare.
935 Duplicate. Fine.
936 GROATS; obv. Madonna and Christ, PRO N. P. M. ORA.; rev. JO–S. DEARA. CO. COTI. PISAVRI. D. Extremely fine. Bust, full face and crown, SANCTVS VOLTVS; rev. arms of Sucensis. Quarter-dollar of Charles II., of Spain, for Naples; FER. I., Parma (1794); Charles III., Sicily; and others of uniform size. Very good. 14 pieces.
937 ROME. Sixtus IV. and Sixtus V., half-scudi; rev. lion with banner. 2 pieces.
938 —— Clement XI., Benedict XIV., and other Papal and Italian coins. Ordinary. Several old and rare pennies, value 6 cts. 12 pieces.
939 —— Benedict XIV., Pius VII., and Gregory X. Extremely fine. 10 baiocchi, &c. 3 pieces.
940 —— Pius IX. "20 baiocchi," "1 lira," "10 baiocchi," "10 soldi," and "5 soldi." Uncirculated. 5 pieces.
941 —— Republic of 1849. "40 baiocchi," 16 do., 8 do., and 4 do. Uncirculated. These have an eagle displayed, standing on a fasces within oak wreath, and the denomination, date, and "Republica Romana" on the reverse. This is a fine set and rare. 4 pieces.
942 —— Miscellaneous. Half-scudi, lira, and smaller. 6 pieces
943 FERRARA. Paul and half-Paul of Clement XI., 1709; rev. St. Maurell standing. Extra fine. 2 pieces.
944 MANTUA. 1702. Obv. bridled horse running; rev. bonfire. Fine and extra rare half-Paul.
945 VENICE. Old groat, broken, and 15 soldi of the provisional governmet of 1848; also old penny of 1722. All uncommon. 4 pieces
946 PARMA and Lucca. 10 soldi, 1815, do. of 1833, do. 1855. Fine. 3 pieces.

## Coins of Italy.—Silver. 57

947 SARDINIA, Sicily, and other States. "10 soldi," "50 centimes," "10 granas," &c. Extra fine, and two medalets with loops. A valuable lot. About dime size.
10 pieces.

948 ITALY (Napoleon.) 10 soldi, 5 do., and 10 centimes. Extremely fine. Rare. 3 pieces.

<small>The fine collection of crowns, under this head, have been reserved for this place, although in some instances, necessitating a repetition of titles.</small>

949 ALOYSIUS CONTARENUS, Doge of Venice, 1676 to 1684. Broad half-crown (size 23); obv. St. Mark, with the Doge kneeling before him holding a banner with the lion of St. Mark on cross staff; rev. inscription and date, 1683.
<small>A cabinet piece. Uncirculated. Excessively rare.</small>

950 SIMILAR half-crown. On reverse a figure standing, guarded by a lion. Very fine. Equally rare.

951 GENOA. Broad crown of the Republic, 1676; obv. a cross with lilies in the angles, above each a winged cherub, "Dux E Gubernatores Reip Gen;" rev. Madonna and Jesus on a cloud. Very fine and rare.
Size 35.

952 TUSCANY. Cosmus III., 1685, "Dux Etruriæ," crowned bust; rev. a fortified harbor in which are ships, &c., PATET ET FAVET. Extremely fine and rare crown.
Size 27.

953 —— Another crown of Cosmus III., 1718; obv. coat-of-arms of the Medeci family (6 balls) under a crown; rev. a double rose tree. Equally fine and rare. Size 27.

954 —— Leopold I., 1787. Scudo; obv. bust undraped; rev. crowned shield with Arms of Austria, Lotharingia and Tuscany, with order chain of the golden fleece, and Star of Maria Therese. DIRIGE DOMINE CRESSVS MEOS. Very fair, rare.

955 —— Ferdinand III. 1799. Scudo; obv. undraped bust; rev. similar to last, except motto, which is LEX TVA VERITAS. Fine, rare.

## Coins of Italy.—Silver.

956 TUSCANY Charles Louis and Aloysia; bust of the former on the latter, which is diademed; rev. arms on a pointed shield, crowned and draped with the order chain and badge of the golden fleece. Mint mark, FLOR. Edge lettered, 1807, Double Thaler. *Extremely* fine, rare.

957 —— Another. Their busts vis a vis. Crown, 1807. Good.

958 PARMA. Odoardus Farnese, Duke. 1626; obv. his bust rev. St. Vitalis holding sceptre. "Scudo." In fair preservation. *Very* rare.

959 —— Another splendid Crown of Odoardus. 1629. Obv. his bust in high collar and ruff; rev. St. Antony with a banner. Uncirculated. Very rare.

960 —— Maria Lucia. 1815. Five Lire. Fine bust with diadem; rev. handsome coat-of-arms. Extremely fine.

961 NAPLES. Ferdinand and Maria. 1772. Their busts conjoined; rev. FECVNDITAS. Mother and infant child. Good scudo, rare.

962 —— Joachim Murat. King. 1810. 12 Carlini, (DODICI CARLINI), his bare curly head to *left*. Unusually fine and very rare.

962* —— Another of Murat. "Five Lire." 1813. Fine head to *right*. Uncirculated. Very rare.

963 SICILY. Ferdinand IV. 1787. Good scudo. 120 granas.

964 —— Ferdinand IV. and Caroline. 1791. Extremely fine crown with their busts conjoined; rev. "Soli reduci." A blazing sun and section of the zodiac. A globe below. Rare.

965 —— Ferdinand II. 1855. Scudo. 120 granas. Fine.

966 —— Frances II. 1859. Scudo. 120 granas. Uncirculated.

967 MALTA. F. Emanuel Pinto, Grand Master. XXX. Tari piece of 1757; obv. Arms of the Order of St. John of Jerusalem; rev. the Good Shepherd, with banner of the cross. Fine and rare Crown.

968 —— F. Emanuel de Rohan. 1781. Extremely fine, thirty Tari piece with his bust; rev. arms on a shield, backed by a crowned eagle. Very rare.

## Coins of Italy.—Silver.

960 MALTA Another Dollar of Rohan. 1796. Different reverse. Very fine.

970 —— F. Ferdinandus Hompesch, M. M. 1798. Fine and rare XXX Tari Crown of he last of the Grand Masters; obv. bust to l.; rev. arms on an eagle displayed.

> The Knights of St. John were driven out of Malta in 1798 by Napoleon. The island which had been in their possession since 1522, when it was given to them by Charles V., of Naples, is now under the Crown of Great Britain.

971 ROME. Hugo and John. COMITES IN MONTFORT, under Ferdinand II. 1621. Uncirculated Crown. Very rare.

972 —— Urban VIII. 1623. Bust in rich robes and regalia. Below AN XII; rev. St. Michael slaying the dragon—the combat in the air. Well preserved and rare Scudo.

973 —— Alexander VII. 1663. Obv. St. Peter supporting Arms of the Popes; rev. man giving alms to a pauper with a wooden leg. Scudo, in good preservation, and very rare.

974 —— Clement X. 1675. Obv. Arms of Rome; rev. interior of a cathedral. A fine and rare Crown.

975 —— Clement XII. Oval medal. FRVSTRA VIGILAT QVI CVSTODIT. Very fine; size, 22x23.

976 —— Pius VI. 1778. Uncirculated Half-crown.

977 —— Gregory XVI. Half-crown. 50 Baiocchi. Ordinary.

978 —— Pius IX. Medal for the soldiers. PETRI SEDE; rev. "Victoria Qvæ vincit mundum Fides Nostra." A ring medal with cross in centre and clasp. Rare. Size 24

979 VENICE. Republic of 1848. "Five Lire." Winged Lion and open book on pedestal. Uncirculated. Rare.

980 BOLOGNA. Scudo. 1796. Obv. shield with arms quartered. "LIBERTAS," and cross repeated in alternate angles; rev. Virgin and child on a cloud above the city. Uncirculated. Extremely rare.

## Medals and Coins of Italy.—Copper.

981 RAGUSA. Scudo. 1793. Obv. female bust; rev. "Libertas." Edge milled. Fine and rare.

982 FRANCIS III. MUT. REG. MIR. DUX (?). 1739; rev. handsome coat-cf-arms. Fine Crown.

983 LUCCA. Republic. Scudo, 1747. Obv. Arms. LVCENSIS; rev. St. Martin on horseback, dividing his cloak with a beggar. Unusually fine for this rare Crown.

984 —— Felice and Elisa, their heads conjoined; rev. "Five Francs." Ordinary.

985 SARDINIA. Victor Emanuel. Five Lire, 1817.

986 SUB ALPINE GAUL. Five Francs of the year 9 of Liberty, (French Revolution). Splendid proof. Rare.

987 —— Same. Year 10. Circulated.

988 —— Mezzo Scudo. Same era. Year 7. Fine.

### Medals and Coins. Copper.

989 MEDALS illustrative of Roman History. The subjects—portraits, historical incidents, views, etc., etc.
Quintius Flaminius; rev. Liberty restored to Greece; Numa Pompilius; rev. Numa, giving laws to the Romans, year of Rome, 39. M. Tull. Cicero; rev. the Triumph of Eloquence, year of Rome, 688. Second Punic War. Conquest of Gaul. The Hortii and the Cureatii. Battle of Pharsalia, year of Rome, 706. Cæsar and his Fortune, etc. Executed in a grand style by Dassier. No duplicates. All uncirculated and in wrappers. Size 20.                52 pieces

990 —— Popes—one of Leo XII. in lead, with two busts in three-quarter face, between them a cross; (of the time). One of Paul III. Alexander I. Boniface I. John I. Silvester I. Leo II. Stephen I. Urban VI., etc. All old and sharp. About size 26, with one exception, bronze.                12 pieces

991 —— With loops. Devotional. Very fine. 8 pieces

992 —— Julianus Medices Magnus; Julius Ligvr, etc. In a very old style. Size 20.                2 pieces

993 ROGER I. Crusader. 1072 to 1101, (Count of Sicily); obv. a knight on horseback. ROGE-RIVS-Comes; rev. Madonna and child. Thick coin, very rare. Size 16

Medals and Coins of Italy.—Copper.

994 CRUSADERS' Coins. Small and irregular in shape; fine and interesting. Rare. One with R., for Raimond, Count of Tripoli, 1109 to 1122, generally with one or more crosses.  5 pieces

995 VENICE. Coins of the Doges. "Sanctus Marcus Venetus." Head and wings of a lion facing; sometimes head of the saint. Reverses, as " Armata et Morea," "Dalma et Alban," "Corfu, Cefalo, Zante." Representing Ludovico Manin, Paulus Rainerus, and many others. A most rare and desirable lot. Very fine.  6 pieces

996 —— Doge Alois Contarenus, 1676, and others. 17 pieces

997 —— Paulus Rainerus, 1779; rev. " Salus imperi." Others, fine and rare (Italian, not Venetian), as "Virgileus Maro;" rev. EPO, etc., etc.  10 pieces

998 TUSCANY. Leopold II. and Louis and Maria.  2 "

999 SARDINIA. Charles Emanuel, 1756; Victor Amadeus, 1782. Varied lot, bringing the dates down to the present year. Fine.  16 pieces

1000 PARMA. St. Hilarius, Protector. From 1790.  4 pieces

1001 GENOA. A great variety. From 1755.  8 "

1002 MALTA. Emanuel Pinto.  1 "

1002*SAN MARINO. Fine and rare. Rep. 1864.  2 "

1003 CORSICA. Pascal Paoli. 1 Soldi, 1768. A hat on a pole, marked R. R.

1004 —— Same. 4 and 2 Soldi. Fine and very rare.  3 pieces

  See Journal of a tour to this island, with memoirs of Pascal Paoli, by James Boswell, Esq. Printed by the Brothers Foulis in Glasgow, 1768.

1005 MANTUA. From Francis II. 1484. "Sesino" and "Soldi." Some with blazing sun; some with cross. Rare.  6 pieces

1006 MONACO. From Louis XIV., 1683, to Honore V., 1838. Some nearly uncirculated.  6 pieces

1007 NAPLES. Murat. 2 Grana and 3 Grana. The former excessively rare.  3 pieces

62    *Medals and Coins of Italy.—Bronze.*

1008 SICILY. Ferdinand IV. (1791) to Francis II. (1859). Tornesi, from 1 to 10. 10 pieces
1009 —— Another lot. Finer. Some of the rarer ones bright. 6 pieces
1010 LUCCA. (Arms, Lily.) 1 Soldi, 2 Quatrini. Very fine. 2 pieces.
1011 LOTHRINGEN. Henry, Duke of. 1648. And Miscellaneous. 15 pieces
1012 FREDERICK I., 1458; Charles I. and Charles II. (1699), Philip III. Extra fine and rare lot. 10 pieces
1013 NAPOLEON. "Regno D'Italia." Obv. bust; rev. crown of Lombardy, 1808–1813. *Soldi.* ½ do. ¼ do. Nearly uncirculated. Rare. 3 pieces
1014 —— Others. 10 "
1015 "LOMBARDO VENETIO REGNO." Uncirculated. Centesimi, etc. 6 pieces
1016 ROME. Urban VIII. 1636. All old. 12 "
1017 —— 5 Baiocchi, 4 Soldi, 2 Soldi, Baiocchi, Mezzo Baiocchi. From 1796. All fine. Generally uncirculated. Superb lot. 12 pieces
1018 —— Others. 7 "
1019 —— Republic. Revolution of 1800. Arms. Cap of Liberty on fasces. Duo baiocchi and Mezzo baiocchi. 2 Soldi. Extra fine. 5 pieces
1020 —— Republic of '48. 3 Baiocchi and ½ Baiocchi. Arms. Eagle displayed. 4 pieces
1021 FERRARA AND GUBBIO. 1622–1750. Rare. 4 "

*Carrara and Other Rare Bronze Medals.*

1022 FRANCESCO SENIOR. Obv. naked bust, shown to the waist; rev. arms (head of a satyr-winged bust, drapery displayed, an ox lying down, and shield bearing ivy?). AN. XXXVII M.VIII. D.V. QVI. SVM. CIVI. BENI. REX. IT. Size 44
1023 NICOLAUS DE CARRARIO II. Territorii Pat. An MCCCXXIII. Bust in cap and close vest; rev. arms, OBIT ANNO DO MCCCXXVI. Size 44
1024 JACOBUS GRANDIS, etc. Obv. bust; rev. arms. All very fine. Rare medals. Size

*Antique Coins, Roman and Greek.*  63

1025 TRIUMPH OF HERACLIUS. Obv. crowned bust on a crescent, rays descending; rev. a triumph.   Size 56

> I take this fine medal to have been the work of one of the great Italian medallists of the fifteenth century—Pisanello, or his successor, Matteo dé Pasti. These men, as well as Sperandio of Mantua, modelled profile busts with great skill and delicacy, and they were fond of introducing horsemen on the reverses of their medals. I have somewhere—I cannot at this moment remember where—seen an engraving of this rare bronze.

1026 COSMUS II., Duke of Etruria. His bust; rev. hooks, DVABVS. Fine copper.   Size 48

> Cosmo II. succeeded his father, Ferdinand, in 1609.

1027 ANTIQUE BUSTS in oval brass mounting. Heads of Roman ladies—Agrippina, and others unknown; with head of Caius Cæsar. All very fine and artistic. Well patinated and probably 200 years old. Size 42 x 52.
5 pieces

1028 OBSCENE HEAD. Rev. head of a satyr; with head of Hercules in the ancient style, etc. Very curious lot.
3 pieces

1029 SIMILAR LOT.   4 "

1030 MEDAL, probably intended as a prize for excellence in learning. Obv. female bust laureated; rev. Pallas and female, with book and civic crown. A splendid impression.   Size 40

1031 —— Another, from the same dies, but with a rim added. Brass. Equally fine.

## ANTIQUE COINS, ROMAN AND GREEK.

*Denarei of Roman Families.*

1032 AEMILIA, Antonia, Antestia, and others.   7 pieces
1033 CALPURNIA, Julia, and Cassia. Extra fine. Valuable.
3 pieces
1034 SCRIBONIA, Rubria, Julia, Sergia, etc. Fair condition. Rare.   10 pieces

## Imperial Denarei.

1035 TIBERIUS. (Tribute Penny). Trajan, Hadrian, Sabina, and Faustina. A lot of good coins. 6 pieces

1036 NERVA. Trajan, Ant.–Pius, and others. Poor. 10 pieces

1037 JULIA DOMNA, Heliogabalus, and others. Same period. Base silver. 12 pieces

1038 MEDALLION OF ANTONINUS PIUS. Obv. draped bust laureated; rev. Hygeia seated on a column, Telesphorus and serpent behind a tree, SALVS in exergue. A piece of exquisite work. Thick solid silver. Valuable, but modern. Size 24

1039 COUNTERFEIT DENAREI. Rare types. 3 pieces

## Greek Silver Coins.

1040 ATHENS. Clump Tetradrachm. Obv. head of Minerva; rev. owl. AΘE. Sharp, but of irregular form. Rare.

1041 ALEXANDER THE GREAT. Tet. Obv. head covered with lion's scalp; rev. Jupiter seated. Very good.

1042 PHILIP, MACEDON, father of preceding. Tet. Good.

1043 PTOLEMY I. Rev. Eagle. Tet. Fine, rare.

1044 DRACHM OF SERIPHUS. Chimera and eagle.

1045 PTOLEMY III. A Tetradrachm of base silver, but genuine.

1046 MEDALLION OF ALCIBIADES. Obv. head in a Greek helmet; rev. two figures and serpent. Medallion of good silver and work, but modern. Fine. Size 24

1047 COUNTERFEIT TETRADRACHMS. Alexander, Ptolemy, etc. 5 pieces

1048 PERSIAN OF SAPOR? Obv. bust with winged cap; rev. fire worship. Very fine. Size 18

1049 —— Of later date. A fine coin of the same size.

1050 —— Obv. rude head; rev. the sacred bull of Brahma, lying down. Silver. Size 12

1051 —— Duplicate of last, and another. 2 pieces

## Roman and Greek Copper Coins.

1052 FIRST brass. M. Aurelius, Maximinus, and Philip I. Fine. 3 pieces
1053 FIRST and second brass. Trajan, Faustina, Jr., Ant-Pius, Philip, Maximinus. Good. 5 pieces
1054 SECOND brass. Domitian, Agrippa, Trajan, Ant-Pius, etc. Fair. 6 pieces
1055 —— Others of the same era. Poor. 4 pieces
1056 —— Justinus. Two nimbused figures seated; John Zimeses, Jesus Christ nimbused; and one of Constantine, with Christian monogram. All in good condition. Rare. 4 pieces
1057 SECOND and third brass. Lower Empire. 10 pieces
1058 —— Similar. Poor. do.
1059 SMALL brass. do. do.
1060 —— Similar. do. do.
1061 —— do. do. do.
1062 —— do. do. do.
1063 —— do. do. 8 pieces
1064 SMALL brass. Patinated and fine. Constantine, Diocletian, Magnentius, Licineus, etc. 10 pieces
1065 —— Patinated. Some fine. 20 pieces
1066 MEDALLIONS and large brass coins, well made and artificially patinated; very dangerous copies of rare types, and some fabrications, such as Otho; some with magnificent reverses, Eg., the Emperor attended by his servants, sacrificing before a temple, on a coin of Augustus. A *Congiarum* on a rev. of Domitian, etc. 10 pieces
1067 —— Similar lot; hardly equal to last. 10 do.
1068 —— Similar, equal to last. 10 do.
1069 ANTINOUS. (Favourite of Hadrian); obv. bare bust; rev. a ram. Copy of an antique. Very fine. Size 22
1070 PYRRUS OF EPIRUS; obv. head of Jupiter Dodonœus; rev. woman seated. Superb work of art. Copy of a tetradrachm.
1071 SIDON. Turreted head of the Province; rev. Eagle. Superb copy of a tetradrachm.

1072 OTHER copies of magnificent Greek Coins. Solid bronze.  
6 pieces
1073 GENUINE Coin of Hiero II. of Syracuse; obv. Diademed Head; rev. Cavalier. Fine. Size 18
1074 OTHERS. Egypt, Greece, Bruttum, Rhodes, Italy, etc. Good and rare lot. Different sizes. 13 pieces

## MODERN GREECE.
### Silver.

1075 DOLLAR of 1833. (Five Drachmi). "Ellados." Uncirculated.
1076 DRACHMA. Same. Uncirculated.
1077 HALF-DRACHMA and Quarter do. Uncirculated. 2 pcs
1078 DRACHMA of 1868. Brilliant.
1079 PHOENIX, Drachma, half do., quarter do., 30 Lepta, small coins of the Ionian Islands. All fine. 6 pieces

### Copper.

1080 TWENTY LEPTA of 1831; Phœnix, above, cross. 10 Lepta, and 5 do. Uncirculated. 3 pieces
1081 —— Repetition. Very fine. do.
1082 TEN, 5, 2 and 1 Lepta of 1833. Brilliant. 4 pieces.
1083 —— Repetition of last. Brilliant. do.
1084 —— 5, 2 and 1 do. 1845. Fair. do.
1085 IONIAN ISLANDS. 1819; obv. Winged Lion; rev. Britannia. 10, 5, 2, and 11 Lepta. 4 pieces
1086 MISCELLANEOUS. Greek. 8 pieces
1087 WAR MEDAL. Victory over the Turks, Oct., 1827. Greek Head; rev. three Crowns. Brass. Fine and rare. Size 22

## COINS AND MEDALS OF RUSSIA.
### Silver.

1088 ANCIENT COPEKA. Oblong, with a Knight on horseback on one side; on the reverse, inscription in straight parallel lines across the *smallest* diameter. From Vladimir. (10th century). 7 pieces

1089 ANCIENT COPEKA Same, with the ins. running on the *longest* diameter. 3 pieces
1090 IVAN IV. 1533. Penny. (Following Abbe Barthelemy). Fine and rare.
1091 IOANOVITCH DMITRE. 1605. Penny. Fine, rare.
1092 SMALL Coins, not understood; some with Cross, some with Double Eagle, some with St. George on horseback. All fine and generally uncirculated. 6 pieces
1093 COINS resembling Rupees, and of the same value. Struck for circulation in Georgia. On one side a Castle and two Branches Crossed. On both inscriptions in Tartar characters. Rare. 2 pieces
1094 —— Exact duplicates. do.
1095 —— One of the same. (Rupee?) Half and Quarter do. 3 pieces
1096 JOHN ALEXIS. 1688. German Dollar (Brabant). Stamped with the Arms of Russia, and date. For circulation in that Empire. Rare.
1097 PETER I. Alexowitz (the Great). 1682 to 1725. Crown; obv. young bust, bare head; rev. double-headed eagle. Letters very long; edge plain; broad, and extremely fine. Rare type.
1098 —— Half-crown. Same type, except that the head is laureated. Equally fine and rare.
1099 —— Crown, laureated bust; rev. double-headed eagle. No date. Nearly uncirculated. Very rare.
1100 —— Crown. Equally sharp and fine. No date.
1101 —— Crown. 1723. Older Bust; rev. Cross good. Rare variety.
1102 —— Crown. 1725, (The year of his death); obv. laureated bust; rev. Cross. Uncirculated. Very rare.
1103 —— Another, 1725, with half-crown, same date. 2 pieces
1104 PETER II., son of Alexis Petrowitz (succeeded the Empress Catherine at the age of 15.) Crown; obv. laureated bust; rev. cross. 1727. Very fine and rare.

1105 CATHERINE I., mother of Peter II., 1725 to 1727. Crown; obv. bust to left, hair bound with fillets of pearls; rev. double-headed eagle. Extremely broad and fine. Rare. Size 27.
1106 —— Crown, 1726; splendid, uncirculated. Same type as last. Very rare.
1107 —— Crown, 1726; bust to right; rev. like the others of this Empress. Very fine, rare.
1108 ANNA IVANOVNE. 1730 to 1740. Crown, 1731. Young bust; rev. double-headed eagle. Uncirculated. Very rare.
1109 —— Crown, 1732. Sharp but stained.
1110 —— Crown, 1740. Bust crowned; rev. like last. Fine.
1111 —— Half-crown. Ordinary.
1112 JOHN III. Antonovitch crown, 1741. Young bust laureated, ribbon and St. Andrew's cross; rev. double eagle. Splendid crown; broad and uncirculated. Rare.
1113 —— Another equally fine. Same date, but from a different die; thicker and less broad. Very rare.
1114 —— Half-crown to match 1112. Splendid, very rare.
1115 ELIZABETH I. Petrovna. Crown of 1757; obv. bust, head-dress of pearls; rev. double eagle bearing two shields, arms of ? Good crown.
1116 —— Half-crown. Same type. Extra fine.
1117 —— Crown of 1759. Fine.
1118 —— Quarter and eighth do. Fine. 2 pieces.
1119 PETER III. Feodorovitch, 1762. Crown; obv. bust in armor, head bare; rev. double eagle. Uncirculated. Rare.
1120 —— Duplicate. Uncirculated.
1121 —— Triplicate. Circulated.
1122 —— Half-ruble. Circulated.
1123 CATHERINE II. Crown, 1769. Fine.
1124 —— Quarter and eighth ruble. Very fine.
2 piece
1125 PETER, Duke of Semigallia. Fine crown, 1780. Rare.

## Bronze Medals of Russia. 69

RUBLE, half and quarter, 1800; obv. inscription on square tablet; rev. arms. 3 pieces.
ALEXANDER I. 1834. Medal; obv. bust; rev. monument (struck by Nicholas); value one ruble. Very fine, rare.
NICHOLAS I. Ruble, 1845. Uncirculated.
—— Obv. bust; rev. equestrian statue on a monument, 1859. Uncirculated. (Ruble.)
MEDAL with loop, 1814, 19th March; obv. laureated bust in rays; rev. ins. in a circle of laurel loop.
Size 16
MEDAL of Peter the Great, to commemorate the battle of Pultowa, 1709. Bust of Peter; rev. battle; has a burnished surface. Thick. Rare. Size 27
MEDAL of Anna. Obv. her bust crowned; rev. Genius of Russia, with crown and palm, leaning on a column, near trophies and captives; in exergue OBSESS ET LIBERAT MENS, Oct., 1727. Extremely fine, rare.
Size 27
MEDALET of 1789, with equestrian statue on a rock.
Size 16
COIN of 33 copecks, one of 25 do., one of 16 do., one of 10 do., and one of 5 do. 5 pieces
SMALL coins from Peter the Great to Nicholas I. One for Georgia. Very fine. Many rare. From 5 to 10 copecks. 15 pieces

### Bronze Medals.

1708. Medal of Admiral? Bust; rev. war-ships in port. Fine proof. Size 34
1724. The Emperor and Empress (Peter the Great and consort); their busts jugata; rev. the Emperor holding a crown above the head of Catherine I. Fine proof.
Size 38
1725. Peter the Great. To commemorate his death. Fine proof. Size 34
1730. Anna. Her bust; rev. the Empress standing with 3 attendants, one with cross, one with anchor, one holding a crown. Proof. Size 38

## Bronze Medals of Russia.

1140 1741. Elizabeth Petrovna. Her bust; rev. "Clementia Augusta." Fine proof. Size 38

1141 1754. The same; rev. PAVLO PRINCIPE JVVENT NATO D XX. SEPT. MDCCLIV. Fine proof. Size 38

1142 1749, 1755, 1757. Medals of uniform size from Roettier's Series. Busts of members of the royal family. Size 29. 3 pieces.

1143 1779. Catherine II.? Fine bust; rev. Pallas and Catherine. Fine proof. Size 35

1144 1783. Obv. bust; rev. map of the Crimean peninsula. Fine proof. Size 58

1145 1784. Catherine II.; rev. three turreted shields surmounted by a caduceus and cap of liberty. Fine proof. Size 44

1146 1784. The same; rev. woman standing amidst a group of nude children. Proof. Size 24

1147 1788. Admiral? Bust, with furled flag; rev. naval column, at its base cannon and flags. Fine proof. Size 50

1148 1793. Bust of Prince Alexander and consort, vis a vis; rev. two shields with monogram (AP and EA) united and crowned; the sun in splendor above. Fine proof. Size 42

1149 1826. Catherine II. On her death. Fine proof. Size 24

1150 1831. Poland; obv. two female figures, one with the attributes of Poland, TU NE MOURRAS PAS.; rev. A L' HEROIQUE POLOGNE, a palm and olive crossed. Fine proof. Size 33

1151 MEDAL in honor of General Vlemincks, Inspector of the Sanitary Service of the army. Inscription to the same effect. Size 38

1152 MEDAL in honor of Paul I. (1796 to 1801); obv. his Bust; rev. Cross. Fine proof. Size 33

1153 MARRIAGE Medal of Alexander Nicholas and Maria Alexandrina. 1841; obv. their busts conjoined; rev. their monogram crowned. Splendid proof. Size 28

## Copper Coins of Russia.

PRIZE MEDAL. University of Moscow, by Alexander I.
Size 33
MORTUARY MEDAL. Obv. female bust crowned with oak.
No inscription; rev. in two wreaths—roses and laurels.
"1776–1826." Fine proof.   Size 24
MEDALS of Marshall Suwarrow and Bishop? Their pictures full face. Size 22.   2 pieces
MEDALS. Square and oblong octagon. Very fine. 2 pcs
MEDALETS. Octagon and round, of Peter the Great, Anna, Peter II., etc. About size 16. Extremely fine, all bright, very beautiful and select, but with Russian inscription, and requiring a knowledge of that language properly to describe.   16 pieces
JETONS. All Russian.   5 pieces

### Copper Coins.

PETER I. (the Great). 1682 to 1725, with St. George on horseback, with cross and with double eagle. With and without dates. Fine lot.   5 pieces
PETER II. 1727 to 1730; rev. cross. Extra fine.  3 pcs
ANNA. Ivanovna. 1730 to 1740. Extra fine. 5 pieces
IVAN III. 1740–1741   2 pieces
ELIZABETH. Petrovna. 1741–1762.   7 pieces
KATHARINE II. 1762 to 1796. Pieces from ten to one quarter Copec. Fine lot.   7 pieces
—— Similar to last. Some earlier.   do.
PAUL I. 1786 to 1801. Rare.   1 piece
ALEXANDER I. 1801 to 1825. (One extra fine). 3 pcs
NICHOLAS I. 1825.   10 pieces
ALEXANDER II. Miscellaneous. Valuable lot. 33 pcs
POLISH REVOLUTION. A set of patterns of 10 Kopecks, 5 Kopecks, 2 Kopecks, and 1 Kopeck. Splendid proof. Very rare.   4 pieces
RIGA. (City). Small Coins. Rare.   4 pieces
MOLDAVIA and WALLACHIA. Two shields. Head of a bull, front face, and bird holding a double cross, united under a crown. Rare coins.   5 pieces
SIBERIA. An old Coin, and two of Catherine II. 1771 and 1773. Large size. Rare.   3 pieces

## COINS OF POLAND.

### Silver.

1176 LADISLAIUS II. 1138 to 1146. Head, front face; rev. double cross? Denarius. Rude coin, well preserved. (Uncertain).

1177 OTHERS without date, and of uncertain attribution. Denarii and Groshen, mostly of cities. All in good condition. 7 pieces

1178 ALEXANDER I. and Sigismund I., 1501 to 1548. Denarii and Groshen. Valuable lot. 6 pieces

1179 SIGISMUND I. (Alone). 1506 to 1548; obv. bust crowned; rev. eagle displayed. 1531–'34, etc. Coins of the Groat and Half-groat size. As fine as when struck. Very rare. 5 pieces

1180 —— Varieties. Groats, etc. Sig. I. and II. 4 pieces

1181 SIGISMUND II. 1566 and 1569. Four Groshen, (about 20 cts.); bust; rev. double shield. "Moneta Magni Ducat Lit." Fine. 5 pieces

1182 STEPHEN BATHORI. 1575 to 1586. (Fine silver coins, dime size); obv. crowned head; rev. III. GROS. ARG. TRIP. M. D. LIT. Also a shield between St. George and an eagle. Another with two towers. CIVI RIGEN. Said by Wellenheim to be very rare. 3 pieces

1183 SIGISMUND III. 1587 to 1632. Coins of the same description as last. Bust crowned. Large collar; rev. as before. Extremely fine. 5 pieces

1184 —— Bust crowned, collar and beard like Charles I. of England; rev. Arms of Dantzig. (GEDANENSIS). Quarter-crown. 1613. Very fine, rare.

1185 —— Similar, and others smaller. Dantzig and other cities. Different dates. 12 pieces

1186 —— Figure standing, shown to the hips, with sword and wand; rev. round shield with elaborate coat-of-arms. 1630. Splendid crown, burnished field. Very rare.

1187 —— Similar, except that less of the figure is shown. Nearly uncirculated Crown. 1628. Rare.

## Coins of Poland.—Silver.

- 1188 SIGISMUND III. Another, the King with different dress and decorations. Equally fine Crown. 1630. Rare.
- 1189 —— Another, slight variety. Extra fine Crown.
- 1190 —— Two Crowns of the earliest issue. 1627. Circulated, but worn. 2 pieces
- 1191 WLADISLAUS IIII. 1632 to 1648. The King's figure to the hips; crowned and with sword and wand; rev. arms of the city of "Thorunensis"? (angel over a gate with three towers), 1637. Uncirculated crown. Very rare.
- 1192 —— Same; rev. arms of Poland. Fine crown.
- 1193 JOHN CASIMIR. 1648 to 1668. Splendid uncirculated crown. 1649.
- 1194 —— Small coin, and ½ crown of "Thorunensis." 3 pieces
- 1195 JOHN III. Sobieski. 1674 to 1696. A variety of his smaller silver coins. Fine. 5 pieces.
- 1196 —— Medal of Sobieski and wife, their busts conjoined; rev. their coronation, 1776, a city and tree. Very *beautiful.* Rare. Size 30.
- 1197 AUGUSTUS II. 1696 to 1733. ⅓ crown, 1707. Uncirculated. Rare.
- 1198 MEDAL in memory of the death of Christina Eberhardina, Queen of Poland, 1727. Pierced. Rare. Size 16
- 1199 CROWN of 1729. Fine and rare.
- 1200 AUGUSTUS III. 1733 to 1763. Coronation medal. Tin. Uncirculated. Size 28
- 1201 —— ⅔ crown. 1736. Uncirculated. *Very rare.*
- 1202 —— Crown of 1755. Extra fine. Rare.
- 1203 —— Small coronation medal (size 18), uncirculated, and medalet of the preceding reign. 2 pieces
- 1204 STANISLAUS, Augustus. 1764 to 1798. Coronation medal. Bare bust; rev. crown in rays, "Coron XXV NOV MDCCLXIV." Very fine and rare. Size 21
- 1205 —— Coronation medal, struck at Warsaw. Uncirculated. Size 20
- 1206 —— Half-crown, with one of Frederick Augustus. Both rare, and well preserved. 2 pieces
- 1207 —— 2 groschen, 1767 (uncirculated), and two others, larger. 3 pieces

## United States.—Gold.

1208  ALEXANDER I. 1815 to 1825. (Kaiser.) Fine crown, 1823 (10 zlot.) Rare.
1209  —— Half-crown (5 zlot), and 2 zlot. Uncirculated. 2 pieces
1210  —— 5 and 2 and 1 zlot. 1815 and 17— Av. value 30 cts. Very rare. 9 pieces
1210a —— For Cracow and other cities. A miscellaneous lot. 21 pieces
1210b COPPER coins of Poland. A valuable collection, all in good order. 38 pieces

## UNITED STATES.

### Gold.

1211 1795. Half Eagle. Fine.
1212 1797. Eagle. Small Eagle reverse. Very good. Rare.
1213 1799. Half Eagle. Fine. Scarce.
1214 1800. " " Very fine. Scarce.
1215 1803. " " " " " "
1216 1804. " " " " Rare.
1217 1804. Quarter Eagle. " " "
1218 1806. " " Fair. "
1219 1807. " " "
1220 1813. Half " Very fine. Scarce.
1221 1818. " " " " " "
1222 1829. Quarter " Extremely fine. Scarce.
1223 1834. " " Equally fine, N. S. Scarce.
1224 1835. " " The same. Scarce.
1225 1836. " " Fair. Scarce.
1226 1854. Three Dollars. Extremely fine.

1227 1849. California Half Eagle. Full weight, without alloy. Very fine. Scarce.
1228 1849. Oregon Exchange Company. "130 grains Native Gold, 5 D." Beaver. Fine and rare.
1229 GEORGIA Gold. 128 grains, 22 carats. C. Bechtler. Five Dollars. Fine. Scarce.

## United States.—Silver.

1230  CAROLINA Gold. 140 grains, 20 carats. 1834. C. Bechtler, Five Dollars. Fine. Scarce.
1231  —— ONE DOLLAR. 30 grains. Extremely fine. Rare.
1232  —— 1 Dollar. 27 grains. Extremely fine.
1233  1849. Mormon gold. Five Dollars. Two hands clasping. Very rare.
1234  1849. Same. Two and a half Dollars. Rare.
1235  1860. Pike's Peak Gold. Ten D. Very good.
1236  1860. " " " Five D. Uncirculated.
1237  CAROLINA Gold. 2½ Dollars. 70 grains, 20. Thick coin Uncirculated.
1238  CALIFORNIA Gold Dollars, 1853 and 1854, different designs Uncirculated. 3 pieces.
1239  CALIFORNIA Half Dollars, 1872, different designs. Proof 2 pieces
1240  " Quarter Dollars, different designs and dates. 9 pieces.

### Silver Dollars.

1241  1795. Flowing hair. Fine. ——
1242  1795. Duplicate. Fair.
1243  1795. Fillet head. Very fine. Rare.
1244  1795. " Small letters and date. Very good.
1245  1795. " Large do. Same.
1246  1795. " Ordinary.
1247  1796. Extremely fine. Very rare.
1248  1797. Seven stars to r. Very good, for date.
1249  1798. Fifteen stars. Small Eagle reverse. Good, for variety. Rare.
1250  1798. Large Eagle reverse. Very good.
1251  1798. Duplicate. Equally good.
1252  1798. Another. Ordinary.
1253  1799. Five stars to r. Good, for variety. Rare.
1254  1799. Six stars to r. Very good.
1255  1799. Another. Same.
1256  1799. Triplicate. Scratched.
1257  1799. With R. C., Portland, Aug. 4, neatly engraved on obv.
1258  1800. Stars on reverse *small*. Fine and rare.
1259  1800. " " Larger. Ordinary.
1260  1801. Ordinary.

## United States.—Silver.

| | | |
|---|---|---|
| 1261 | 1802. | Better. |
| 1262 | 1803. | Uncirculated. Rare. |
| 1263 | 1803. | Very good. |
| 1264 | 1804. | Stained and somewhat rubbed, but still in very good condition. |

[Accompanying this coin is the following note: "Obtained through great personal exertions from Dr. Liebig, from the collection of his intimate friend, the celebrated traveler, Prof. Schledehausen, now deceased." This information is interesting, yet the great traveler may have been imposed upon. The motive to do it was large, on account of the extreme rarity and great value of a dollar of this date. It would be rash to decide absolutely against its authenticity, but the purchaser must exercise his own judgment.]

| | | |
|---|---|---|
| 1265 | 1836. | Pattern Dollar. A little circulated. Rare. |
| 1266 | | Planchet, with edge milled. Without impression on either side. |
| 1267 | 1840. | Circulated. |
| 1268 | 1841. | " |
| 1269 | 1850. | "      N. O. Mint. |
| 1270 | 1859. | "           " |
| 1271 | 1860. | Very fine.       " |
| 1272 | 1860. | Equally fine.    " |
| 1273 | 1861. | Very fine. |
| 1274 | 1872. | Uncirculated. |
| 1275 | 1872. | Duplicate. |
| 1276 | 1872. | Another. |
| 1277 | 1873. | Brilliant proof. Rare. |
| 1278 | 1873. | Trade Dollar. Brilliant proof. Rare. |
| 1279 | 1873. | "       "     Uncirculated. Rare. |

### Half Dollars.

| | | |
|---|---|---|
| 1280 | 1794. | Unusually fine. There are scratches on the head yet it has been but little circulated. Rare. |
| 1281 | 1795. | With scratches, as before, appearing to have been mainly in the planchet. Scarce. |
| 1282 | 1795. | Much rubbed. |
| 1283 | 1803. | Nearly uncirculated. Extremely rare in this condition. |
| 1284 | 1803. | Circulated. 2 pieces. |
| 1285 | 1806. | Very fine. But little circulated. |
| 1286 | 1806. | Others. One very fine. 2 pieces. |
| 1287 | 1807. | Head to r. Very good. |

1807. Head to l. Fine.
1807. Duplicate. Head to l. Ordinary.
1808. Fine.
1810. Circulated. 2 pieces.
1811.    "
1812. Extremely fine.
1813. Very fine.
1813. With one of 1812. Ordinary. 2 pieces.
1815. Ordinary. Scarce.
1821. Very fine.
1822.    "
1824. Good. With "Houck's Panacea, Baltimore," stamped on obv.
1824. Others. Fine. 2 pieces.
1826. Fine. 2 pieces.
1827.    "       "
1831.    "
1834.    "   Large date.
1834.    "   Small date.
1835.    "
1836. Very fine.
1836. Fine. New die.
1836. Old and new die. 3 pieces
1837. Extremely fine.
1839. Very fine.
1853.    "
1860.    "
1867.    "
1873. Brilliant proof. Rare.

## Quarter Dollars.

1796. Very fine. Rare.
1804. Extremely fine; quite superior to any heretofore known to exist. Fifty dollars has been offered for this piece at private sale. Very rare.
1806. Very fine. Scarce.
1806. Ordinary.
1818. Very fine.
1821.    "    But little circulated.
1825. Fine.
1835.    "
1853, 1856 and 1857. Ordinary. 3 pieces.
1861. Very fine.

## Dimes.

| | | |
|---|---|---|
| 1326 | 1796. | Extremely fine. Rare. |
| 1327 | 1796. | Nearly as fine; a variety. |
| 1328 | 1798. | 13 stars. Poor, but rare. |
| 1329 | 1803. | Extremely fine. Rare. |
| 1330 | 1805. | Twice pierced, but little rubbed. |
| 1331 | 1805 and 1807. | Much rubbed. 3 pieces. |
| 1332 | 1814. | Fair for date. Scarce. |
| 1333 | 1820 and 1824. | Poor. 2 pieces. |
| 1334 | 1827, '29, '30, and '31. | Ordinary. 4 pieces. |
| 1335 | 1832. | Extremely fine. |
| 1336 | 1833. | Poor. 2 pieces. |
| 1337 | 1834. | Fine. |
| 1338 | 1835. | " |
| 1339 | 1837, '41, '44, and '46. | Ordinary. 4 pieces. |
| 1340 | 1851, '53, '54, '56, and '57. | Fine. 5 pieces. |
| 1341 | 1859, '60, '61, and '72. | Fine. 4 pieces. |

## Half Dimes.

| | | |
|---|---|---|
| 1342 | 1794. | Fine. Rare. |
| 1343 | 1795. | Uncirculated; tarnished. |
| 1344 | 1795. | Nearly as fine. Broken die. |
| 1345 | 1795. | Nearly uncirculated. 2 pieces. |
| 1346 | 1796. | Uncirculated. Very rare. |
| 1347 | 1800. | Very fine; a scratch on face of head. Rare. |
| 1348 | 1800. | Fine. 2 pieces. |
| 1349 | 1803. | Extremely fine. Rare. |
| 1350 | 1829. | Uncirculated. |
| 1351 | 1830 and '31. | Fine. 2 pieces. |
| 1352 | 1832 and '33. | One pierced. 2 pieces. |
| 1353 | 1833 and '34. | Very fine. 2 pieces. |
| 1354 | 1835, '36, and '37. | Very good. 4 pieces. |
| 1355 | 1839, '42, '43, '44, and '49. | Ordinary. 5 pieces. |
| 1356 | 1850, '53, '54, '55, and '57. | Fair. 6 pieces. |
| 1357 | 1858, '59, '60, '61, '70, and '72. | Very fine. 6 pieces. |

## Three Cents.

| | | |
|---|---|---|
| 1358 | 1851, '52, '53, etc. | 9 pieces. |

United States.—Copper.      79

### Cents.

| | | |
|---|---|---|
| 1359 | 1793. Liberty cap; head much rubbed. Rare. | |
| 1360 | 1793. Wreath; Liberty and date small. A good cent; but dark, and hair rubbed. Rare. | |
| 1361 | 1793. Similar to last; much rubbed. | |
| 1362 | 1794. Uncirculated; the color fine and original, in part red. As fine as any known. Rare. | |
| 1363 | 1794. Very ordinary. 3 pieces. | |
| 1364 | 1795. Nearly uncirculated, but not bright; the color a fine olive; edge plain. | |
| 1365 | 1795. Similar, but "one cent" higher in the circle, on the reverse. Nearly uncirculated. | |
| 1366 | 1795 and 1796. Same type; only fair. 2 pieces. | |
| 1367 | 1797. The edge battered slightly, but little rubbed. Dark. | |
| 1368 | 1798. Uncirculated, but not bright. Very desirable. Rare. | |
| 1369 | 1798. A variety nearly as fine; a narrow, milled rim. Rare. | |
| 1370 | 1799. Remarkably fine; it shows traces of a black rust, which has been nicely removed, and appears to have been quite uncirculated before oxidation. I think nearly, if not quite, equal to the Abbey Cent. Very rare. | |
| 1371 | 1800, 1801, and 1802. Poor. 5 pieces. | |
| 1372 | 1801. Uncirculated. Color, a light olive. Very rare. | |
| 1373 | 1804. Broken die. Very good. Rare. | |
| 1374 | 1803 and 1805. Ordinary. 3 pieces. | |
| 1375 | 1806 and 1807. Ordinary. 2 pieces. | |
| 1376 | 1808 and 1809. Fair and scarce. 2 pieces. | |
| 1377 | 1810. Fine. Scarce. | |
| 1378 | 1810, '11, and '12. Ordinary. 3 pieces. | |
| 1379 | 1813, '14, '16, '17, and '18. Ordinary. 6 pieces. | |
| 1380 | 1818 and '19. Fine. 2 pieces. | |
| 1381 | 1818, '19, and '21. Ordinary. 3 pieces. | |
| 1382 | 1820. Bright and uncirculated. | |
| 1383 | 1822. Uncirculated. Olive. Rare. | |
| 1384 | 1822, '23, and '24. Ordinary. 3 pieces. | |
| 1385 | 1825, '26, and '27. " 5 " | |
| 1386 | 1828, '29, and '30. " 4 " | |
| 1387 | 1831 and '33. " 5 " | |
| 1388 | 1834 and '35. " 3 " | |
| 1389 | 1835, '36, and '37. Fair. 3 pieces. | |
| 1390 | 1837 and '38. Poor. 6 pieces. | |

| | | |
|---|---|---|
| | 1391 | 1838. Very fine. |
| 1392 | 1838 and '39. Very fair. 2 pieces. |
| 1393 | 1840, '41, and '42. A very good lot. Varieties. 6 pieces. |
| | 1394 | 1843, '44, and '45. Ordinary. 4 pieces. |
| | 1395 | 1846, '47, and '48. Fair. 4 pieces. |
| | 1396 | 1849, '50, '51, and '52. Very good. 4 pieces. |
| | 1397 | 1853, '54, and '55. Fine. 4 pieces. |
| | 1398 | 1856 and '57. (Large and small date.) Fine. 3 pieces. |
| | 1399 | CENTS of various dates. 27 pieces. |
| | 1400 | NICKEL Cent of 1856. Fine. Rare. |
| | 1401 | " Cents of 1857 to '64, inclusive. Fine. 8 pieces. |
| | 1402 | " and Copper, Nickel size. 5 pieces. |
| | 1403 | " 5 and 3 cents, 1873. 2 pieces. |

### Half Cents.

| | | |
|---|---|---|
| | 1404 | 1795. Nearly uncirculated. On the edge, *two hundred for a dollar*. Rare. |
| | 1405 | 1797. Very fine, for date. |
| | 1406 | 1803, '4, '6, and '8. A good lot. 4 pieces. |
| | 1407 | HALF CENTS, various dates. A good lot. 23 pieces. |

### COLONIAL AND STATE COINS AND TOKENS.

| | | |
|---|---|---|
| | 1408 | 1652. Pine-Tree Shilling. Quite uncirculated. Rare. |
| | 1409 | 1652. " " Clipped and battered. |
| | 1410 | 1652. " " Poor. |
| | 1411 | 1721. "Colonies Francoises," for Louisiana. Fine. Scarce. |
| | 1412 | 1722. Same, except date. Equally fine and rare. |
| | 1413 | 1721 and '22. A good example of each. 2 pieces. |
| | 1414 | Repetition of last. 2 pieces. |
| | 1415 | 1767. Colonies Francoises, L. XV divided by two sceptres crossed. Without countermark. An uncirculated example. Rare. |
| | 1416 | 1767. Same, with the usual countermark. R F in a circle of dots. Very good. |
| | 1417 | 1773. Virginia Half-penny, nearly bright. |
| | 1418 | Same, dark and rubbed. 3 pieces. |
| | 1419 | 1783. Georgius Triumpho. Very good. |
| | 1420 | 1787. Franklin Cent in Silver and Copper. 3 pieces. |
| | 1421 | 1787. Nova Eborac. Fair. |
| | 1422 | 1787 and '88. Vermont and Connecticut Cents. Ordinary. 4 pieces. |

| | | |
|---|---|---|
| 1423 | 1787. New Jersey Cent. Good. | *Haseltine* |
| 1424 | 1788. Massachusetts Cent. Good. | " |
| 1425 | 1788. Massachusetts Cent and Half Cent. Good. 2 pieces. | " |
| 1426 | 1783. Nova Constellatio. Good. 2 pieces. | |
| 1427 | Kentucky Cent, edge engrailed. Uncirculated. Rare. | *Parmelee* |
| 1428 | Same, edge plain. Rather poor; battered. | *Haseltine* |
| 1429 | 1776. Continental Currency. Tin. Uncirculated. | |
| 1430 | 1722. Rosa Americana Penny; Half-penny size. Poor. | *S R* |
| 1431 | 1779. Rhode Island Token; obv. Map of R. I.; rev. ship. Very fine. Brass. | *Mitchell* |
| 1432 | 1781. North American Token. Good. | *Trumbull* |

## AMERICAN MEDALS AND TOKENS.

| | | |
|---|---|---|
| 1433 | Washington, Liberty, and Security Token. The large size. Copper. Uncirculated. | *Mathew* |
| 1434 | —— Liverpool Half-penny. Obv., head; rev., ship. 1793. As good as usually found. | *Haseltine* |
| 1435 | —— Double-head Cent. Fine. | *Evans* |
| 1436 | —— Success to the United States. Large size, in brass, silvered. Very fine. | *Bahamas* |
| 1437 | —— Duplicate of last, with medal struck and distributed in civic procession on his birthday. Philadel., 1832. In bronze. Both fine. 2 pieces. | *Payne* |
| 1438 | —— Sansom Medal. Obv., military bust; rev., chest supporting fasces and sword. 1797. Silver. Very fine. Dollar size. | *Bir* |
| 1439 | —— Temperance Medalet. "We serve the tyrant Alcohol no longer." Silver. Extremely fine. Pierced. Rare. Dime size. | *Haw* |
| 1440 | —— Obv., head; rev., Gerdt's, coin-dealer, card. Silver. Fine. Same size. | *C* |
| 1441 | —— Demorest's Mt. Vernon Factory Medal. Obv., bust; rev., tomb. Brass gilt. Made in shells and joined. Size 48. | *C* |
| 1441* | —— Head; rev., Edward Cogan's card, 1859, Phila., with medalet Baltimore Monument. Both uncirculated. Tin. Sizes, 20 and 13. 2 pieces. | *C* |
| 1442 | 1796. Franco-Americana Token. Copper. Uncirculated. | |
| 1443 | BAR Cent. U. S. A., in Silver. Very fine. Rare. | *Hale* |

82                    *American Medals and Tokens.*

1444  MEDAL. To commemorate the Armed Neutrality of Russia, Denmark, Sweden, and Holland, during the Revolutionary war. Obv., mailed arm holding suspended four shields; rev., under an eye with rays, inscription in eight lines, "In exergue, MDCCLXXX., A. V. BAERLL. Extremely fine silver medal. Half-dollar size. Rare.

1445  MEDAL. To commemorate the services of William I., King of Holland, as umpire between England and America. 1829. Bronze. Magnificent proof. Size 26. Rare.

1446  LIBERTAS AMERICANA. Obv., head of Liberty, 4 Juil, 1776; rev., Pallas opposing a panther; on the ground, young Hercules. Fine uncirculated medal. Bronze. Size 30.

1447  ——— Fine copy of same, double thickness of the original.

1448  ——— 1783. Rev., "Communi consensu;" Pallas holding 5 shields. Uncirculated. Tin. Rare. Size 29.

1449  GENERAL LAFAYETTE Medal. "The Defender of American and French Liberty." Fine bronze proof. Size 30.

1450  COM. EDWARD PREBLE, for the naval engagement before Tripoli, 1804. Splendid proof in bronze, with guard surmounted by eagle and loop, the guard finely chased and gilt. Awarded by Congress. Very rare. Size 40.

1451  MEDAL. Presented by N. Y. State to Volunteers in the Mexican War. In tin box. Silver. Nearly 3 oz.

1452  AMERICAN Institute Prize Medal. Silver. Weight, about 3 oz.

1453  NEW YORK STATE Poultry Society Medal. Large silver medal awarded as a prize in 1869. Nearly 2 oz. Size 28.

1454  SALISBURY, N. C., Court of Equity Seal. Thick silver. Justice holding scales, etc. A relic of the War. Unique. Weight, about 2 oz.

1455  WEST VIRGINIA. War Medal, 1861, '65. Liberty crowning Valor. Bronze. Size, 24. Rare.

1456  SCHILLER Medal. 10 Nov., 1859. Silver. Size 26.

1457  N. Y. STATE Agricultural Society Prize Medal. Silver. Size. 20.

1458  FIRST product by the Mill process in the Pah-Ranagat mining district, Nevada. Fine proof. Silver. Size 20. Rare.

1459  WOOD'S Minstrel's Token. Silver. Fine. Size 16.

## American Medals and Tokens. 83

1460 JACKSON Medal. Obv., military young bust; "Andrew Jackson, President of the United States, 1829;" rev., within a wreath of laurel and oak, "Hero of New Orleans." Tin, silver-plated; pierced. Uncirculated. *Very rare.* Size 24.

1461 JACKSON Medal. "General Jackson, the gallant and successful defender of New Orleans, and candidate for the Presidency of the United States of America, 1828;" rev., eagle displayed, with U. S. shield covering his body; around, circle of stars. Pierced. Tin, silver-plated. Uncirculated. *Very rare.* Size 24.

1462 ——— Silver Medalet, struck at U. S. Mint. Size 12.

1463 HON. JAMES BUCHANAN. By S. B. S. and H., N. Y. Tin. Size 22.

1464 DANIEL WEBSTER. Rev., E. Hill's card. Tin. Size 19.

1465 W. H. HARRISON. Rev., "Go it, Tip. Come it, Tyler." Abraham Lincoln; rev., splitting rails, with original colors, red, white and blue, as worn in procession. Fenian Brotherhood token; "Ireland and America," two hands clasping. John C. Fremont, James Buchanan and Henry Clay medalets, in brass, nearly uniform size. A good lot. 6 pieces.

1466 GEN. GEO. B. MCCLELLAN. Pioneer Base Ball Club, Great Air Ship City of New York. Rev. John Wesley and Rt. Hon. Wm. Pitt. In white metal. All fine. 5 pieces.

1467 JEFFERSON DAVIS, 1861; man hanging. Franklin Pierce, Millard Fillmore, Louis Kossuth, and Winfield Scott. 6 pieces.

1468 NEW YORK and Harlaem R. R. Co. octagon check; Brimlow's card, in nickel and copper; Columbia Farthings. Washington Copperheads, etc. An excellent lot to purchase. 20 pieces.

1469 SILVER BADGE (Odd Fellows'), 5 x 4 inches, with gilt medallion centre. Faith, Hope, and Charity. Fine.

1470 "CUSTOM HOUSE CART, S. Draper, Collector," Badge, with pin. Silver. Rare.

1471 TRUCKEE Mine Silver Bar, 5.25 oz., $6.64. 979 FINE.

1472 INTERNAL Revenue. Ingot pure silver, 4.60 oz., $7.34. 980 FINE. Handsome square bar, with handsome border. Rare.

84                    *Coins of Mexico.*

1473  GOLD-BEARING Quartz and Nuggets from California Mines.
                                                          3 pieces.
1474  PATTERN Cent of 1855. Tarnished proof.
1475  EBLING's Columbian Garden, Bowery, N. Y., Card, stamped
        on a Spanish quarter dollar. Very rare.
1476  SHIN Plasters and Cents, with countermarks 15.
1477  ANTI-SLAVERY Tokens, Cards, etc. 39 pieces.
1478  CALENDER; half cent worth of pure copper. Model Dollar
        California, etc. Very fine. 8 pieces.
1479  COPPERHEADS. No duplicates. 125 pieces.
1480  —— Others. 60 pieces.

## COINS OF MEXICO.

1481  COB Dollar. 1771. Nearly round; thick; diameter, 1 inch.
        Very fine.
1482  —— 1778. Thicker; regular lump. Very fine.
1483  —— 1772. Thick, long oval. Fine.
1484  —— 1739. Oblong square, counter-stamped for Rio de la
        Plata. Unusually good example.
1485  —— 1759. Coin of even thickness, but irregular form;
        full weight.
1486  —— Long, narrow plate cob dollar.
1487  COB Half Dollar. Full weight.
1488  SET Cob Money. 1, ½, ¼, ⅛, and 1/16 dollars. Counter-
        stamped Rio de la Plata. Fine. 5 pieces.
1489  —— Similar to last. 5 pieces.
1490  —— Another set. 5 pieces.
1491  —— Dollar and Half Dollar; counter-stamped. Fine.
        2 pieces.
1492  —— Quarters and Eighths. 8 pieces.
1493  CUT Money, formerly much used on the Spanish Main. The
        Quarter covered with marks of circulation among the
        Chinese. 3 pieces.

  [" Cob" money conformed to the lawful standard in weight and
  fineness, but was struck with the hammer, without much regard
  to regularity of form or impression. The date shows that the
  larger portion of it was issued before the year 1740; but in this
  collection is a dollar bearing the date 1772 (or, as written, 772,
  the thousandth place being omitted), which is very remarkable.
  The "8," which is so conspicuous on the dollars, signifies 8 reals,
  and, combined with the two columns which always appear rising
  out of the water on one side of these coins, becomes our dollar
  mark—thus $.]

## Coins of Mexico.

1494  Cob Dollar of Philip V.; counter-stamped; struck on a round planchet large enough to receive the full impression of the dies, or very nearly so. Pierced, but well preserved. Very rare.

1495  Vargas Dollar. Struck with a hammer in the year 1811 or '12. Obv., Vargas and date (indistinct); in centre; LUS; rev., crowned shield, ROAXA DE SOMBRETE. Very rare.

1496  ——— A rare variety, apparently coined when the General's facilities were unusually limited, his name being stamped upon the plain surface of the piece with a punch.

1497  Morelas Dollar, struck in copper. Obv., a bow and arrow below, SUD; rev., M° 8 R. 1812. Uncirculated. More rare than the silver dollar.

1498  Dollar. Obv., star of five points; below, IP; rev., plain (Chili).

1499  Ferdinand VI. Shield crowned; rev., pillars of Hercules crowned, between them two globes supporting a crown. 1796. Fine Dollar.

1500  Charles IV. 1789. Obv., similar to last; rev., double-headed eagle between the pillars of Hercules. Dollar size, but less thick. Fine.

1501  Ferdinand VII. Obv., bust to the waist; rev., eagle and lion opposed; behind them flags and arms; "Busta maut Erigio." M. Ano, 1808. Fine Silver Medal, about 3 oz. weight.

1501*  Square plate of pure silver. Size 24. It is a piece of Necessity, resorted to by Ferdinand VII., having its value, "⅛," stamped upon it without other mark. Intrinsic value, $2 (⅛ doubloon). Very rare and valuable.

1502  ——— Oblong, oval Gilt Medal, with ribbon. Obv., laureated head on a leaf; rev., "Regal Colleg aven Palafoxio Angelopoli erect Tessera et inviolat fidei Moniment."

1503  Republic. 1824. Crooked-necked eagle tearing serpent. Very rare and in good preservation. Dollar.

1504  ——— Dollar, with the eagle upright. Fine.

1505  Augustus I. (Iturbide). Obv., military bust; rev., two wolves rearing against a tree; "Guadalaxara," etc. 1822. Fine and rare dollar.

1506  ——— Obv., bare bust; rev., crowned eagle on cactus. 1822. Fine and rare dollar.

86 . *Coins of Central America.*

1507 AUGUSTUS I. Similar obv.; rev., eagle on cactus; from a different design. Fine dollar.

1508 —— Similar, in all but date, to 1506. Fine dollar. 1823.

1509 —— Quarter dollar, same date; pierced, but very fine.

1510 —— Eighth and Sixteenth do. Rare. 2 pieces.

1511 LIBERTAD Half Dollar. " Jura de la Constitution Mexicana en 1843." Fine.

1512 MAXIMILIAN (Emperor) Dollar of 1866. Mint-mark M̊. Extremely fine. Scarce.

1513 —— Dupliate. Very fine.

1514 —— Dollar of same date. M. MM. P$^I$. Extremely fine.

1515 —— Dollar of 1867. M. M̊M. Very fine.

1516 —— Duplicate. Equally fine.

1517 —— Half Dollar. 1866. M̊. Fine. Rare.

1518 —— Duplicate.

1519 REPUBLIC of 1866 Dollar. Very fine.

1520 —— of 1867 Dollar. Uncirculated. *Extremely rare.*

1521 QUARTER Dollar of Philip V., 1735. Of the Republic, 1822 and 1854. Uncirculated. 3 pieces.

1522 EIGHTH and Sixteenth. 1832 and '28. Uncirculated. 2 pcs.

1523 IMPERIAL of 1864, and Republican of various dates, from 25 to 5 cents. Very fine. 14 pieces.

1524 COPPER Coins of Chihuahua, Tuxpango, etc. A good lot. 20 pieces.

## CENTRAL AMERICA.

1525 DOLLAR. 1824. Obv., a range of mountain peaks at sunrise, REPUBLICA DEL CENTRO DE AMERICA, and date; rev., a tree, 8 R., LIBRE CRESCA FECUNDO; below, mint-mark and quality of the silver. Uncirculated.

1526 —— Same, except date. 1826. Not as fine.

1527 QUARTER Dollar. 1831. Very fine.

1527* COSTA RICA Half Dollar. 1865. Obv., Central American arms on shield bristling with armor; rev., same as 1525. Nearly uncirculated.

1528 —— Small; from 20 cents to 5 cents. Rare. 5 pieces.

1529 HONDURAS Provisional Coin. 1 R. Obv., mountain peaks at sunrise; MON. PROVISIONAL, DEI. EST. DE.

## Coins of South America.

HOND.; rev., same as reverse of 1525. Copper coin, silver-plated; edge milled; size of United States copper cent. Fine, and very rare.

1530 HONDURAS. Another, obsidional. Copper. Twice the size of last; much worn. Very rare. 2 pieces.
1531 ——— Siege coins, struck from gun-metal. Very broad. Size 24. Excessively rare. 2 pieces.
1532 ——— Similar, in copper. 2 pieces.
1533 ——— Others, large and smaller. 2 pieces.
1533a GUATEMALA Dollar, of Carrera. 1863. "Un Peso." Fine.
1533b ——— Dollar, Half Dollar, and Real. 3 pieces.

## SOUTH AMERICA.

1534 NEW GRANADA. Medal Dollar of Ferdinand VII., struck at Bogota 11th Sept., 1808. Obv., bust; rev., cross and crown, two lions supporting. Fine and *extremely* rare.
1535 ——— Un Peso (Dollar), 1858. Also struck at Bogota. Rare.
1536 ——— Ocho Dineros (Dollar), 1840. Scarce.
1537 ——— Dos Reals (25 cents). 1 Real (12 cents), and 2 dime size. 4 pieces.
1538 ——— Decimo and Half Decimo de Real. Copper. 2 pieces.
1539 ECUADOR. Two Reals. Obv., head of Liberty, 1848; rev., Arms of Ecuador. Coined at Quito. Very rare.
1540 VENEZUELA. Obv., head of Liberty, 1858; rev., Arms. Two Reals. Fine and rare.
1541 ——— and Caracas Coppers. 9 pieces.
1542 CARACAS. Four and two Reals of Ferdinand VII. Cob money. Rare and fine. 2 pieces.
1543 ——— Two Reals. Same.
1544 COLOMBIA and POPAYAN coins of different denominations, from 2 Reals to smaller. Some very rare. 6 pieces.
1545 ——— Farthings. Obv., head without inscription; rev., Mercury running, no inscription. Obv., head MAXIMUS; rev., NON PLUS ULTRA. Obv., head Columbia; rev., Justice seated. The first two exceedingly rare. Fine. 3 pieces.
1545* ——— Mints of Bogata and Popayan. Gold coins alloyed with silver. Two dollar size. 1831, 1833. Rare. 2 pieces.

## Coins of South America.

1546 CARTHAGENA. Small copper coin. Obv., figure seated under a tree, pointing to a bird; rev., ESTAD DE CARTA-GENA, 1812. All very rude and struck by hand. Fine and rare.

1547 SURINAM. Rev., Tree, 1764. Exceedingly rare. Small copper.

1548 PERU. Dollar of Ferdinand VII., 1808. Struck at Lima. A proclamation piece. Fine and rare.

1549 ——— Dollar of the Republic (1830). Counter-stamped with monogram of F. T. under a crown. Rare.

1550 ——— First Dollar of the new Republic, still at war with Spain, 1822. Obv., Arms of the Republic and date; rev., column and scroll, to r. a figure of Virtue, to l. Justice. Uncirculated. Very rare.

1551 ——— Dollar of 1825. Goddess of Liberty, with staff and shield; rev., Arms of the Republic quartered on a shield; above, oak wreath; to r. and l. laurel and palm. Uncirculated, but stained. Rare.

1552 ——— Dollar of 1827. Same type. Fine.

1553 ——— SOUTH PERU. Cuzco, 1837. Obv., sun and four stars; rev., castle and volcano; in background a ship ih foreground a cornucopia. Very fine; rare.

1554 ——— Similar, 1838. Equally fine.

1555 ——— Duplicates of 1550 and 1554. Dollars. 2 pieces.

1556 ——— Proclamation and Republican Half Dollars. 2 pieces.

1557 ——— Dollar of 1855. New dies. Uncirculated.

1558 ——— Un Sol (dollar) of 1864. Obv., figure of Liberty seated. Uncirculated. Rare.

1559 ——— Half Sol (50 cents); Quarter do. (25 cents); undino (10 cents); half dino (5 cents), and quarter do. Fine set. Uncirculated. 5 pieces.

1560 ——— Copper and small Silver Coins. 6 pieces.

1561 ——— Copper Tokens. Very interesting and fine; must be seen to be appreciated. Farthing size. 8 pieces.

1562 ——— OMNIBUS TICKET. Hotel, Lima. Octagon. Fine.

1563 PERUVIAN Medal half dollar of Simon Bolivar. Obv., military bust; rev., arms of Peru. 1824. Extremely fine and rare.

1564 ——— Dollar in honor of Bolivar, without his bust. Fine, and very rare.

## Coins of South America. 89

1565 BOLIVIA Dollar. Obv., bare bust of Bolivar; rev., two Lamas lying under a palm tree; above, six stars. 1851. Very well preserved, and rare.

1566 ——— Half dollar. Military bust to r.; rev. as before. Ordinary.

1567 ——— Medal dollar of the Department of Potosi, 1852. Obv., circular temple in rays, 6 Sept., 1850; rev., Fame flying, VIVA BOLIVIA, 1852. Uncirculated. Rare.

1568 ——— Dollar of Gen. Melgarejo, "Pacificador of Bolivia." Obv., his bust; rev., inscription and date, 1865. Fine and rare.

1569 ——— Half dollar of Generals Melgarejo and Munoz, with their busts. 1865. Very fine and rare.

1570 ——— Duplicates of 1568 and 1569. 2 pieces.

1571 ——— Dollar of 1858. New pattern. "La Union es la Fuerza" within oak wreath; "1. Boliviano 500 G' 9 DFINO" in ex. date. Rev., Arms of the Republic. Uncirculated.

1572 ——— Similar dollar, 1872, the Arms slightly changed. Uncirculated.

1573 ——— Duplicate. Splendid.

1574 ——— Quarter, with Simon Bolivar's bust. Uncirculated. Rare.

1575 ——— Silver tokens and coins, 25, 10, and 5 cts. value. 4 pieces.

1576 LA PLATA, or Argentine Confederacy. Dollar of 1813, from the Potosi Mint. Obv., the sun, PROVINCIAS DEL RIO DE LA PLATA; rev., Arms of the Confederacy, EN UNION Y LIBERTAD. Very fine.

1577 ——— Similar dollar of 1834. Very fine.

1578 ——— Dollar of Rioja. Obv., a mountain, military emblems below, 1839; rev., Arms of the Confederacy, ETERNO LOOR AL RESTAURADOR ROSAS. Fine and rare.

1579 ——— Copper coins—penny, half-penny, and farthing size. Quatro, dos, and un centavos. Very fine. 3 pieces.

1580 ——— Half, quarter and eighth dollars. 3 pieces.

1581 ——— PROVINCE of Cordoba. Obv., a sun, "Confedera 8 R', 1852. Dollar and half dollar. Rare. 2 pieces.

1582 CHILI. Dollar of Santiago. "Un Peso." Obv., a volcano; rev., a column supporting a globe, above the globe a star. 1817. Very fine.
1583 ——— Same type, different die. 1834. Dollar.
1584 ——— Dollar. Obv., Condor with a broken chain and shield, 1855; rev., Arms of the Republic within a laurel wreath. "Un Peso." Very fine.
1585 ——— Plate dollar of Copiapo. Obv., COPIAPO—CHILI. I P.; rev., 1865. Uncirculated. Rare.
1586 ——— Duplicate. Very fine.
1587 ——— Dollar of 1868; similar to 1584, but improved. Extremely fine.
1588 ——— Half and quarter dollars; both types unlike any described above. Fine. 2 pieces.
1589 ——— Quarter and three smaller coins. 4 pieces.
1590 ——— Medal half dollar of 1828. Fine.
1591 ——— Centavo and Medio Centavo. Uncirculated. 2 pieces.
1592 ——— Other copper coins. 4 pieces.
1593 URUGUAY. 40, 20, and 5 centesimos. Copper. Uncirculated. 3 pieces.
1594 BUENOS AYRES. A variety of copper coins. 10 pieces.
1595 BRAZIL. Dollar of Carolus IV. (Mexican dollar). Counter-struck with the arms of Portugal and Brazil. The stamp very pretty. Rare.
1596 ——— 3 Patacs, or 960 reis (large dollar). 1812. Obv., arms of Portugal crowned; rev., a belted globe on a cross. Fine.
1597 ——— Same. 1817. Extremely fine.
1598 ——— Patacs, or 320 reis. 1820.
1599 ——— Three patacs, or 960 reis. 1821. Rev., belted globe on a cross. Fine.
1600 ——— Two patacs, or 640 reis. Very fine.
1601 ——— Peter II., Emperor, 1868. 2000 reis. New standard (1 dollar). With bust. Very fine.
1602 ——— Dollar, or 2000 reis of Peter II., without his bust. Fine.
1603 ——— Half dollar (1000 reis), quarter dollar (500), and piece of 200 reis. All very fine. 3 pieces.
1604 ——— 1000 and 500 reis, new standard, half and quarter dollars. 2 pieces.

*West Indian Coins.* 91

1605 BRAZIL. (Old Standard). 320 reis, 160 reis, and 80 reis. Nearly uncirculated. Intrinsic value, 1 dollar. 4 pieces.
1606 ——— Copper coins illustrating the several changes in the standard value of reis. An extra lot. Many large. 14 pieces.

## WEST INDIES.

1607 HAYTI. Boyer, President. Dollar, half dollar, quarter dollar. Uncirculated. 3 pieces.
1608 ——— Small coins, including President Petion's. Obv., head over II.; rev., martial implements and a tree, surmounted by a liberty cap. 4 pieces.
1609 ——— Republican copper coins of 1831, etc. Deux Centimes and un Centime. Obv., a fasces surmounted by a liberty cap; rev., Deux Centimes between two palms. 4 pieces.
1610 ——— Similar coins of 1846. Six, two, and one centime. Very fine. 3 pieces.
1611 ——— Coins of Soulouque, under the title of Faustin I. Obv. crowned head, 1850; rev., coat of arms, lions supporting. A fine coin, size of English penny. Very scarce. 2 pieces
1612 ——— Copper coin of President Geffard, 1863. Obv., bust; rev., coat of arms. Fine. 3 pieces.
1613 ——— Faustin and Geffard. 5 pieces.
1614 BRITISH POSSESSIONS. Quarter dollar. Obv., British Coat-of-Arms; Georgus IV., D.G; BRITANNIARUM . REX F.D. Rev., anchor and crown; IV.; COLONIAR . BRITAN MONET . 1822. Fine.
1615 ——— Bahama (Island). Halfpenny of George III. 1806. Obv., bust; rev., ship. Fair.
1616 ——— Jamaica (Island). Penny, copper, Kingston currency. Coat-of-Arms supported by two Indians, another, man holding a horse. Very good. 2 pieces.
1617 ——— Do. Penny in Nickel. Obv., Victoria's bust, 1869; rev., arms. Fine.
1618 ——— Bermuda. Splendid proof penny of George III. 1793. Rare.
1619 ——— Do. Circulated.
1620 ——— Antigua Farthing. Obv. tree, 1836; rev. in wreath of laurel and oak, the denomination. Pretty and scarce. Fine. 2 pieces.

1621 BRITISH POSSESSIONS. Barbadoes Penny. Obv. negro head, with Welsh feathers; rev. pine-apple, 1788. Very fine. Scarce.
1622 —— Same, with three tokens. Rare. 4 pieces.
1623 —— British Guiana (in South America and not regularly under this head). Three Guilders of Demerara and Essequibo. Obv. bust of George III. laureated; rev. "3," surmounted by a crown and inclosed by two oak branches, 1832. Silver coin, dollar size. Pierced, but very good. Rare.
1624 —— Guilder, Half Guilder, and Quarter Guilder. Fine. 3 pieces.
1625 —— Another lot, similar. Geo. III. 3 pieces.
1626 —— Guilder and Half Guilder of William IV.; also another Guilder and Half Guilder. Very good. 4 pieces.
1627 —— Stiver and Half Stiver of B. G. Uncirculated. Rare. 2 pieces.

[The stiver varies but little in size and value from the penny. The guilder was worth 20 stivers.]

1628 —— Duplicates of last. Dark. 2 pieces.
1629 FRENCH POSSESSIONS—Windward Islands. Obv. head of Louis XV.; rev. **ISLES DU VENT**, 1731. Small silver coin, pierced.
1630 —— Various French Colonial Coppers, containing a little silver. 4 pieces.
1631 DANISH POSSESSIONS. Piece of twelve skillings. Obv. the royal monogram crowned; rev. ship, 1740, DANSK AMERIC, etc. Fine.
1632 —— Ten Cents of Frederick VII. Obv. bust; rev. sugar-cane, 1859. Five Cents; rev. ship, with various designs and dates. Small coins. Fine. 9 pieces.
1633 DOMINICAN REPUBLIC. Copper Coins of 1844. Very rare. 2 pieces.

## AFRICA.

1633* SIERRA LEONE One Dollar Piece. Obv., lion; rev., two hands clasped. Poor.
1634 —— Penny of 1791. Obv., lion; rev., two hands clasped. Splendid proof. Rare.
1635 —— Cent, same date and type. Splendid proof. Rare.

*Coins of the Provinces under British Crown.* 93

1636 SIERRA LEONE Penny, same date. Different from 1633; equally fine. Smaller die. Rare.
1637 —— Ten Cents and two Penny pieces. Poor. 3 pieces.
1638 HAWAIIAN ISLANDS. 1847. Hapa Haneri (Cent). Obv., full-face military bust of the king, Kamehameha III., ka moi; rev., Aupnrri Hawaii. Extra fine and rare. 2 pieces.
1639 ST. HELENA Half-penny, 1821. Fine. Scarce.
1640 GUINEA Half-penny. Obv., lion, 1813; rev., within wreath of laurel, Britannia seated. With two of St. Helena. 3 pieces.
1641 LIBERIA. One Cent, 1833; Colonization Society founded 1816. Five Cents, 1847: obv., head of Liberty; rev., palm tree. One Cent, same type. Very good lot. 3 pieces.
1642 —— Two and One Cent, 1847. 2 pieces.

## COINS OF PROVINCES UNDER THE BRITISH CROWN.

1643 CEYLON. George III. Rev., elephant. One Rix Dollar, 1821. Fine and rare.
 [Of the value in silver of the rupee.]
1644 —— "Ceylon Government, '48"; rev., elephant, 1802. And a similar coin in tin, but smaller, and very thick. 1803. Rare. 5 pieces.
1645 INDIA STRAITS. "One Cent," Victoria. 2 pieces.
1646 HONG-KONG. Obv., crowned bust of "Victoria, Queen?" rev., "One Dollar, Hongkong, 1867." Uncirculated. Scarce.
1647 —— The same. Very fine. Scarce. 2 pieces.
1648 —— Half Dollar. Very fine. Scarce.
1649 —— "Ten Cents" and Copper. Very fine. Scarce. 6 pieces.
1650 EAST INDIA Co. William IV. 1835. Rupee and Half Rupee. Very fine. 2 pieces.
1651 —— Victoria, 1840, with the Queen's bust uncrowned. Rupee, Half Rupee, and Quarter Rupee. Very fine. Rare. 3 pieces.

1652 EAST INDIA Co. Victoria, with her bust crowned, 1862. Rupee and Quarter Rupee. Very fine. 2 pieces.
1653 —— (With some native coins). 5 Rupees.
1654 —— Half Rupee and Hongkong silver coins. Average value, 12 cents each. 5 pieces.
1655 —— United E. I. Co., 1794. Figure 4 above a heart; rev., the Company's arms; the Company's issue in 1803 of XX, X, and V cash, with Half and Quarter Annas. A very fine representative lot of Copper coins, in fine condition. 10 pieces
1656 —— Copper coins in great variety. Very fine. 34 pieces.

## Australia.

1657 ADELAIDE Penny Tokens, with cards of Wm. Morgan, John Howell, Crocker & Hamilton, Harrold Brothers Martin, & Sach, Alfred Taylor, John Martin. Very fine. 1858, etc. 7 pieces.
1658 NEW ZEALAND. Various towns. Penny tokens of S. Hagur Smith, E. De Carle & Co., J. M. Herrington & Co., H. J. Hall. Very fine. 4 pieces.
1659 NEW SOUTH WALES. Pennies and Half Pennies of Sydney tradesmen. Fine and rare. 5 pieces.
1660 QUEENSLAND. Tradesmen's tokens of 1863 and '64: Stewart & Hemmant, Brisbane; T. Zenyer, J. Pettigrew & Co., Ipswich; D. T. Mulligan, Rockhamp'on. Fine. 5 pieces.
1661 TASMANIA. Penny Tokens: W. D. Wood, Joseph Buckhill, Andrew Mather, E. De Carle & Co. Rare. 4 pieces.
1662 VAN DIEMAN'S LAND. R. Joseph's New Town Toll-Gate Pennies. Fine and rare. 2 pieces.
1663 VICTORIA Pennies: T. F. Merry & Co., J. R. Grundy, J. Booth, Miller Brothers, Thomas Stokes, Annand, Smith & Co., Hide & De Carle. Very fine. 7 pieces.
1664 —— Pennies of Melbourne tradesmen. Very fine. 5 pcs.
1665 Australian Pennies. Various. 4 pieces.
1666 —— Half Pennies. Some rare. 7 pieces.

## Canada.

1667 PENNIES. Upper and Lower Canada. 4 pieces.
1668 —— Various. 5 pieces.

*Oriental Coins.* 95

1669 Half Pennies. 7 pieces.
1670 —— Similar lot. 7 pieces.
1671 —— Rare lot. 7 pieces.
1672 VICTORIA 50 Cents, 25 Cents, 10 Cents, and 5 Cents, 1871.
   Very fine. 4 pieces.
1673 —— Similar set. 4 pieces.
1674 VICTORIA 20 Cents, 1858 and '65. Fine. 2 pieces.
1675 —— 10 and 5 Cents. 5 pieces.
1676 —— One Cent. Fine. 2 pieces.

*Nova Scotia.*

1677 VICTORIA Penny, and a variety of Half-pennies. 9 pieces.

*New Brunswick, Newfoundland, Etc.*

1678 PENNY of Magdalen Islands, and Half-pennies N. B. and N.
   F. 8 pieces.

*Gibraltar.*

1679 VICTORIA. Two and One Quarto. Poor. 2 pieces.
1680 ROBERT KEELING & SONS. Value, two Quartos; with 3
   towers, gate; 1810; and lion guarding key. Very good.
1681 —— One Quarto, same type, with one obv. rock; rev.
   3-tower gate. Fine. 2 pieces.
1682 —— Others. 4 pieces.

## ORIENTAL COINS.

1683 CHINA. "Chopped" Spanish Dollar, 1813, bearing the
   private marks of nearly 100 merchants.
1684 —— Mexican "Chopped" Dollar, 1857.
1685 —— "Chopped" Dollar of Bolivia, 1859. Fine.
1686 —— Tokens, with and without hole in centre; square and
   round. Copper. Very curious. 4 pieces.
1687 ——— Cash; brass coins, with hole in centre. 13 pieces.
1688 ——— Coin of fine silver of the intrinsic value of the half
   dollar. Chinese characters, and square hole in centre.
   Made in the style of Chinese cash. To me an unknown
   coin, but fine and interesting.
1689 ——— Others in the same style, one gilt. Intrinsic value,
   25 cents each. 2 pieces.

1690 CHINA. Porcelain token or coin. Size 14.
1691 ——— Silver medal of the Han-Lin College (?). First a thin medal of the dollar size, with the usual hole in the middle; joined to this a sort of ornamental yoke. Very fine.
1692 ——— Medals in fine brass gilt; hole in centre; dollar and half dollar size. Covered with Oriental figures. 2 pieces.
1693 ——— Stack of brass coins, from size 10 to 40, graduated. Very fine and desirable; thick hole in centre. 9 pieces.
1694 ——— Similar. 6 pieces.
1695 MOROCCO. Small silver coin, with the year of the hegira (1187) in European figures.
1695* ——— Silver rupees, 1749 and 1802. Fine. 2 pieces.
1696 ——— Copper; on one side, double triangle; on the other, date; anno hegira 1268. 7 pieces.
1697 JAPANESE gold coin (Obang?) Oval, 6 x 3 inches. Weight 67 gold dollars; worth 75 dollars in currency to melt. A cast bar, the upper surface presenting a waved appearance. It bears impressions from several small stamps. Black India ink caligraphy on one side. A striking and extremely rare coin. 966 thousandth fine.
1698 ——— Gold bar. Oblong square. Stamped on both sides. Weighs 23 dollars. Kingdom of Anam.
1699 ——— Gold Cobang, two and a half inches long, and half as broad. Plate with various stamps. Intrinsic value, about six dollars.
1700 ——— Gold piece, 20 yen ($20). Obv., a dragon; rev., a sun within a wreath crossed by two flags. Edge reeded. Extra fine and rare.
1701 ——— Five yen. Same type. Equally fine.
1702 ——— Yen, in gold. Fine and rare.
1703 ——— Silver half-yen, same type as the gold. Value, 50 cts. Fine and rare.
1704 ——— Parts of yen, corresponding to U. S. dime and half-dime. 3 pieces.
1705 ——— Gold itzebu. Uncirculated. Intrinsic value, 1.11.
1706 ——— Same, alloyed with silver. 3 pieces.
1707 ——— Silver itzebu, and parts of do., one very long. 4 pieces.
1708 ——— Tempo, long oval, with square hole in centre. 3 pieces.

## Oriental Coins.

09 SIAM. Old bullet money. Tical (60 cts.) and parts of same. 5 pieces.

1710 ——— Two ticals ($1.20), silver coin, dollar size. On the principal side three pagodas; rev., an elephant in the centre of several ornamented and reeded circles. Very fine.

1711 ——— Tical (60 cts.) Equally fine.

1712 ——— Quarter tical. "

1713 ——— Eighth tical. "

1713* ——— Gold coin, dollar size. Rare and fine.

1714 ——— Tical in silver, and a collection of base coins of the same type. Their denomination unknown. Probably in no other collection in the country. All in good preservation. 7 pieces.

1714* BURMAH. A specimen of their old currency. A lump of brass. Rare.

1715 ——— Modern silver rupee. Obv., peacock; rev., Cufic inscription. Very fine. Rare.

1716 COREA. A large curious copper coin in the Chinese style, but with the characters on only one side. Diameter 2 inches.

1717 ——— Smaller. Same type. 1 inch.

1718 GOA. Small tin coin. G A divided by a rude shield; rev., cross. Rare. Size 8 inches.

1719 BORNEO. A copper piece resembling the work of the Japs. Fine and rare.

1720 SUMATRA. Obv., Arms of the E. I. Co.; rev., inscription in native characters. Very fine. Copper. 2 pieces.

1721 MALACCA. Similar. On one side a rooster. One very fine. 2 pieces.

1722 PERSIA. Scrook (about half rupee). Obv., sun and lion; rev., Persian letters. Thick silver coin. Very fine and rare.

1723 ——— Copper coin, same type. Thick. Fine. 2 pieces.

1724 ——— Others. Two sizes. 2 pieces.

1725 ——— Gold pagoda, 5-pointed star. Rev., naked figure. Value about 1½ dollars.

1726 ——— Silver half pagoda. Obv., tower and stars; rev., a king crowned. Fine.

1727 ——— Quarter pagoda. Very fine.

## Oriental Coins.

1728 RUPEE. Old Cufic coin. Square. Very rare.
1729 RUPEES. Indian and Persian. 8 pieces
1730 HALF-RUPEES. Indian. 5 pieces
1731 —— Indian and Persian. 5 pieces
1732 MISCELLANEOUS. From ¼ to 1/16 rupee. 10 pieces
1733 PONDICHERRY. Fleur de lis and star. Small silver. Coined by the French. 5 pieces
1734 INDIAN coppers. Thick coins. Great variety. 20 pieces
1735 TRIPOLI. Thick coins. Struck in collars, with milled and plain edges. A series, nearly all uncirculated From size 25 to 16. Rare. 5 pieces
1736 —— Similar. Mixed lot. 6 pieces
1737 TURKEY. Yermilik in gold. 20 piasters. Fine.
1738 —— Onlik. Equally fine. 10 piasters.
1739 —— Beshlik. do. 5 piasters.
1740 —— Double piaster.
1741 —— Piasters. 2 pieces.
1742 —— Silver dollar; obv. *Toghra* of the Sultan; rev. place of mintage. Engrailed edge. Uncirculated.
1743 —— Quarter-dollar. 2 varieties. 5 pieces
1744 —— Small silver coins. Paras, &c. 13 pieces
1745 —— Thick base piaster. Extra fine. Size 30
1746 —— Silver medal of ASMI ACHMET EFFENDI; obv. turbaned bust; rev. inscription in 8 lines. Struck in 1791. Extremely rare. Size 20
1747 —— Base coins. Quarter-dollar size. 3 pieces
1748 —— Uncirculated silver coin. Egyptian. Same size.
1749 —— Small coins. Fine silver. 4 pieces.
1750 —— Base coins. 15 do.
1751 —— Uncirculated copper coins. 2 do.
1752 —— Coppers. Thick and thin. 4 do.
1753 —— Repetition. 4 do.
1754 RING MONEY. A string of minute metallic rings, said to pass from hand to hand as a measure of value among certain islanders. It is a curious and not inconvenient currency, as will be seen upon examination, and to a contemplative mind suggests a question as to the relative merits of "ring money" and "stamps."

# DENMARK.

### Silver Coins.

1755 SVEN ESTRIDSEN, 1047 to 1076. Denarius. Two angels standing; rev. cross and gothic letters. Fine, and extremely rare.
1756 WALDEMAR I. 1157 to 1182. Rude bust with sceptre; rev. St. Peter. Denarius.
1757 ABEL. 1250 to 1252. Obv. A; rev. R. Billon penny. Black. Very rare and fine.
1758 —— Duplicate.
1759 ERICH V. 1259 to 1286. Very fine penny. Rare.
1760 CHRISTOPH II. 1319 to 1334. Obv. R crowned, CRISTOF; rev. cross and shield. Rare penny.
1761 CIVIL WAR to 1340. Penny. Rare.
1762 CHRISTIAN I. 1448 to 1481. Small silver pennies? Very rare. Well. 9,849.   3 pieces
1763 JOHN. 1481 to 1513. Penny. Billon money; obv. JOH, Gothic L crowned; rev. cross and shield. Very rare.
1764 CHRISTIAN III. 1534 to 1539. "2 skill." Arms of Denmark (3 lions).
1765 FREDERICK II. 1559 to 1588. Crown of 15—72; his bust to left; rev. coat-of-arms, DEVS REFVGIVM ET FIDVCIA MEA. Fine and rare.
1766 CHRISTIAN IV. 1588 to 1648. With his figure to the hips; rev. shield with three lions. No date. "1 marck danske" (nearly 40 cts.) Marked varieties.   3 pieces
1767 —— 1606-7-8. "8 skill danske." Crowned bust. Rare. Good silver, about ½ thaler each.   3 pieces
1768 —— Marks and half-mark. 1608 to 1617.   4 pieces
1769 —— Rare crown of 1618. The King at full length, walking, with sword and sceptre; rev. large crown in the area of the coin, CORONA DANSKE. Broad and fine.
1770 —— The same type, 1620. Less broad. In splendid preservation. Very rare.

*Denmark.—Silver.*

1771 CHRISTIAN IV. Remarkable crown of 1624. The King's bust, crowned, to the waist; below in three straight lines his name and titles; rev. cordon of 13 shields around the arms of Denmark. Extra fine. Rare.

1772 —— Thaler of extra thickness. Size 20; rev. large crown. Very fine and rare.

1773 —— Collection of his small coins. 4 pieces

1774 —— Ducat, with the inscription, JUSTUS JUDEX, 1646. Hebrew characters. Rare.

1775 —— Siege coins. Square, 1648 (klippingers.)
2 pieces

1776 FREDERICK III. 1648 to 1670. Crown, without date, "3 marck danske," arms without bust. Good crown. Rare.

1777 —— ½ daler and small coins. Rare lot. 7 pieces

1778 —— Crown of 1653. Crowned bust with long hair; rev. lion. Splendid, broad piece.

1779 —— Another; obv. same; rev. cordon of shields around arms of Denmark. Equally as fine as last.

1780 —— Crown of 1659. Cypher of his name crowned; rev. two hands, one holding sword, the other severed from the arm by same. Very fine, rare.

1781 —— Crown of 1666. The finest of the series in design. Slightly circulated. Bare bust laureated; rev. arms on a cross. Broad and fine. Rare.

1782 CHRISTIAN V. 1670 to 1699. Crown of 1675. The King on horseback—the horse trotting.

1783 —— Small Coins of this and other types. "1 Marck," and other denominations. (av. 16 cts.) Valuable lot. 5 pieces

1784 —— Crown. CV., crowned; rev. arms. 1679. Uncirculated.

1785 —— With others of Christian IV., and Fred. III. and IV. Fine little coins, intrinsic value, small. 10 pcs

1786 —— Thaler. 1693. Mailed bust, bare head; rev. large crown. PIET ET JUST. Fine.

1787 —— 1 Mark. 1675. A little gem as thick as a Dollar. Diameter of a Half-dime. Uncirculated. Rare.

*Denmark.—Silver.*

1788 FREDERICK IV. 1699 to 1730. Crown of 1723. The King on horseback, pointing forward with his sceptre; rev. coat-of-arms within two royal order chains. Fine, rare.

1789 —— Crown of 1725. Arms on a heart-shaped shield crowned; rev. cypher of the King, also crowned. Very fine, rare.

1790 —— Many varieties. "XVI. Skilling." "Tolf Skilling." "XII. Skilling," etc. Fine. 6 pieces

1791 —— Head; rev. head of Christian V. Fine Coin. Dime size. Very rare.

1792 CHRISTIAN VI. 1730 to 1746. Half-thaler of 1732. Bust; rev. arms.

1793 FREDERICK V. 1746 to 1766. Base coin. Size 20

1794 CHRISTIAN VII. 1766 to 1808. Dollar of 1771. Pillars of Hercules; between them two shields crowned; rev. arms crowned. Uncirculated. Very rare.

1795 —— Thaler of 1776. Letter C and 7 interlinked; rev. oval shield. Crowned. Uncirculated.

1796 —— Specie Ducat. 1178. (Crown). Same type as last. Uncirculated. Rare.

1797 —— Same. 1788. Bust; rev. lion. "Rigs Daler Courant." Uncirculated. Rare.

1798 —— Same. 1796. Bust; rev. arms crowned. "Sixty Schilling Schlesw-Holst." Fine.

1799 —— For American Provinces. Base. 2 sizes

1800 FREDERICK VI. 1808 to 1839. His cypher crowned; rev. within wreath of oak FRIVILLIGT OFFER TILL FÆDRENELANDET, 1808, MF. Base. Size 18

1801 —— Three and eight Rigs Bank Schillings, and others. Uncirculated. A pretty lot. 5 pieces

1802 CHRISTIAN VIII. 1839. Small coins. Base. 3 pieces

1803 FREDERICK VII. 1863. (Christian IX. on the reverse). "Two Rigs Daler." One do. Uncirculated. 2 pieces

1804 MISCELLANEOUS. Including two and one "Royaliner" of Christ, 7 (1776). Several old and rare. 18 pieces

## SWEDEN.

*Silver Coins.*

1805 CHRISTIAN I. 1470. Half-groat. (Similar to the English of the same period). CHRISTIANVS D. G. DANOR GO. REX. Three lions; rev. Agnus Dei. Fine, rare.

1806 GUSTAVUS I. Vasa. 1523 to 1560. Crown; obv. the King standing, a shield by his side; rev. the Saviour standing. 1544. Extremely fine. Has never been in circulation. Very rare.

1807 —— Half-crown ; rev. two shields under a crown. Very rare, but rubbed.

1808 ERICH. 1560 to 1568. Base money. On each side a shield, one on a cross. ERIC. Half-groat. Rare.

1809 —— Seige Piece. 1563. E. R. on a shield crowned; rev. arms crowned. Diamond-shaped, extra thickness. (Dollar). Very rare.

1810 JOHN II. 1568 to 1592. Base coin; obv. the King standing; rev. arms. Very fine. Size 18

1811 JOHN III.; obv. the King with sword and mund; rev. SALVATOR MVNDI. SALVA NOS., 1573. The Saviour standing. Crown. Rare and fine.

1812 SIGISMUND. (King of Poland). Like John II. Base coin.

1813 CHARLES IX. 1604 to 1611. Quarter-crown. Fine.

1814 —— One-eighth crown, and small. Base. Very fine. 2 pieces

1815 GUSTAVUS ADOLPHUS. 1611 to 1632. Bracteate and Penny. Extra rare. 2 pieces

1816 —— Quarter-crown. Bust laureated. Hebrew word for Jehovah and rays. Below, three shields ; rev. crown and sceptre under a blazing sun. Fine and rare.

1817 —— Crown " Gustavus Adolphus Magnus." Laureated bust in rich dress. ÆTA-TIS SVÆ, 38; rev. inscription and crown; in Ex. OSNABRV. Beautiful and rare.

1818 GUSTAVUS ADOLPHUS. Medal (Crown size). Bust three-quarter face as a medallion, in garnished frame; rev. sword with myrtle and palm, the point entering a crown. Double circle of inscription. Fine, rare.

1819 —— Another, laureated bust to the waist; rev. arms quartered on round shield under a Crown. 1632, the year of his death. Extra fine and rare.

1820 —— Same year. A rare and valuable Crown, showing figure, with sceptre and crown in suit of mail; rev. the Saviour standing. Nearly uncirculated.

1821 —— Medal, struck to commemorate the victory at Leipzig? 1631; obv. the King riding hard; in background, battlefield; rev. four round shields and military symbols. Has been suspended by loop, now removed. As fine as when struck; or perhaps cast and burnished. Size 30

1822 —— Crown on the same victory. Long inscription in straight parallel lines. Remarkably fine. A rare Crown.

1823 CHRISTINA. 1632 to 1654-89. Two of her small Coins (Or's). 1633. As fine as when struck. Rare.

1824 —— Medal. Young laureated head, bare bust. REGINA CHRISTINA; rev. three Crowns. Il-M. Thick. Beautiful, and extra rare. Size 21

1825 —— Crown of 1640. The Queen's figure in large collar and full dress, shown nearly full length; rev. the Saviour standing. Very fine and rare type, and better than usually found; in this condition very rare.

1826 —— Another Crown, 1644; the same type, but a larger bust to the shoulders. Equally fine, rare.

1827 —— Small Coin, with examples of several of the preceding reigns. 5 pieces

1828 CHARLES X. (Gustavus). 1654 to 1660. Laureated bust; rev. three crowns. Size 20

1829 —— Medal to commemorate his death; hand holding sword upright; others to right and left. Very fine, rare. Size 27

1830 CHARLES XI. 1660 to 1697. "2 M," (about half-thaler). Laureated bust l.; rev. 3 crowns. 1668. Good.

Sweden.—Silver.

1831 CHARLES XI. 12 eine richs daler. Base. 2 coins.
1832 —— Small medal. A gem. Size 10
1833 CHARLES XII. 1697 to 1718. "2 M," (about half-thaler), 1762. Young bust. Fine.
1834 —— 1707. Beautiful medalet and coin. "5 O." (re.) 2 pieces
1835 —— 1706 medal; obv. bust to r.; rev. between 2 shields, FELICITAS, "Sardinia Saxoniæ." Proof. Thick medal. Size 16
1836 —— "X M" (thaler), 1718. Two letter C's entwined; rev. shields arranged as a cross. Very little circulated. Rare.
1837 —— Medalet to commemorate his birth and death. Splendid proof. A gem. Size 12
1838 —— Crown Medal. Splendid bust in rich robes, head bare; rev. lion rampant, PAR ANIMO ROBVR. Fine, nearly proof. Lettered edge. Rare.
1839 —— Another brilliant proof crown medal on the treaty of Breslau, 8th February, 1709; obv. splendid bust; rev. lion erect, one paw on a monument. Very rare.
1840 —— Coins of 1716 and '18. Extra fine. Size 16. 2 pieces
1841 FREDERICK IX. 1720 to 1751. Broad crown, 1723 bust; rev. shield; lions supporting. Fine and rare.
1842 —— Coin (5 ore) of 1747. Fine.
1843 ADOLPHUS FREDERICK II. 1751–71. Fine crown, 1752. Arms in an order chain. Rare.
1844 GUSTAVUS III., 1771–92. Medal. Splendid crowned bust of "Augustus Adolphus Filius Rex." Rev. inscription in 7 lines. Uncirculated. Size 20
1845 —— Crown of 1776; obv. bare bust; rev. arms crowned, encircled by an order chain with the star of Maria Therese. Uncirculated.
1846 —— ⅓ do.
1847 GUSTAVUS IV. (Adolphus), 1792 to 1809. Crown of 1792. Naked bust; rev. arms as before, GUD OCII FOL-KET-I-R P. Uncirculated. Very rare.
1848 —— Similar crown of 1796. Fine.
1849 —— Small coins. Quarter-dollar size. 2 pieces

1850 CHARLES XIII. 1809-18. 2 base coins.
1851 CHARLES XIV. Splendid uncirculated dollar (I. S P$^s$), 1824. Bare bust, curly hair; rev. arms (lion) on square escutcheon.
1852 —— 4 R SP$^s$ (30 cts.) "2¼ skilling," and "4 skilling."  3 pieces
1853 CHARLES XV. Half-dollar, 1862. Bust and arms; like coins of Charles XIV. Extra fine.
1854 —— With several of the small coins of Oscar. A pretty lot. Different denominations.  8 pieces
1855 OSCAR. 2 skilling, 1843, $\frac{1}{32}$ RDR–SP and 10 ore, 1855. Very fine.  3 pieces

### Copper.

With a few copper coins of Denmark.

1856 DANISH West Indian Possessions. "1 cent," proof, and two others.  3 pieces
1857 DANISH coins. Examples of many dates and denominations. Fine  48 pieces

All following under this head are Swedish.

1858 CITY OF STOCKHOLM. 1573. Arms of the city; rev. arms of Sweden. Very rare.  2 pieces
1859 CITY OF ARBORG. 1627; obv. griffon; rev. handsome coat-of-arms. Large coins. Size 24. *Very rare.*  2 pieces
1860 GUSTAVUS ADOLPHUS. Two arrows crossed, crown, "I.OR" MONETA CVPREA DALERENSIS. Uncirculated.  Size 28
1861 —— Thick siege piece. "I.OR." Square. 1726. Extra fine and rare.
1862 CHRISTINA. Uncirculated specimen of the new copper money of the period.  Size 30
1863 —— Another extra thick. Very fine. Rare. Size 30
1864 —— Medal, 1640. *I C M.* Her bust as Pallas; rev. owl on pile of books. Uncirculated.  Size 20
1865 CHARLES X. (Gustavus). 1634-50. ¼ or; rev. 3 crowns.  3 pieces

## Sweden.—Copper.

1866 CHARLES XI. 1660–97. Medal; obv. bust in royal robes; rev. Pallas standing, 1663. Uncirculated.
Size 20
1867 —— "Or" of the large size (30), and 2, ½ do. 3 pieces
1868 CHARLES XII. Medal to commemorate his landing in Udstadt, 1715. Bright and uncirculated. Very rare.
Size 28
1869 —— Medalet worn at the time, retaining a piece of silk from which it was detached. His bust; rev. lion holding a palm and sword, *inclined to both peace or war.* Size 12
1870 —— Variety of his copper coins, and a rare medalet. A good lot. 6 pieces
1871 —— Coins of Necessity issued by Baron Goerck. "1 daler," 1718, with figures of pagan deities: as Jupiter, Saturn, Mars, Phœbus, Mercury, etc. Uncirculated. Full set with portions red. 10 pieces
1872 —— Another full set. Fine. " "
1873 —— Repetition of last. Fine " "
1874 —— Do  do " "
1875 —— 8 varieties. Fine. 8 "
1876 —— Do " "
1877 —— 6 Do 6 "
1878 —— Not assorted. 8 "
1879 —— Plate of copper, 6 x 6 in., value 1 dollar; with stamp of the mint. Very rare.
1880 FREDERICK IX. 1720–51. Small coin, "1 or." Reduced in size. 4 pieces
1881 —— Plate of copper. Value half-dollar. Stamped at the mint. 4 x 3 inches. Very rare.
1882 ADOLPHUS FREDERICK II. 1751–71. Medal; obv. bust; rev. a spider's web and merchandise. Uncirculated.
Size 20
1883 —— Medalets. Very fine. 1763. 2 pieces
1884 —— Coins. "2 or," "1 or," "12 cinen reiche thaler." 3 pieces
1885 GUSTAVUS III. 1771–1792. Medal, bust; rev. REGIA. SOCIETAS. PATRIA. SVECA. Caduceus sustaining a helmet, wreath, weapon, and banner. Very fine. Size 26

*Netherlands.—Silver.* 107

1886 GUSTAVUS IV. (Adolphus). 1792 to 1809. A fine lot
of coins. 4 pieces
1887 CHARLES XIII. 1909 to 1818. "1 Skilling." ½ do.
 1/12 do. Varieties. Uncirculated. 5 pieces
1888 OSCAR. 1845. "5 Ore." 2 do. ⅔ Skilling. ⅓ do.
 ½ Ore. Nearly all uncirculated. 6 pieces
1889 CHARLES XIV. A fine lot of uncirculated coins.
 9 pieces
1890 MEDALETS, Tokens, and Coins. Fine and valuable.
 19 pieces

## NETHERLANDS.

### Silver Coins.

The territories comprising the kingdoms of the Netherlands and Belgium' formerly existed as distinct principalities under the names, Guelders, Brabant, Luxemburg, and Limburg—Duchies; with the counties of Antwerp, Holland, Zealand, Zutphen, Flanders, Arlois, Hainaut, and Nemur; and the Lordships of Utrecht, Groningen, Overyssel, Friesland, and Mechlin. Having passed into the house of Austria, and through the Emperor Charles V. into the hands of Philip II. of Spain, seven of these provinces revolted, and their independence was finally acknowledged under the name of the "United Provinces." Things continued pretty much in this shape until Napoleon created the "Kingdom of Holland," and subsequent revolutions have established the present kingdom.

1891 PENNIES. Head; rev. Cross. Many other varieties; Gothic legends. Can all be assigned to their proper places—10th and 11th centuries. Good coins.
 10 pieces
1892 —— Similar lot. 8 pieces
1893 GUELDERS. (Principality). *D* GELRIÆ, 1756; rev. arms crowned. Uncirculated. Size 16
1894 —— Another. 1752. Size 16
1895 BRUSSELS (City). "Moneta Bruxellencis." An angel. Groat, very fine, of John, Duke of Brabant 1282—1294. Rare.
1896 ALBERT and Elizabeth, Duke and Duchess of Brabant. 1619. Crown, busts jugata; rev. arms upheld by lions; above them, a crown. Obv. fine. A rare piece.
1897 —— ½ Crown; same heads. Very fine. Rare.

## Netherlands.—Silver.

1898 MARIA, Princess of Brabant. 1480. Quarter dollar. Very fine and rare.

1899 ANTON, Duke Limberg. 1405 to 1415. Groat. Lion; rev. cross. Very rare.

1900 CORNELIUS (LUTTICH). 1538 to 1544. Large thin coin; as broad as a half dollar. Well preserved. Very rare.

1901 ERNST. 1581 to 1612. Luttich. Similar.

1902 JOHN THEODORE (Cardinal Luttich). 1744—1768. Very fine coin. ⅛ dollar. 1751. Nearly uncirculated. Rare.

1903 CHARLES V., Emp. Germany. "Urbis Imperialis Novi Magen Insignia." His bust with crown and sceptre. Well preserved and very rare.

1904 PHILIP II. (Spain). Duke of Brabant. 1550 to 1598. "Dominus Michi Adiutor." The King's bust and cross of Brabant. Extra fine. Groat.

1905 —— Similar to last. Varieties. Groats. 3 pieces

1906 —— ⅓ dollar, with his bust. Rare.

1907 PHILIP IV. (Spain). 1621 to 1665. Duke? 1645. Lion upholding a shield; ½ crown. Fine and very rare.

1908 BALERN. Tournois of Marguerite, wife of Louis V. (Struck at Valenciennes). Horseman galloping; rev. cross. Extra fine and rare.

1909 BURGUNDY and Flanders. Charles (der Kuhne). 1467 to 1477. Groat. Two sceptres crossed, fleur de lis in the angles; rev. coat-of-arms; motto of France; fine and very rare; and one, rev. cross. Wellenheim, 8819. 2 pieces

1910 —— Groat; rev. two lions *regardant*. Date of Charles der Kuhne. KAROLVS : Dei : Gra DVX : BV : COM : F. As it came from the die. Rare.

1911 —— Groat of Philip III. (the Good). 1419–67. Rev. Long cross, in the midst a lily--in the angles, lions and lilies. Extra fine and rare.

1912 —— Groat of Maria. 1477 to 1482. Arms; rev. cross fleurie. MARIA (DUC) ISSA BG CO FL. Very fine.

1913 —— David V. 1457 to 1496. Fine and rare groat.

## Netherlands.—Silver.

1914 FLANDERS. Broad groat of Louis I. 1322 to 1346. (Called by Wellenheim, "Lion.") LVDOVICVS : DEI : GRA : COMES : Z DES. (Sic) FLANDRIE ; rev. two circles; ins. and cross fleurie. Very fine and rare.

1915 —— Lion of Louis II. 1346 to 1389. (Tournois). Fine and rare.

1916 —— Groat of Magaretha. 1404 to 1405. Extra fine and rare.

1917 HOLLAND. Crown of 1621. Bust of the Emperor of Germany; rev. lion upright with a drawn sword. MON. ARG. PRO. CON. BELG. HOL. Fine and rare.

1918 —— 1659. "Campensis." Soldier standing, one leg behind shield; rev. like last. Very fine crown.

1919 —— Half-crown. (1650). Ordinary.

1920 —— Splendid crown of the Emperor Charles V. 1555. His bust crowned and with drawn sword ; rev. 3 shields. WOLLENSIS DAVENTRIENSIS and CAMPENSIS. Very rare.

1921 —— One Gulden (40 cts.) and X Stivers (20 cents). 1749. Fine. 2 pieces

1922 —— For Batavia. 1 Gulden ; rev. ship. Two varieties 1802–07. Very fine. 2 pieces

1923 —— For same. $\frac{1}{8}$ & $\frac{1}{10}$ "G." Extra fine. 2 pieces

1924 —— One hundred S(tivers). 1794. Piece of necessity with date, denomination, and star. Very rare.

1925 —— Duplicate.

1926 —— Piece of the City of Rotterdam. 1689. View of the City under a palm tree ; rev. a Convention. Fine and undoubtedly rare. (Of the value of 1 Gulden).

1927 —— Pieces of 1746 and 1764. Lion in a ring, holding staff and cap of Liberty, and 2 stivers. 2 pieces

1928 —— Breda. Piece of necessity. 1573. Square Klippe. B above a round stamp, shield crowned. Very rare.

1929 —— Siege piece of 1625. (Klippe). "20" (Stivers). Fine and rare.

1930 HOLLAND. Klippe. "20" (Stivers.) Bust. M.DES-VRVILLA.
1931 ―― "Lodew I. King von Hol." Bust of L. Bonaparte. 1808 50 S. Dollar. Uncirculated. Rare.
1932 ―― Small coins, many varieties. Several fine old denarii. 8 pieces
1933 ZEALAND. Half-crown of 1620. Bust of the Emperor; rev. arms crowned. Fine.
1934 ―― Crown of 1661. Mailed cavalier; rev., arms supported by two crowned lions. Good preservation. Rare.
1935 ―― Piece of 30 stivers (60 cts.) Soldier standing, one leg behind a shield; rev. 7 shields. 1682.
1936 ―― Crown of 1779; obv. same; rev. arms crowned. Fine and rare.
1937 ―― Small coins (6 and 2 stivers.) Fine. 3 pieces
1938 WEST FRIESLAND. 1583. Half-crown. Cavalier; rev. arms (2 lions.) Good, rare.
1939 ―― Crown. 1591. Man in fur cap and coat, with drawn sword; rev. double eagle. In remarkably good preservation for date.
1940 ―― Similar piece. 1601. (14 stivers).
1941 ―― Half-crown. 1619. Bust of the Emperor; rev. lion upright. Fine.
1942 ―― Half-crown. 1662. Knight on horseback; rev. like last. Very fine.
1943 ―― Ship; rev. arms. 6 stivers. 1677. Fine.
1944 ―― Piece of 1686. (14 stivers). Old soldier in cap, as before. Rare
1945 ―― Crown of 1690. (28 S.) Same as last. Counterstamped, JOII. Rare.
1946 ―― Crown, 1792, or 3 gulden (120). Liberty standing, one arm on book resting on altar; the other with staff and cap. Extremely fine. Rare.
1947 ―― Small coins. 3 pieces
1948 DAVENTER (city). Pieces of 6 stivers. Knight on horseback, galloping. 3 pieces
1949 MAGENSIS (city). Similar Device. 6 stivers. 3 "

## Netherlands.—Silver.

1950 ZUTPHEN (county). Half-crown. Knight riding hard, as before; rev. arms on cross fleurie. Broad. Well preserved. Rare.

1951 OVERYSSEL (county). Crown of 1685. Counter-stamped JOH. 28 stivers. Rare.

1952 UTRECHT (county). David V. (Burg.) 1487-96. Rare and fine groat. David seated, front view; rev. arms.

1953 —— Groat, MCCCCLXXVIII (1478). Very fine and rare.

1954 —— Small coins. 1759-89.  2 pieces

1955 —— Splendid crown. 1758. Knight galloping, under the horse a shield. " Mo. No. Arg. Con. foe, Belg. Pro. Traj;" rev. arms crowned, 2 lions supporting; " crescunt concordia resparvai." 3 gulden ($1.40.)

1956 —— Another crown of 1785. Knight standing, one leg behind a shield; rev. like last. Very fine.

1957 —— Crown, 1808. Similar to last. Extremely fine.

1958 GRONINGEN. Groat, 1477 (MCCCCLXXVII.) Double eagle; below 2 shields, " Moneta Nova Groningen;" rev. long cross, 2 circles ins. Fine and very rare.

1959 —— Another. Nearly same.

1960 —— Larger coin of 1568. Very elaborate. Fine and remarkable.

1961 —— Crown of 1692. Counter-stamped JOH. (Notice several crowns, before described, with same counter-stamp). This has the motto of France. Very rare.

1962 —— Another of these rare crowns.

1963 NAMUR. Struck in 1745 for Francis I. " Co Regenti Imp." A very fine coin. Handsome bust and coat-of-arms. About half-crown. Nearly proof.

1964 PIECES overlooked of several of the foregoing duchies and counties, and of the Belgic Confederacy. Small coins. Fine.  6 pieces

1965 BELGIAN CONFEDERACY. 1790. Bundle of darts, fan-shaped at both ends, held by two hands; rev. lion upright. 1 Florin, and X sols. Nearly uncirculated. Value 40 and 20 cts.  2 pieces

## Netherlands.—Copper.

1966 BELGIUM (Kingdom) Leopold "Premier Roi;" rev. busts of the Duke and Duchess of Brabant. 21 and 22 Aug., 1853. Value of 5 francs. Very fine. Rare.

1967 NETHERLANDS (Kingdom). 1 gulden of 1824. William, King. Uncirculated.

1968 —— Small coins of Belgium and Netherlands. Generally uncirculated. 9 pieces

1969 OCTAGON piece of silver. S. P. Q. R. within wreath of two branches oak; rev. shield crowned, no inscription. Value about half-dollar.

1970 COINS of the City of Magensis of the year 1682, with the reverses erased, and political or other pasquinades skillfully engraved thereon. Size 22 and 18. 3 pieces

### Copper Coins and Medals.

*In alphabetical order.*

1971 ALKMAAR (city in Holland). Token. Uncirculated. Fine brass. Size 16

1972 ANTWERP (Anvers). From 1630, 1700, 1708, and 1814. Open hand over a three towered gate. 10–5 cent, 1 sol, &c. Siege coin and klippe. All rare. No duplicates. 8 pieces

1973 AMSTERDAM. Large and very remarkable token of "Petrus Lourentius, 1781." (A mighty medicine). Esculapius standing; rev. monument. Cast, work in high relief. Size 30

1974 ARNHEIM (city.) Single coin. Said to be rare. Pierced.

1975 BATENBURG (Count). 1657. Bust; rev. arms. Never in circulation. Size 16. 5 pieces

1976 BELGIUM (Confederacy and Kingdom, with a few prior to either). From 1511. A great variety. Many very fine. 28 pieces

1977 —— (Kingdom.) Medal. Bust of Leopold; rev. busts of Duke and Duchess of Brabant. One on the anniversary of his coronation (21 July, 1856) and another Extremely fine. Size 20–18–16. 4 pieces.

## Netherlands. Copper.

BELGIUM. Waterloo Medalet. June 18, 1815. "Crown Prince of Orange—Holland's glory." Proof. Size 16
—— Obsidional coins of the City of Lille (now in France). "Pro Defensione Urbis et Patriæ." 1708. Arms of Lille. From size 12 to 18. Extra rare.
            3 pieces.

BREDA (city in Holland). Obsidional. 1625. Square. Fine.

CAMPAN (city). 1644. Arms. Rare.

FRISIÆ (or West Friesland). Province. Great variety. See silver coins from 1633.   9 pieces

GUELDERS. Province from 1757–94. GELRIÆ. Divided shield, two lions upright. Fine.  7 pieces

GORKUM (city in Holland). 1 coin. Rare. Size 16

GRONINGEN (Province).     6 pieces.

HASSELT (Count). Arms (3 clevices); rev. cross; in the middle a rose.

HOLLAND. (Province). "Hollandie." Lion with pole and cap in an enclosure, and E. I. Co. VOC from 1611. Several remarkable types. A very rare lot.
            14 pieces

—— E. I. Co. for Malabar, Java, Batavia, etc., etc., and two pieces pure copper, cut from a bar. (Two Stivers). Very fine and rare lot.  12 pieces

—— Rare tokens from 1595 to 1603, witty political medalets, with apt illustrations; Eg., the fable of the fox and cock, etc. Many local to cities, as *Breda*, and personal, as *Maurice*, Count of Nassau. Very fine. About size 19. Embracing a great variety of subjects, and interesting.     18 pieces

—— Coins of various sizes. Uncirculated. With large letter W.       14 pieces

—— War Cross and Medals, W. Fine.  3 pieces

—— "Bonaparte Op. St. Helene." The exile on a rock. WA. AR. ZAI. IK., ONTKOMEN. Size 16. Very rare, with badges worn at the fiftieth anniversary of the Battle of Waterloo; struck in tin, and enameled or painted in red, white, orange and blue. Valuable lot.
            4 pieces

114     *Netherlands.—Copper.*

1993 HOLLAND. Medal of Count Egmont. Obv. splendid bust by Simon; rev. birth and death. 1568. Proof, but for a slight abrasion.  Size 30

1994 —— Medal of the Seven United Provinces in honor of Prince W. C. H. F. AVR. ET ANNA MAG. BRIT. Their busts jugata; rev. arms of the United Provinces. A similar one of the Prince of Orange. (William Charles Henry Fritzo). The last pierced. Fine and rare.  Size 25. 2 pieces

1995 MEDAL of Philip II., Spain and "Margarita Austria." One of a Turk, and others.  5 pieces

1996 HUISSEN (City). HVESSEN; rev. arms.  5 coins

1997 LIEGE (Luttich), city in Belgium. (LEOD.) St. Lambert Patron. A great variety of excellent Coins. Some rare church tokens 1653 with skull and cross bones below.  16 pieces

1998 LUXEMBERG. (Duchy). 10, 5, 2½ Centimes. 1855–1860.  4 pieces

1999 MAESTRICHT (City). Siege Coins. 1579. (Arms five-pointed star). Ins. in four lines across the coin. A naked sword dividing the lines. TRA–INC AB. HIS–OBSES PROVIS–CAVSÆ DEFE–SION. An in exergue XXXX. In some, XVI., and XII. Several types from size 22 to 16.  5 pieces

2000 NARMUR. (City in Belgium). One coin.

2001 NETHERLANDS. Patterns for gold coin. 1826. In copper and tin. 10 G. (ulden); 10 G., rev. incused; and 5 G.; rev. plain. Excessively rare. Uncirculated.  3 pieces

2002 —— East India Coins. 1857 to 1825.  6 pieces

2003 OBERYSSEL. (Province).  5 coins

2004 RECKHEIM (Count). Province of Utrecht.  2 pieces

2005 ROTTERDAM. Medal of the City. 1823. Fine proof.  Size 23

2006 RUREMOND (Fortress of). A rare coin.

2007 STEVENSWORTH. (City of Holland).  5 pieces

2008 UTRECHT. (Province).  8 pieces

2009 VLISSINGEN. (City). Siege piece—square.

Bavaria.—Silver.

2010 ZUTPHEN. (City). Coin. CIV ZVTFEN. Rare.
2011 ZEELAND. (Province). Very fine. Seventeenth and eighteenth centuries. 8 pieces
2012 ZWOLLE. (City). 1618. Rare. 2 pieces

## BAVARIA.

### Silver Coins.

2013 BRACTEATES, city of Munich and others, 3 pieces
2014 RUDOLPH and ADOLPH SIMPLEX. 1319-1327. Rude figure. R.-A.; rev. bust in a lozenge. Denarius. Very rare. (Wellenheim, 1696).
2015 DENARIUS. Pyramid and cross. Gothic letters. Beautiful. Unknown.
2016 OTHO PHILIP. 1508 to 1518. Count Pfals. Groat. 1517. Fine, rare.
2017 THALER, without date. Arms of Bavaria, and motto of France. "Moneta Nova Bavarica." Very old. Good.
2018 FREDERICK III. 1573. Crown. Bust in mail; front face. Sword. Very rich decorations. Extremely rare, fine.
2019 JOHN II. 1623. Duke; obv. bust; rev. coat-of-arms, with five crests. Fine Crown.
2020 WOLFGANG (WILLIAM). Count Pfalz. 1623. Extremely fine Crown. Bust in high collar. Arms within chain of the Order of the Golden Fleece. Rare.
2021 —— The same for 1624. Fine Crown; not equal to last.
2022 MAXIMILIAN I. 1625. Double Dollar; on one side coat-of-arms; the other Madonna, as queen, with infant Christ. *Ex. fine and rare.*
2023 —— Fine Crown. 1626. Lions supporting arms of Bavaria.
2024 CHARLES LOUIS. 1659. Fine crown. Bust to the waist, head bare.
2025 —— The same. Thaler, 1673. Very fine.

116  *Bavaria.—Copper.*

2026 PHILIP WILLIAM. 1675. Thaler. Hair (wig) long. Very good. Rare.

2027 JOHN WILLIAM. 1700. Thaler. Edge milled. Rare.

2028 CHARLES PHILIP. 1740. Double crown. Bust, head bare, double-headed eagle on rev. Fine border and milled edge. Splendid, nearly proof. Very rare.

2029 CHARLES ALBERT and Charles Philip. 1740. Busts of both, one on the other. Equal to last. Double Thaler.

2030 CHARLES THEODORE. 1742 to 1799. Crown. 1751. Fine.

2031 —— The same, two-third Crown. 1754. Good.

2032 MAXIMILLIAN JOSEPH. 1799 to 1825. Broad Crown of 1803. Ins. in Dutch, "Got und das Vaterland." Fine; has been worn as a medal. Loop removed.

2033 —— Medal Crown. 1818. Laureated bust; rev. a square column. CHARTA MAGNA BAVARIA. Splendid proof. Rare.

2034 —— Medal by Losch; bare bust; rev. within wreath. DIELKIRCHEN. Crown size. Very fine, rare.

2035 MAXIMILIAN II. Rev. "Patrona Bavaria," Thalers.
2 pieces

2036 —— Similar. "Friedenschluss Zer Frankfurt, 10th May, 1871." Rare.

2037 MEDALS and Coins of Bavaria, some in *fine* silver, others base; average size, sixteen. From 17th century. Heads of Charles IV. (1658), John William (1689), Cardinal Louis, Elector, etc. (1660). Extremely fine lot and valuable.
14 pieces

2038 MEDALET MAX. Jos. on the Constitution of 1806-1818. A little gem, and small coins of various dates. Fine and rare varieties.
10 pieces

2039 MISCELLANEOUS silver coins—base.
11 pieces

*Copper.*

2040 SIEGE Klippe of Wolfgang William. (W.W. interlinked). Newburg, 16-14. Small size.

Anhalt.—Silver.

| | | |
|---|---|---|
| 2041 | WORKHOUSE Coins. (Paltz). 1745–1747. Ins. on one side. "One Churf Abcitshaus," half and quarter do. Under Max. Jos. II. Rare. | 3 pieces |
| 2042 | —— Another set, same in all respects. | 3 pieces |
| 2043 | COINS of the 17th and 18th centuries. W. W. (Wolfgang William), and others. Rare and fine. "Zall Pfenning," "Luchter Kreutzer," etc., etc. | 10 pieces |
| 2044 | COINS of late dates, bright and uncirculated. | 10 pieces |
| 2045 | COINS of various denominations and dates. | 37 pieces |
| 2046 | HELLERS. Late dates. | 35 pieces |
| 2047 | BAVARIAN CROSS. 1866. Length of limbs, 1½ inches. | |

## ANHALT.

*Silver Coins.*

2048 BRACTEATES and indifferent coins. 15 pieces

2049 CHRISTIAN AUGUSTUS. 1622. 24 Krs. 4 pieces

2050 —— Hammered Crown. 1623. Nearly uncirculated. Very rare.

2051 WILLIAM (Bernburg). 1670 to 1709. Duke. "I. D. ⅔," (one Daler, two-third). Crown 1673. Nearly uncirculated; bust; rev. arms. Rare.

2052 JOHN GEORGE. 1674. (Dessau)? Two-third Crown. Uncirculated; bust with long hair; rev. coat-of-arms, arms of Anhalt (bear walking on the turrets of the city wall) in two corners.

2053 JOHN LOUIS and Christian Augustus. Two-third Crown. 1742. Their busts facing to right; rev. coat-of-arms. Fine.

2054 AUGUSTUS LOUIS (of Saxony), Prince of Anhalt. Two-third Crown. 1747. The bears of Anhalt prominent on both sides. Fine.

2055 FREDERICK ALBERT I. 1765 to 1796. Prince of Anhalt and Berneburg. Crown, 1793. X. EIN FEINE MARCK. Fine.

2056 ALEXIS FREDERICK CHRISTIAN. 1796 to 1834 XX. and XL. EIN FEINE MARCK. Bear on a turreted wall. Very fine. 2 pieces

*Copper.*

2057 COINS of many denominations and dates. A good collection. 17th and 18th century. 10 pieces

2058 ——— Similar. 18th and 19th century. 12 pieces

2059 MEDAL of Fred. Hecker, "the man of the people." Fine proof. Size 24

## BADEN.

*Silver.*

2060 FREDERICK, (Marquis). 1628. Crown, with his figure to the hips. Fine and rare.

2061 CHARLES FREDERICK, (Marquis). 1766. Crown. Uncirculated. Very handsome reverse.

2062 CROWN DOLLAR of Baden. 1816. Fine.

2063 GULDEN of 1857 on a particular occasion, and several older and smaller coins. Several for Anhalt. Fine lot. 10 pieces

*Copper.*

2064 MISCELLANEOUS collection of coins. 26 pieces

2065 COIN in commemoration of the 50th jubilee of the Constitution. Others struck by the Prince Regent, his father being insane; and several bright uncirculated pieces. A rare selection. 11 pieces

2066 MEDAL of Federick Magnus. 1639. Tin war medal of 1849, and token of *Itystein*, leader of the ; revolution of the same date. 4 pieces

2067 MISCELLANEOUS. Some of Sweden, Bavaria, Hungary, and many German cities; several of France. 50 pieces

Attention is invited to this lot. In a smaller collection these coins would very probably be made to occupy fifty lines.

2068 ANOTHER miscellaneous lot. Inferior. 64 pieces

2069 A LOT of curious old coppers and counterfeit silver coins. (Several Dollars). 30 pieces
2070 BASE coins unclassified. do.

## HESSE.

*Silver.*

2071 LUDWIG II. 1413 to 1458. LVDWICVS DEI GRA-CIA. Broad groat, as fine as when struck. Very rare.
2072 WILLIAM IV. 1567 to 1592. W. L. Z. H. 1567. VIII.; rev. lion. Ex. fine and rare. (Small coin.)
2073 MAURICE I. 1592 to 1632. Small coin. EIN MA-TIER: 1616. Rare. 2 pieces
2074 WILLIAM VI. 1637 to 1663. Double letter W., crowned, 1656; rev. lion. Size of English half-groat. Rare coins. 2 pieces
2075 CHARLES, Landgrave. 1670 to 1730. Small coins, with cipher of his name; sometimes C. L. No dupli-cates. Fine. 4 pieces
2076 FREDERICK I. and II. 1740 to 1765. And others. Base. 7 pieces
2077 ERNEST LOUIS, Darmstadt. Thaler of 1693. Bust in rich dress; rev. arms on round shield, under crown. Uncirculated. Rare.
2078 —— X. K. Pices. 1728. Fine silver. Rare.
2079 HESSE DARMSTADT. Small coins. H. D. About 1722. Very scarce. 6 pieces
2080 LOUIS, Grand Duke, Hesse. 1809. Splendid uncircu-lated crown. Bare bust; rev. arms of Hesse—lion holding a sword on a spade-shaped shield under a crown; below laurel and palm crossed. Rare.
2081 —— Crown. 1819. Bust; rev. arms as before, on ermine. "Kronenthaler." Uncirculated. Rare.

2082 HESSE-CASSEL. Philip (Der Grossmüthige). 1509 to 1567. Crown, much worn. Curiously counterstamped. 1552.

2083 —— Louis V. 1596 to 1626. Brilliant uncirculated Crown of 1623. Bust royally draped; head bare; rev. coat-of-arms. Rare, according to Appel, Madai, and Wellenheim.

2084 —— Maurice Landgrave. 1625. Two sceptres crossed, branches of a willow tree above; hour glass below; rev. lion. Uncirculated. Crown. Very rare.

2085 —— Repetition of last, except date. 1626. Equally fine.

2086 —— William, Landgrave. 1628. Storm and thunderbolt beating against a willow tree. The sun in splendor above; rev. fine coat-of-arms. Uncirculated Crown, rare.

2087 —— Same. Crown of same type. 1630. Different coat-of-arms. Uncirculated and splendid. Rare.

2088 —— Same. Crown of 1631. More scenery shown with the tree. Edifices and houses. Equally fine.

2089 —— Same. Crown of 1637. Same obverse; rev. lion. Fine, but dark.

2090 —— Repetition of last, except date. 1638. Very fine.

2091 MARIA AMALIA. Fine medal by *Kohler*. 1711. Obv. draped bust. PLACIDE MURTE VILLA MONAST; rev. crown above two coat-of-arms. According to Wellenheim and Madai, very rare. Size 22

2092 CAROLUS, Landgrave. 1727; rev. sacrifice. Extra fine little medal. Size 18

2093 FREDERICK, Landgrave. 1737. (King of Sweden.) VIII. ALBVS. Very fine and rare. Size 17

2094 FREDERICK II., Landgrave. 1766. Bust; rev. arms of Hesse within English Garter, with the motto, "Honi soit," &c. Splendid crown. *Very* rare.

2095 —— Varieties. Crowns of same type. Fine. 2 pieces

2096 —— Half-thaler. "40 stuck." Same type. Fine.

2097 FREDERICK II. EIN HALB THALER. 1776. Struck from silver received from England for the services of Hessian soldiers during the American war, called "subsidy money." It has on the obv. the Landgrave's bust; rev. lion on a round shield covering a star of eight points. Motto, VIRTUE ET FIDELITATE. 1776. The edge is milled. Uncirculated.

2098 —— Another. Same in all respects.

These remarkable coins' are as thick as the ordinary THALER, and only size 18. They will, no doubt, be highly appreciated by American collectors, as, so far as I know, this is the first time they have appeared in a catalogue in this country.

2099 SIX and eight Einen Rix Thalers. 2 pieces
2100 MEDALETS of Louis IX. and Carolus. Fine silver. Size 14 and 15; fine. 3 pieces
2101 GULDEN, Half-gulden and Six-krs. Fine. 3 pieces
2102 LUDWIG X. Bust in armor. By VOIGHT; rev. within oak wreath ½ Gulden. 1838. Proof.

### Copper.

2103 A SELECTION, said to be rare, consisting of 8, 4, and 3 Hellers, 1727 to 1777. 8 pieces
2104 ANOTHER lot, which from their denomination must represent silver coins, such as "VI. Einen Reichs Thaler." "60-Stuk Eine Feine Mark," &c. 7 pieces
2105 —— Same, of various denominations. All of Hesse. 25 pieces
2106 —— Same. Various. 40 pieces

## LIPPE.

### Silver.

2107 BERNHARD. 1241 to 1270. Denarius, but little worn. Full face; rude; rev. cross in the angles. L. I. P. E. Ex. rare.

## Lippe.—Silver.

2108 SIMON. Under Emperor Rudolf. 1600. Obv. arms with the rose of Lippe; rev. arms of Roman Empire. Half-groats, one in gilt, one uncirculated. Silver. 2 pieces

2109 —— Same of 1604 and 1593. Very fine. 2 pieces

2110 —— Same of 1604 and 1607. Uncirculated. do

2111 —— Same of 1600. Very fine. do

2112 GROAT. Without date; under Mathias, Emperor, 1612. Large size, and uncirculated.

2113 SIMON LUDWIG. 1626 to 1636. Silver pennies. 2 pieces

2114 HERMAN. Bishop. 1666. Half-groat. Fine and rare.

2115 SIMON HENRY. 1666 to 1677; "I Matti, G. Lippe, L. M., 16–72." Full blown rose, with wreath. Several varieties. Rare. 4 pieces

2116 —— IIII. Mari. Gro. 1672, with S. H. in Monogram. One of "III. Mari Gro." Same type. Fine and rare coins. 2 pieces

2117 FREDERICK ADOLPHE. 1697 to 1718. "I. Mari Gro." Rev. full blown rose; as it came from the die.

2118 —— Thaler (⅔ Crown). 1714. Uncirculated.

2119 SIMON HENRY ADOLPH. 1718 to 1734. "2 Pfen." Uncirculated.

2120 —— Splendid Crown. 1719. Bust in robes; rev. coat-of-arms, with 5 Crests; the rose of Lippe in two Quarters. Rare.

2121 —— Equally fine Thaler (⅔ Crown.) Same type.

2122 SIMON AUGUSTUS to 1785. ⅙ Thaler. Fine.

2123 FREDERICK WILLIAM LEOPOLD. 1789 to 1802; beautiful medal thaler of 1793. Rare.

2124 —— ⅙ Thaler 1794. Very fine.

2125 PAUL FRED. EMIL. LEOPOLD. 2½, 1, and ½ silver Groshen of 1860. Uncirculated. 3 pieces

2126 BASE silver small Coins. Many old. 12 pieces

## LIPPE—SCHAUMBERG.

### Silver.

2127 WILLIAM I. Broad thin Thalers of fine silver. 1761. Bust, under it a rose; rev. fine coat-of-arms, with 3 crests. Rare. 2 pieces

2128 —— Extra thick Thaler. 1765; rev. coat-of-arms on St. Andrew's cross. Fine silver. Rare.

2129 PHILIP of Schaumberg, and Julia of Hesse; on their marriage. Their busts jugata; rev. a knight holding two shields, with arms, &c. A very fine medal, but bent. Size 24

2130 MEDAL of William Fred., Count of Schaumberg and Lippe. Struck on the 24th Sept., 1748. Very fine. Size 22

2131 CROWN OF "X. MARK." 1802. Very fine.

## LIPPE—DETMOLD.

### Silver.

2132 SIMON HENRY. Bust in the Roman style; rev. coat-fo-arms. 1672. Extra fine broad crown. Rare. Size 28.

2133 SIMON AUGUSTUS. Medal struck on the 12th June, 1767. QUEM QUADRACESIES SEMEL PA- TRIAE NATUM ESSE GRATUL AMUR. Rubbed. Size 62

### Copper.

2134 SET ½ Heller, 1 do., 2 do., 3 do., and 6 do., with the full-blown rose of Lippe. Very fine. 5 pieces
2135 —— 1 Heller, 1½ do., 2 do., 3 do., and 6 do. do.
2136 —— of 1 Pfenning, 1½ do., and 2 do. Extra fine. 3 pieces
2137 PFENNINGS AND HELLERS. Great variety. 20 do.

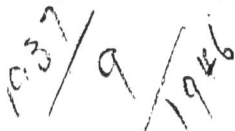

## MECKLENBERG—STRELEITZ AND SCHWERIN.

### *Silver.*

2138 HENRY. Grand Duke from 1503 to 1552. Groat 1525. Military bust; rev. arms. Extra fine, rare.

2139 —— Duplicate. Equally fine.

2140 ALBERT. 1543. Crown. Bust of the Grand Duke full face, on his neck a heavy chain; rev. 5 shields; on one the bull's head, which is the crest of Mecklenberg. Very fine and rare.

2141 JOHN ALBERT. 1549. Crown. Bust with high hat, military coat and chain, as before; rev. coat-of-arms quartered on a shield with 3 crests. Extremely fine and rare.

2142 —— Duplicate. Fine.

2143 —— Denarius. 1552. A mask with a tongue thrust out; crowned. Rare.

2144 ADOLPHUS FREDERICK. 1592 to 1658. "Halb-Reichs Orth," (about the size of an English Groat of same date). Bust to right. Extremely fine, rare.

2145 ALBERT of Wallenstein. Obv. bust in rich suit, with belt and insignia. 16—21. HANS ALBRECHT, etc.; rev. coat-of-arms with 3 crests. A splendid uncirculated Crown, rare.

2146 Half-orth and small.                                3 pieces

2147 CHRISTIAN LUDWIG, Grand Duke. Dollar of 1678; bust, with long curly hair; rev. arms, with angels for supporters. Fine and rare.

2148 CHRISTIAN LUDWIG. Administrator 1725; 8 GUTE GROSHEN COURANT 1754. About one-third thaler.

2149 —— The same when Grand Duke; a fine uncirculated coin of pure silver. His bust; rev. PER ANGVSTA AD AVGVSTA. Quarter crown.

2150 FREDERICK WILLIAM, Grand Duke. Thaler of 1870. Very fine.

## Oldenburg.—Silver.

2151 PAUL FREDERICK, Grand Duke of Mecklenberg-Schwerin. Uncirculated thaler of 1840. Rare.
2152 —— Medalet of same; VOLLENDET D' 7 Marz, 1842.
2153 FRED. FRANCIS, Grand Duke Mecklenberg-Schwerin. Thaler struck on the 25th anniversary of his rule, 1867. Fine proof.
2154 SIXTEEN "Schilling Courant," 1764.
2155 ONE, TWO, and FOUR "Schilling Courant"; uncirculated. 3 pieces
2156 1 GROTE. Three pfenny. One schilling. Six pfenny. 48 einen thaler. Uncirculated. 5 pieces
2157 VARIOUS denominations, old and new. 12 pieces

## OLDENBURG.

### Silver.

2158 ANTON GUNTHER, 1603 to 1667. Broad dollar, "48 Grot." 1660. Bust three-quarter face to right; rev. Arms crowned. AUXILIUM MEUMA DOMINO. On each side of arms a flower. Very fine and rare.
Size 30
2159 —— Another, same in all respects.
2160 —— The half or "24 Grot." Equally fine.
2161 —— Repetition of last.
2162 —— Half-mark or "16 Grot." 3 shields and inscription in 6 straight lines. Rare.
2163 —— Repetition of last—pierced.
2164 —— Quarter-mark or "8 Grot." Fine.
2165 —— Others same size—pierced. 3 pieces
2166 PAUL FRED. Augustus 1844. Thaler. Fine.
2167 NICHOLAS FRED. PETER, Grand Duke 1866. Fine medal, with loop, silver gilt. Bust; rev. date within wreath. Proof. Size 20
2168 THIRD THALERS. 2 pieces
2169 "TWELVE GROTS" and smaller. Base. 13 pieces

*Copper.*

2170 "BACKER MARKE." "Schwaren," "Quarter Grote," "Half Grote," "Three pfenning," etc.   20 pieces

## BRUNSWICK AND LUNEBURG.

*Silver.*

2171 HENRY DUKE 1537. Crown. Obv. Arms surmounted by crown and horse; rev. Seated figure in armor with drawn sword; under his feet a wild animal (Lion?) JUSTUS NON; uncirculated and brilliant. (In Madai rare.)

2172 —— Crown. Bearded bust, wearing a cap; rev. wild man. IN GOTS. GWALT; uncirculated. Equally rare.

2173 —— Crown. Obv. the same; rev. wild man within two circles of inscriptions; 1547. Fine and rare, but not uncirculated.

2174 PHILIP. 1595. Crown. Mailed bust to the waist; sceptre and helmet; rev. Coat-of-arms. GOT GIRT. *Nearly* uncirculated, and rare.

2175 ERICH II. 1584. Groat. Rare.

2176 JULIUS. 1568 to 1589. Bust of the Duke holding a battle-axe and helmet; under the bust cypher of his name; rev. Wild man leaning on a square shield, with inscription and date 1599 (the last of his life.) See Madai 5,287; Willenheim 4,768. Very fine and rare crown.

2177 HENRY JULIUS. 1589 to 1613. "*Wahrheitsthaler.*" Crown of 1597; within a circle of 12 shields, a glorified figure standing on two prostrate bodies; VERITAS VINCIT OMNIA, etc.; rev. RECTE FACIENDO NEMINEM, etc., in parallel lines. Fine and rare.

2178 —— Duplicate; fine.

*Brunswick and Luneburg.—Silver.* 127

2179 HENRY JULIUS. Crown of (15) 99 (mücken thaler.) Shield with wild man supporting; rev. A pelican feeding her young; motto and four bundles of rods. Uncirculated. Very rare. Madai 1,113. Wellenheim 4,776.

2180 —— Crown. Arms; rev. dates of his birth and death, and length of his reign. Very fine, rare.

2181 ELIZABETH. Crown of 1626. On the reverse a short biography in straight lines. Fine and rare.

2182 FREDERICK ULRICH. 1613 to 1634. Half Dollar 1621; rev. wild man. DEO ET PATRIAE. Ex. fine.

2183 —— Set of his Coins, dated 1624; his monogram FV crowned; rev. the denomination and date, from one Marien Groshen to one Marien Gulden. DEO. ET. PATRIAE. Fine and rare. Size 9 to 22. 5 pieces

2184 —— Uncirculated coin, dated 1621. Wild man and double-headed eagle. Groat size.

2185 —— Duplicate, with "half Rix. Ort."  2 pieces

2186 WILLIAM (son of Otto II.). 1641. Uncirculated Crown. His figure in mail to the hips; rev. coat-of-arms, with five crests. DOMINUS. PROVIDEBIT. A rare and beautiful coin.

2187 —— Groat, under Matthias, Emperor. 1616. (16) fine.

2188 GEORGE. 1637. Arms; rev. wild man. AVFF. GOTT. TRAWE ICH. Ex. fine and rare Crown.

2189 AUGUSTUS. 1636 to 1666. Bust, bare head; on his left shoulder a rose; rev. seaport with ships. ALLES MIT. BEDACHT. No date. *Schiffsthaler.* Fine and very rare.

2190 —— Bell Dollar. (Glockenthaler). Coat-of-arms; rev. bell ringing, three hands shown; below, the city of Wolfenbuttel. 1643. Fine and rare.

2191 —— Bell Dollar. The Duke standing; rev. SED. under a square and yoke, inscribed 13 Mai.? Ex. fine, rare.

2192 —— Bell Half-Dollar. (The bell hanging); obv. fine bust of the Duke. Rare.

2193 —— Duplicate of last. Fine.

Brunswick and Luneburg.—Silver

2194 AUGUSTUS. Crown of 1657. Wild man and coat-of-arms. Extremely fine.
2195 —— Crown of 1662. The wild man carrying an uprooted pine tree. Fine and rare.
2196 —— Superb and unusually broad Crown of 1664. Laureated bust in the Roman style. Very rare. Size 29
2197 —— Mortuary Medal. (Half Dollars). An old tree with a human skull at its foot. SIT. TRANSIT GLORIA MUNDI; rev. short biography. Uncirculated. Size 32
2198 GEORGE WILLIAM. 1661. Beautiful uncirculated Crown. The area burnished. Coat-of-arms, and wild man. Rare. Size 29
2199 —— A Medal, size 1¼ Crown. Burnished and gilt; rev. Piety and Justice. Uncirculated and splendid. Size 33
2200 CHRISTIAN, Duke. 1622. Broad and fine Crown. An arm thrust from a cloud holding a drawn sword; rev. GOTTES FREVNDT DER PFAFFEN FEINDT. *Nearly* uncirculated.
2201 —— Mortuary Medal Dollar. 1626. Ex. fine and rare.
2202 CHRISTIAN LOUIS. 1649. Broad Crown. Coat-of-arms; rev. horse galloping. Very fine. Size 29
2203 —— Small Coin with his cypher. 1665. Other fine coins of dime size, of the preceding Dukes; among them rare medalets. 10 pieces
2204 JOHN FREDERICK. Duke. Broad Crown with draped bust, hair tied with a fillet; rev. St. Andrew. 1674. Very fine and rare.
2205 —— Medal Dollar of 1676. Fine bust with long flowing hair; rev. "Ex. Duris Gloria," in a harbor, a rock and palm tree, ships leaving port. Fine and rare. Size 33
2206 —— Two-third Crown. 1679. Same type. Fine and rare.
2207 —— One-third do. do. do.
2208 —— XII. Marien Gros. Wild man. Ex. fine.
2209 —— IV. and II. Marien. Gros. IIis and others. Fine. 8 pieces

2210 JOHN FREDERICK. Mortuary Medal Crown. 1689. Fine and rare. Size 30

2211 ERNEST AUGUSTUS. 1665 to 1697. 4, 2, and 1 M. Groshen. Some with his name, others monogram. SOLA BONA HONESTA. Very fine. 6 pieces

2212 —— Fine coins, varying from one-third to one-sixteenth of a Dollar in size. St. Andrew, wild man, horse, etc., on reverses. In condition extremely fine. Rare lot. 6 pieces

2213 —— Two-third Crown. 1676; rev. hat and crown; between two crescents, a horse galloping. (XXIV. M. G.) Uncirculated. Rare.

2214 —— Bust in mail with long hair. Coin of the same size. Brilliant. Very rare.

2215 —— Medal. Obv. the same as last; rev. a horse in an enclosure, galloping; at the entrance of the enclosure tower and crown. Very fine. Size 18

2216 —— Medal. Fine bust; rev. a harbor with ships in the offing; in the foreground a palm-tree; above the harbor, Æolus sending a blast in the direction of a ship, and conducting by a line, a wheel (arms of Osnaburg). VARIS IN MOTIBVS EADEM, 1680. Thick heavy medal. Size 40

2217 —— Crown. 1689. Draped bust; rev. Arms of Brunswick and Osnaburg. Very fine and rare.

2218 —— Selection of fine coins. II. Marien Groschen die. Not all of Augustus. 12 pieces

2219 RUDOLPH AUGUSTUS. 1666 to 1704. Crown or Medal struck in 1671. Bust in loose dress, with long hair in curls; rev. open book lying on military weapons, and flags crossed. JURE & ARMIS. Fine. Size 30

2220 —— Twenty-four M. Groschen (two-third Crown). 1690; rev. a horse. Another, rev. wild man, both very fine. 2 pieces

2221 —— The same, with a mortuary medalet, with his bust. 1704. Both uncirculated. 2 pieces

2222 ANTHONY ULRICH. 1704 to 1714. A very beautiful Medal Crown, with busts of Anthony Ulrich and Rudolph Augustus. 1695; obv. two busts conjoined; rev. two stands of arms and flags under one crown. Nearly proof. Rare. Size 30

2223 —— XII. M. Gros. Set in a border of volutes, with heart pendant and loop. Very fine.

2224 —— One-sixth Crown; rev. horse. 2 pieces

2225 GEORGE WILLIAM. "XVI. Gute Groschen." (Two, third Dollar). 1694; rev. horse. Fine.

2226 —— Beautiful uncirculated mortuary medal. 1705. 28th August. Size 20

2227 —— Same. Value of a Crown. Ex. fine.

2228 —— Duplicate. Very fine.

2229 —— Small Coins. Medalets and jetons. A fine lot, not confined to this Duke. 8 pieces

2230 ELIZABETH JULIA. Medal to commemorate her birth and death. Her bust; rev. the Duchess ascending; below, view of her palace. Struck in 1704. Fine and rare. Size 30

2231 MEDAL without name or date. One side divided by a cross; in the four angles, scenes representing the usual modes of seeking for wealth and pleasure. On the rev. a figure in light drapery standing on a globe. The legend in Dutch, to the effect that what is vainly sought on one side is found on the other. Valuable. Size 32

2232 AUGUSTUS WILLIAM. 1714 to 1731, second Centenary Jubilee medal. 1717. Bust; rev. ECCLESIA TERRAR WOLFFENS, etc. Jubilee scene, with many figures. Extremely fine. (Thick medal). Size 32

2233 —— Crown. 1715; rev. wild man. PARTA TVERI. Very fine. Size 29

2234 ELIZABETH CHRISTIANA. Obv. bare bust; rev. the celestial globe; below, mariner's compass. *Extremely* fine. No date. Size 24

2235 CHARLES. 1748–1779. Four and two Marien Gros. Uncirculated. Rare. 5 pieces

## Brunswick and Luneburg.—Silver.    131

2236 CHARLES. "Eight Gute Gros." 1759. C. Crowned. Uncirculated.

2237 —— Two-third and one-third Thaler. 1779. Fine.
                                                                                          2 pieces

2238 CHARLES WILLIAM FERDINAND. 1780 to 1806. VIII. Gude Grosch, 1801. Very fine.

2239 —— IIII and II. M. Gros. .    3 pieces

2240 MAX. JULIUS LEOPOLD. Fine medal on his death. 1752; rev. eagle.    Size 24

2241 GEORGE LUDWIG, (in 1814 made King of England as George I.) Broad Crown. Wild man. IN RECTO DECUS; rev. garnished coat-of-arms crowned. "George Lud. D. G., Br. & L. S. R. I. AR. THES. EL., 1715." Uncirculated. *Rare.*    Size 30

2242 —— Two-third Crown, with horse galloping instead of wild man. Uncirculated.

2243 —— Uncirculated Coins without duplicates. Four and two Marien Groshen. Wild man, St. Andrew and horse. Fine.    6 pieces

2244 —— Similar.    8 pieces

2245 GEORGE I. (England). Broad Crown, (size 30). Arms of England on square shield within the garter; rev. wild man. 1723. *Uncirculated.* Rare.

2246 —— Crown of same date; rev. St. Andrew. Milled rim. Very fine and rare.

2247 —— Half Crown, with arms on four shields, arranged in form of a cross; rev. wild man. Fine and extremely rare.

2248 —— Twenty-four Marien Groshen. 1702; rev. wild man. Fine.

2249 —— One-sixth Crown; bust; rev. arms in a cross; and another. Fine and very rare.    3 pieces

2250 GEORGE II. Spendid uncirculated Medal Crown. Struck in 1752, from silver of Cronenburg's mines. "First worked in 1706." Coat-of-arms and picture of the mines. Said to be very rare.    Size 26

2251 GEORGE III. Beautiful Medal. Obv. female seated, one arm raised, the other resting on a shield crowned. On an altar a bishop's mitre and sword. SPES PVBLICA; rev. Latin inscription in nine lines, ending in POSTVLATVS EPISC. XXVII. FEB., 1764. Ex. fine and rare. Size 27

2252 A collection of Brunswick Coins, with varieties said to be very rare in Europe, such as "IIII Schill. Lauenb." IIII Marien Groschen, with English Coat-of-Arms, 1746, etc., etc." Some with monogram of George Rex. in script letters. Fine and rare lot. 25 pieces

2253 PATTERN Half-pfenney, 1792, struck in silver. Very fine and rare.

*Copper (Coins and Medals).*

2254 A COLLECTION of curious copper coins—one and one and a half Pfennings of the 17th century. Rare. 10 pieces

2255 —— Pfennings from 1700. Generally uncirculated. 50 pieces

2256 —— Same. A collection, as I believe without duplicates, made by a resident of the Duchy of Brunswick, with the same zeal that Americans display in collecting cents of different dates. All fine. 88 pieces

*The collector referred to informed the writer that many of these pennies are very rare, and command the price of rarity at home.*

2257 DOUBLE Pennies or Pfennings. Very fine. 16 pieces

2258 RARE Miners and other Tokens. "Gluck Auf. dem Harz. Gluck Auf. Unsallen." With square and other coins. 10 pieces

2259 MEDAL OF DUKE FRED. WILLIAM, by Hascher. Killed at Waterloo (Quatre-bras), in 1815, bronze. Rare. Size 22

*Byron alludes to him in "Childe Harold" as "Brunswick's faded Chieftain."*

2260 —— Charles William Ferdinand. (Duke). 1787. His bust; rev. view of Amsterdam. Proof, tin, with copper plug inserted. Rare. Size 30

Coins and Medals of Hanover.—Silver.   133

2261  WEIGHTS or Patterns for gold coins. (Half Louis). Fine and rare.   2 pieces
2262  IMPRESSIONS in copper from dies for a gold coin, issued in 1827, by Duke Charles, who lost his throne in 1831, (recently deceased, leaving his estate to the City of Geneva). Splendid proofs, and extremely rare.

---

## HANOVER.

### Silver Coins and Medals.

2263  GEORGE III. King. 1788. Twenty-four Marien Groschen; bust; rev. Arms of Great Britain and Hanover. "$\frac{2}{3}$" and Crown. Uncirculated.
2264  ——— Splendid proof set. Dollar, Half Dollar, Third Dollar, and Sixth Dollar, with bust. 1800. Not easily duplicated. Very beautiful.   4 pieces
2265  ——— Laureated bust; rev $\frac{2}{3}$. "18 Stuck Eine Mark Feine 1802." Very fine and *rare*.
2266  ——— Same; with titles of "Koneg und Churfurst." Uncirculated ½ thaler. Rare.
2267  ——— Same; rev. arms in the garter. 1807. Brilliant proof, $\frac{1}{8}$. Very rare.
2268  ——— Pattern Five Thaler piece in silver. Brilliant proof. Very rare.
2269  GEORGE IV. 1827. Laureated bust to left; rev. $\frac{2}{3}$. Brilliant proof. Very rare.
2270  ——— 1828. Same repeated. Brilliant proof.
2271  ——— Medal Crown (X Marks fine silver.) Small laureated bust; rev. DES BERG. WERKS WOHLFAHRT. 1st DES HARZES GLUCK. Another ins. in 5 lines, and date 1830. Brilliant proof. Very rare.
2272  ——— Bust; rev. $\frac{2}{3}$. "18 Stuck Eine Mark Feine."
2273  WILLIAM IV. Bare bust to right. Splendid uncirculated thaler of 1837.
2274  ——— Same; rev. $\frac{2}{3}$. Without arms. Brilliant.
2275  ——— Without bust. Two reverses—arms; rev. "$\frac{2}{3}$." Brilliant. Rare.

134    *Coins and Medals of Hanover.—Copper.*

2276 WILLIAM IV. Same; rev. "Ausbeute der grude Bergwerks Wohlfahrt Bei clausthal." Uncirculated ⅔ thaler. Rare.

2277 ERNEST AUGUSTUS. 1838. Splendid uncirculated Thaler and ⅔ thaler. 2 pieces

2278 —— Thaler to commemorate his visit to the mines in 1839. "Gluckauf Clausthal Thaler." Splendid. Very rare.

2279 GEORGE V. Thaler struck on the 50th An. of the Union of East Fresia with Hanover, 15th Dec., 1865. Bare bust to left; rev. Knight armed "Cap a pie" standing under an Oak Tree. "Up stall boom." Brilliant proof. Extremely rare.

2280 —— Different thaler for the same occasion. The inscription within an oak wreath. Ex. fine, rare.

2281 —— Waterloo Medal Thaler struck on the 18th June, 1865, for presentation to the survivors. Brilliant proof. Very rare.

2282 —— Same, with silver ring. Has been worn. Very fine and rare.

2283 MEDAL of the Army of Hanover. A NAPOLEON EMPEREUR DES FRANCAIS 1804, for protecting the mines and miners of the Hartz during the war. Splendid proof, and extremely rare. Size 28

2284 MINERS' TOKENS. "Glück Auf." Mining Implements. Little beauties, dime size. 2 pieces

2285 1-6 THALER. 3 Marien Grosch., 1 do., 24 Einen thaler, etc. Uncirculated. 6 pieces

*Copper Coins and Medals.*

2286 "GLUCK AUF" penny. "4 Pfenning Scheede Muntz," etc. Ex. fine and rare. 4 pieces

2287 SIMILAR lot. 3 pieces

2288 WILD MAN pennies and other variety pfennings and double pfennings. No duplicates. Uncirculated lot. Very rare. 33 pieces

2289 SIMILAR lot; intended to be without duplicates; but not as carefully examined. Fine.

## Coins of Saxony.—Silver.

2290 SIMILAR to last. [The number of pieces in this and last lot will be given at the time of sale. Erased from manuscript by an accident.]

2291 GEORGE LOUIS (afterwards Geo. I. King of England). Medal in tin. Struck 24th Sept., 1707; obv. bust; rev. Trojan Horse. Proof. Size 28

2292 GEORGE IV. On his visit to Hanover in 1821. Size 24

2293 ERNEST AUGUSTUS, Duke of Cumberland. (On the accession of Victoria he succeeded William IV. as King of Hanover); obv. bare bust; rev. within a beaded circle, a plain field. Magnificent proof; bronze. Size 32

2294 SAME in all respects.

2295 ANOTHER. Splendid proof.

2296 GEORGE IV. of Hanover, the last King. Medal on his marriage with Marie, Duchess of Saxe. Their busts accolated; rev. An arch. Fine proof. Bronze. Size 24

### SAXONY.

*Silver.*

2297 "KLAPPMUTZEN THALER" (The oldest Saxon Crown.) Busts of Frederick, with John and George, all wearing caps; the former on the obv. with drawn sword; the others *vis a vis* on the rev. From 1486 to 1525. Very fine and rare.

2298 QUARTER DOLLAR of the same Dukes. (Winged figure supporting shield.) Fine and rare.

2299 GEORGE. 1500 to 1539. Bare bust to l. 1534. BABB AKSCII counterstamped before the face; rev. bust of John to r. RECK FOTZE counterstamped in the field. Extremely fine and rare Crown.

2300 —— Same Crown. 1536; without countermarks. Equally fine and rare.

2301 JOHN (Elector), with George. Same period; bust of the former with bonnet and drawn sword; rev bust of George wearing a cap. Very fine and rare crown.

2302 —— Half-crown. Christ standing. Rare.

## Coins of Saxony.—Silver.

2303 JOHN FREDERICK and his son. Their effigies wearing caps; rev. festival in a temple. Long inscription. Struck to commemorate the Augsbury Confession 1503. Fine and rare medal.    Size 30

2304 MAURICE. 1546. With bust of John on reverse. Nearly uncirculated crown. Rare.

2304* —— Quarter-crown of 1552. Very fine.

2305 —— Small coins (two having been gilt.) All in fine preservation; dime size.    3 pieces

2306 PHILLIP LANDGRAVE HASSI? 1546. Bust in rich dress, head bare; rev. Bust of John Frederick, with drawn sword. Fine and rare crown.

2307 AUGUSTUS. 1553 to 1586. Crown, dated 1567. Ins. in 8 lines. GOTHA CAPTA SVPPLICIO, &c. Very fine.

2308 —— Quarter crown. His bust, three-quarter face, with drawn sword. Rare.

2309 JOHN FREDERICK II. 1554 to 1595. Fine crown of 1565. His bust to the middle. Rare.

2310 —— Half crown. 1570. Fine.

2311 FREDERICK WILLIAM AND JOHN. 1585. Beautiful crown. A long figure in full regalia on each side; surrounding each a circle with inscription broken by 6 shields. Hardly circulated. Very rare.

2312 CHRISTIAN II. 1591 to 1611. Bust of Christian between John George and Augustus. 1593. Extremely fine crown.

2313 —— Crown of 1603, with long figure of Christian; and on the reverse in a medallion centre, busts of John George and Augustus. Nearly uncirculated.

2314 —— Similar crown of 1606, the figures on the reverse being much larger. Very fine.

2315 —— One-third crowns, with busts of the three brothers on each. 1599 to 1603.    2 pieces

2316 —— Half crown tastefully mounted with button and loop; busts of the brothers as before. 1610. Fine.

## Coins of Saxony.—Silver.

2317 ERNEST. 1610 to 1675. Duke Saxe Gotha. Medal with his bust in high relief, three-quarter face; rev. female seated; in exergue, Pietas, 1673. Medal cast and finished with care by C. S. Entirely perfect in preservation. Size 30

2318 DOLLAR of Eight Dukes. VIII FRAT: DVC: SAX. Four busts, full face on each side. 1610 Fine, rare.

2319 ANOTHER. 8 FRAT: DVC: SAAXON JVL: CLI: MONT. The busts as before, but arranged more nearly in a horizontal line. Ex. fine. 1813.

2320 DOLLAR, with busts of four brothers, Dukes of Saxony. 1624. Their figures to the hips in full regalia, heads bare. IOHN PHIL: FRID: JOHN WILLIAM: ET: FR. WILLIAM. Splendid crown.

2321 CROWN of 1622. MONETA FRATRVM DVC: SAXON LIN VIII. No busts, but a full length figure standing, with shield and banner; rev. coat-of-arms. Uncirculated and brilliant. Very rare.

2322 JOHN CASIMER AND JOHN ERNEST. 1613. Their busts face to face, their hands joined; rev. knight on horseback within two circles. Very fine crown.

2323 —— Crown of 1625. Bust of one of the Grand Dukes on each side. Ex. fine, rare.

2324 —— Half crown. 1605. Two busts. Rare.

2325 WILLIAM, from 1600 to 1662. A medal with three hands meeting above the point of a drawn sword upright; rev. 1547, 1641, and 1650; two hands from the clouds holding a crown above a coat-of-arms; less than dollar size. Uncirculated, rare.

2326 JOHN ERNEST. 1638. Bust to the middle. Fine and rare crown.

2327 JOHN GEORGE 1st. 1611 to 1656. Square dollar, the date found in the tall letters of legend; bust and coat-of-arms. Ex. fine, rare.

2328 —— Thick Dollar. Quarter dollar size, full weight. 1614. Never in circulation; busts of John George and Augustus, brothers. Ex. rare.

2329 —— Double dollar. 1615. On each side bust as before. Splendid and uncirculated, rare.

## Coins of Saxony.—Silver.

2330 JOHN GEORGE 1ST. Extra broad crown of 1619. John George on horseback; rev. long inscription in 12 lines. Ex. fine, rare.

2331 —— Broad crown of 1627. Bust with drawn sword; rev. handsome coat-of-arms. Ex. fine.

2332 —— Another, same date. Equally fine.

2333 —— Double dollar in Commemoration of the first centennial festival of the Augsburg Confession. 1530–1630. Busts of John and John George. Uncirculated and brilliant. Ex. rare.

2334 —— Dollar of the same type. Uncirculated, rare.

2335 —— Medalet on the same occasion. 1630.  Size 16

2336 —— Two-third dollar. 1651. Uncirculated, rare.

2337 —— One-half dollar, one-quarter dollar, one-eighth dollar, and another. 4 pieces

2338 JOHN GEORGE II. 1656 to 1680. Broad medal crown, struck at the beginning of his reign. 1657. The Duke on horseback, DEO ET PATRIÆ; rev. inscription in 12 lines. Very fine, rare.

2339 —— One-third crown, same type and date. Uncirculated.

2340 —— One-third crown, with his bust. 1668. Rev. coat-of-arms. Uncirculated, rare.

2341 —— One-third and one-sixth crown. Fine. 2 pieces

2342 —— Square dollar. 1679. Rev. Hercules on a cloud. VIRTVTE PARATA. Uncirculated, very rare.

2343 —— Broad piece; within the garter and motto of England—Fame and two shields over a prostrate figure; rev. inscription in 16 lines. Extremely fine and rare medal. Size 32

2344 JOHN GEORGE III. 1680 to 1691. Broad crown of 1682; large bust to the hips; rev. arms with 8 crests. Ex. fine, rare.

2345 —— Two-third crown of 1684. Bust; arms crowned. Very fine.

2346 —— Crown. HEROS DEFENSOO-IMPER A TVRCIS GALLISQ; arm holding a banner. IEHOVA VEXILLVM MEVM. 1691. Very fine, rare. (Not in Wellenheim.)

Coins of Saxony.—Silver.

2347 JOHN GEORGE III. Two-third crown, same type. In Wellenheim, No. 5824.

2348 —— Broad medal crown, on his death; bust within 3 circles of inscription; rev. inscription in 15 parallel lines. Uncirculated, rare.

2349 —— Medalet. "Presses Auxilles." Sword and banner crossed. Size 10

2350 JOHN GEORGE IV. 1691 to 1694. "12 Einen Thaler;" rev. 4 shields in the form of a cross; sword and banner crossed before the shields; resembling a testoon of Scotland. Rare.

2351 —— Two-third crown, bust; rev. like last. Rare.

2352 —— Medal. Mailed bust, long, curly hair, ermine over his armor; rev. the Duke standing between Minerva and the Goddess of Peace. FELICITATIS PUBLICÆ CVSTOS ET VINDEX. A very remarkable medal for the time. Perfect and brilliant proof. Very rare. Size 28

2353 MORTUARY MEDALETS of Ernest and Magdalene—1686 and 1729—with a selection of fine groats of the 14th, 15th, and 16th centuries. All nearly uncirculated.
10 pieces

2354 FREDERICK AUGUSTUS. Mailed bust to l.; rev. "John George Filio, born 1662, died 1684." Part of the inscription in Scripture. Medal. Size 24

2355 FREDERICK 1st, Duke. 1690. ⅙ Crown.

2356 WILLIAM ERNEST. Medal. "In memoriam Natalis Principes Nova Egpiæ Fundationis. De XXX. October, MDCCXVII." Obv. bust; rev. edifice. Reformation Jubilee Medal. Uncirculated and beautiful.
Size 24

2357 —— Another Jubilee Medal — the second after the Reformation; Oct. 31, 1717; rev. a hand from above lighting a candle placed on an open book. On the table cover $\frac{W}{E}$—William Ernest. SIE DÆMPFFN NICHT DES WORTES LICHT. Crown. Very fine and rare.

140                Coins of Saxony.—Silver.

2358 MEDALS AND COINS about ¼-dollar size; one in proof condition, dated 1616; another 1780 "Gluet der Repdenstadt Meiningsn." One of Chas. VI. Very fine lot.                                  5 pieces

2359 FREDERICK III. 1732 to 1772. A regular series corresponding to 1, ½, ¼, and ⅛ Thaler, all with bust—also a Jubilee Medalet and one on his death. Fine.
                                                                                                    4 pieces

2360 XAVIER, (of Poland). Duke of Saxony. Medal of X. Marks (Crown) with his bust; rev. view of mines with miners at work. By the Academy of Freyburg, 13th Nov., 1765. Very fine.

2361 —— Crown of 1766; rev. coat-of-arms. Fine.

2362 JOSEPH FREDERICK. 1781. Crown. Bust in rich dress, chain of the Order of the G. Fleece; rev. young warrior, with arms of Saxony. Very fine.

2363 "FATHERLAND MEDAL" of 1814. Inscription in German text; bundle of rods.                           Size 25

2364 REFORMATION JUBILEE MEDALET. 1817.                 Size 15

2365 SILVER CROSS, iron inclosed. F. C. in monogram, and on rev. XX., with ring and loop. Very fine.

2366 SILVER CROSS, with gold and enamel work; gold head in relief. ALBERTVS ANIMOSVS; rev. arms of Saxony. Extremely fine.

2367 ANTON AND FREDERICK AUGUSTUS, King and Regent. Crown. 1831. Two busts, scroll. Very fine.

2368 JOHN AND AMELIA. Their busts jugata. 1822–1872. Beautiful medal; thick.                           Size 26

2369 FREDERICK AUGUSTUS II. 1854. Uncirculated Thaler. Bust; rev. shield, with arms of Saxony between two seated females with attributes of Justice and Hope.

2370 —— ⅓ Thaler; rev. arms of Saxony and Prussia. Very fine.

2371 —— Smaller Coins. ⅓ and ⅙ Thaler. Fine. 2 pieces

2372 ERNEST. Thaler of 1869. Uncirculated. "29th January."

2373 —— Duplicate. Fine.

2374 —— Smaller Coins. 2 Groschen and 20 Krs. Uncirculated.                                           2 pieces

## Coins of Nassau.—Silver.

2375 JOHN V. 1871. Brilliant uncirculated Thaler. Bust; rev. winged male figure on a horse.

2376 —— Small Coins of John and Ernest; 1 and 2 Groshen and 10 Krs. Fine. 4 pieces

2377 EARLY Saxon and Cleves Coins. Penny size, without date. Rare. 8 pieces

2378 SAXON Coins, about 1550. Rare. 4 do.

2378* MISCELLANEOUS, of small size, with Medalets. Fine lot. 12 pieces

2379 —— All kinds. 44 pieces

### Copper.

2380 HENNEBURG. Arms; a hen. 2 pieces

2381 KLIPPINGERS. Square coins. 3 do.

2382 JOHN GEORGE III. and Anna Sophia—beautiful Monogram. Rare.

2383 MEDALETS. "Gute Schaupfenigs," with curious devices. Little Medalets. Thick Pieces. Very fine, rare. 10 pieces

2384 MEDALET of Fred. Aug. of Nassau, on his visit to the mint at Ehrenbriechtine in 1808.

2385 —— Lead Token. 1,000 years' festival at the City of Brunswick. Rare. Size 18

2386 Miscellaneous Saxon Coins. A very fine lot. 110 pieces

---

## NASSAU.

### Silver.

2387 JOHN, Francis, Henry, William, and Maurice; broad crown, 1681. 5 busts, with names of 5 Dukes of Nassau, etc.; rev. coat-of-arms, lions supporting. Madai, 1365. Wellenheim, 3772. Described as rare. Very fine. Size 30

2388 HENRY. 1680. Bust; underneath XV. (Kreutzer); rev. arms of Nassau. Appel, 2284. Fine and rare.

2389 —— "II. Albus." 1683. Rosettes. Rare.

142 *Coins of Holstein.—Silver.*

2390 FREDERICK AUGUSTUS. Crown. 1812. Bust; rev. arms of Nassau. Uncirculated.

2391 —— Waterloo Medal of 1815. Frederick Aug. Bare bust; rev. Fame crowning Valor. June 18, 1815. With loop. Rare.  Size 19.

2392 WILLIAM. King. Medal Dollar of 1831. "Erbante munzstatte zu Wiesbaden, den 28 Dec." Very fine, rare.

2393 ADOLPHUS. King. 21 Aug., 1864. Uncirculated Thaler. On his accession. Rare.

2394 SMALL Coins. Base silver.  6 pieces

## HOLSTEIN.

*Silver.*

2395 FREDERICK I. 1533. "XVI. Reis Dal." VIRTVT GLORIA MER. Fine and rare.

2396 —— Others. Same.  3 pieces

2397 CHRISTIAN IV. 1588 to 1648. "3 Schilling." Bust in robes, collar and crown. Ex. fine and rare.
Dime size

2398 FRANCIS II. (In Lauenburg). 1603 to 1619. Splendid uncirculated Crown. 1609. Bust in collar and robes, bare head. Brilliant, rare.

2399 ERNEST. Brilliant Crown, without date. Bust with fringed collar, head bare. ERNESTVS D. G. HOL-SATIÆ, etc. A magnificent piece.

2400 FERDINAND II. (Emperor.) 1622. Arms of Holstein and Germany. Brilliant uncirculated Crown. Very rare.

2401 FREDERICK III. 1616 to 1659. Brilliant uncirculated Crown. 1622. Mailed and royally draped bust, fringed collar; rev. coat-of-arms. Superb, rare.

2402 —— Series of his Coins. "VIII. and XVI. Reis Dal," etc.  5 pieces

## Coins of Reuss (Duchy).—Silver.

CHRISTIAN ALBERT. 1659 to 1691. XVI. Reis Dal.
4 pieces
—— In memory of the death of Maximillian, Emperor. Thaler Medal. 1678. Fine and rare.
JULIUS FRANCIS. (In Lauenberg.) 1678. Fine Thaler ($\frac{2}{3}$ Crown), with his bust. Rare.
CHARLES FREDERICK. 1712. (Dime size.) 2 Coins.
CHRISTIAN VII. (Denmark). "Twenty Schilling Schles: Holst. Courant, 1789." Rare.
FREDERICK VI. (Denmark). Two-third Crown. (Lauenburg). Very rare, fine.
WAR MEDAL. Schles. Holstein against Denmark. Iron cross, silver clasp. Rare.
NASSAU AND HOLSTEIN Coins and Medalets. Several of Kings of Denmark. Fine lot, to be closely examined by purchaser. 18 pieces

### REUSS (Duchy).

*Silver.*

HENRY XXIX. 1739. Twenty-four Einen Thaler.
HENRY III. 1751. Quarter Specie Thaler. View of mines.
—— 2752. Quarter Specie Thaler. Proof.
HENRY XXIV. 1765. Two-third Crown. Fair condition. Rare.
HENRY XI. 1769. Beautiful Crown, and rare.
HENRY XII. 1764. Two-third Crown. Nearly uncirculated. Very rare.
HENRY III. 1807. Splendid uncirculated Crown. Very rare.
SMALL Coins. Good lot. 6 pieces

The chronology of the Princes of Reuss, as exhibited above, appears to be slightly confused, but the titles and dates will be found on the coins as described. As similar descriptions in Wellenheim's Catalogue pass without comment, it is to be presumed that however inscrutable to us, the system is understood, and approved in the "Fatherland."

## Copper.

2419 FOUR, three, two, one and half Pfenning and Heller. Fine and rare. 6 pieces
2420 SIMILAR lot. 10 pieces

## PRUSSIA.

### Silver.

2421 ALBERT. Margrave Brandenburg. 1144. Bracteats. 2 pieces
2422 OTHO. Margrave Nebenlinie in Brand. Pennies. Wellenheim, 6343. Rare. 2 pieces
2423 —— Another. Well. 6348.
2424 SIGISMUND (Luxemberg). 1378 to 1417. Pennies. 2 pcs
2425 FREDERICK (Silesia). 1543. Bust; rev. Eagle; Groats. Very fine. 2 pieces
2426 ALBERT (Margrave Brandenburg). 1525 to 1565. Crown. 1549. Figure of Albert to left; rev. cross fleuri. Four shields in angles. Fine and rare.
2427 —— "III Gross-Ar.-Triplex Prussie." Guilloche border and loop. Worn as a medal. Fine and rare.
2428 —— without the m...... 5 pieces
2429 —— three Grossus; rev. eagle. Fine and rare. 3 pcs
2430 —— GEORGE and ALBERT. 1544. Their figure face to face; rev. like Albert's Crown. Extremely fine and rare.
2431 JOHN GEORGE. (Saxony). Three Grossus and others of this period. 12 pieces
2432 PENNIES of very early date. Fine silver. 6 pieces
2433 GEORGE. (Margrave Brandenburg). 1567. Crown under Maximillian, Emperor. Rare.
2434 GEORGE WILLIAM. 1619 to 1640. Hammered Crown of 1631, two-third length figure in mail to right; rev. immense shield with coat-of-arms. Very fine, rare.
2435 —— One-third Crown. 1623. Bust on ermine. Bril-

## Coins of Prussia.—Silver.

2436 GEORGE, LOUIS, and CHRISTIAN, brothers. Three busts. Other small coins. 3 pieces

2437 CHRISTIAN (DUKE SILESIA). One-third Crown. 1667.

2438 FREDERICK III. Elector. (The same as Frederick I., King), from 1688 to 1701, and 1701 to 1713. Medalet on his accession, 1688. Thick. Size 18

2439 —— Another. Coronation Medal. Uncirculated and beautiful. (Rev. Crown). Size 18

2440 —— Twelve Einen Thalers. Various. 14 pieces

2441 —— Two-third Crown. 1689. Guilloch milling. Very fine and rare.

2442 —— Two-third Crown, milled in the usual way. 3 pcs

2443 —— Crown of 1695. F. III. repeated, the letters F. back to back. Fine and very rare.

2444 —— One-third Crown; with same of Sylvi, Frederick, and John Frederick, of Brandenburg. An interesting and rare lot. 5 pieces

2445 SMALL Coins of this period, average dime size. A rare lot. 10 pieces

2446 —— Similar lot, smaller. 20 pieces

2447 FREDERICK WILLIAM. (Elector.) Eminent in the war against Sweden. Splendid proof Crown, 1645. His bust, with sword and sceptre to right; rev. large and beautiful coat-of-arms. (Twenty-four divisions). Broad, and very rare. Size 29

2448 —— Bust with long hair. One-third Crown. 1668. Very broad. Uncirculated.

2449 —— Laureated bust. Edge milled. One-third Crown. Uncirculated.

2450 —— Others different. 2 pieces

2451 —— Two-third Crown, (Dollar size). Bust with long hair in curls. Uncirculated. Splendid, rare.

2452 —— Similar. The year of his death. 1688. Uncirculated. Splendid. Rare. Size 24

2453 —— Another. (Two-third Crown). 1675. Fine.

2454 —— About Quarter-dollar size. 6 pieces

10

## Coins of Prussia.—Silver.

2455 MEDAL on the Birth of Frederick the Great's Father (4th Aug., 1688). Winged Hippogryph; rev. FAVST NATALIB FRED. WILHELMI BRAND. FRED. II. ELECT EX. SOPHIA CAR BRYNS. FIL II. Fine and very rare. Size 18

2456 FREDERICK II., the Great. 1740 to 1786. Medalet on his accession. VERITATI ET. JVSTITIA. 3 AVC., 1740. Fine and very rare. Size 18

2457 —— Thaler. 1741. Young bust, broad milling. Fine and rare.

2458 —— (XV). Quarter Dollar. 1743. Another similar. 2 pieces

2459 —— Thaler, Half-dollar, Quarter-dollar. 1850; rev. eagle, etc. Two last uncirculated. 3 pieces

2460 —— Half Thalers of 1750. Quarter and twelve Ein Thal. 4 pieces

2461 —— Thin Medal, in case. Extremely fine and rare. Size 32

2462 —— Brilliant Thaler. 1782.

2463 —— Thaler in Memory of his death. 1786. Fine and rare.

2464 FREDERICK WILLIAM II. 1786 to 1797. Medals on his accession, 1786. Bust; rev. NOVA SPES REGNI. 28th Oct. Fine. Two varieties. Size 20. 2 pieces

2465 —— Bust, royally dressed, face to left; rev. within wreath, of laurel "Nova Spes Regni"; in ex. FIDES. 13 Nov., 1786. Thick medal by Looz; splendid work and condition. Rare. Size 32

2466 —— Equally beautiful Medal; rev. Prussia seated with arms, an eagle with olive branch and thunderbolt hovering above. AIVIS EXPVG CAROLI BRUNSV. D AVSPICTS, 1787. Size 32

2467 —— Medal by Looz; brilliant proof; bust ¾ face; rev. semi-nude figure seated under a palm tree, on which his armor is hanging, in the act of receiving a caduceus from the Angel of Peace. PARATA BASILEAE, 5 April, 1795. Size 32

2468 —— Thaler. 1792. Fine.

Coins of Prussia.—Silver. 147

2469 FREDERICK WILLIAM III. 1797 to 1840. Medalet and coin. Size 18. 2 pieces
2470 —— Medal by Looz. Paderborn, 1802; very fine. Size 32
2471 —— Medal by *Abramson*. F. William III., Alexander X., Napoleon I.—26 June, 1807; obv. their busts, the two former facing the latter; rev. Sun rising. Proof. Very rare. Size 32
2472 —— Medal on his death, 1840. Obv. bust; rev. Fame and History. Size 32
2473 FREDERICK WILLIAM IV. 1840. Medal on the Confederation; 39 shields charged with arms of German states. EIN MANN, EIN BUND, EIN FREIES DEUTSCHES VOLK; Man with Lion skin robe standing on heap of armor. Beautiful and rare. Size 27
2474 —— Gulden and ½ Gulden. 1852. 2 pieces
2475 —— Thaler on his death, 1861. Proof. Rare.
2476 WILLIAM, King. 1861. (The present Kaiser.) Thaler. with William and Augusta crowned facing to r.; rev, small eagle displayed. W-R-A-R-W and A crowned. Uncirculated. Rare. (Struck on their coronation.)
2477 —— Others. Very fine. 2 pieces
2478 —— Thaler of 1866. Bust *laureated*. Uncirculated. Rare.
2479 —— Others. Equally fine. 2 pieces
2480 —— Thaler of 1871. Germania seated. Brilliant. Rare.
2481 —— Duplicate. Fine.
2482 —— Medal (Double thaler) to commemorate his victorious war against France. Column and inscription in rays. 1870–1871. Brilliant proof. Rare.
2483 DOUBLE Thaler. 1744. Frederick W. C. FURST ZU HOHENZ HECH, *by Voight*. 1844. Ex. fine.
2484 —— Duplicate. Fine.
2485 DOUBLE Thaler, same date,—1744. "Carl ZU Hohenzollern Sigmaringen." By *Doell*. Fine. Rare.

2486 CROSS of the Order of the Crown, instituted by the Kaiser William, on his accession to the Crown of Prussia in 1861; fine gold and enamel. Size 32. Fine and rare.

2487 CROSS. Order of the Iron Cross; iron, with silver mounting. Fine and rare.

2488 WATERLOO Medalet. "Sieg Bei Belle Alliance Durch Herzog V. Wellington und Fursten Blücher, 18 June, 1815." Owl standing on a helmet. Very fine and rare.   Size 12

2489 MEDALETS and Coins. Fred. the Great and other Prussian Kings—one-fourth, one-sixth, and one-twelfth thaler. Some so old as to be without date; well worthy of specification; massed to avoid tediousness.
    15 pieces

2490 ANOTHER lot similar, smaller size. Base.   56 pieces

### Copper. (*Coins and Medals*.)

2491 KINGDOM of Prussia and Duchies Nassau and Mecklenburg; several old and very rare.   20 pieces

2492 MEDALETS and Coins. Extra fine and rare lot.
    12 pieces

2493 WEIGHT (Double Louis d'or) and medalets from 1545. Rare.   12 pieces

2494 WAR Medals, 1813 and 1849. Loops; fine.   2 pieces

2495 MISCELLANEOUS Coins.   53 pieces

2496 WAR Medals of Frederick the Great—Prague, Rosbach, and others; one, "Gall, Austr. Russ et Succ." another, "Famæ-Prudenticæ et Virtute." Size 25
    8 pieces
    This lot of medals is very desirable.

2497 BLUCHER Medal, struck in Berlin 1816. Bust of Blucher in the character of Hercules; rev. 1813, 1814, 1815; St. Michael slaying a dragon with the head of Napoleon Bonaparte. Berlin Iron; in the style called *cavo relievo*. Fine, and very rare.   Size 48

2498 MEDAL by Looz. Bust of Fred. the Great; rev. his monument. 1840. Fine proof.   Sixe 32

## Coins and Medals of Prussia.—Copper.

2499 LEOPOLD II. and Fred. William II. 13 Aug. 1791, and one of Fred. William III.; also, one very thick in lead "18th March 1849." Av. Size 30.   3 pieces

2500 MORTUARY Medal in honor of Prince De Hardenburg. Obv. bust; rev. Galley, May, 1750—May, 1810. Fine proof.   Size 32

2501 BISMARCK; Bust of Prince Bismarck in Helmet, KAISER DES DEUTSCHEN REICHS; rev. The Genius seated with sword and olive branch; in the field a torch and caduceus; 1870. 1871. POSCIMUR; a very beautiful proof in dark bronze. By Bovy.   Size 32

2502 VON MOLTKE. Bust; rev. Victory, with palm and crown borne through the air by an Eagle. 1870. 1871. Fine bronze proof.   Size 32

2503 JUBILEE Medal by Looz. GESCHLOSSENEN EHEBUNDES, Sept. 16th, 1792. Busts of JOHEN BARTELS JU DR MAR. ELLIS V. RECK; rev. JUBEL FEIER. 1842, Oct. 6. Busts of AMAND AUGUST ABEND ROTH J. U. Dr. JOH. MAGD V. RECK. Lettered edge; in the *cavo-reliveo* style (rim raised, field sunk). A superb bronze proof.   Size 36

2504 SPLENDID Medal by Looz and Pfeuffer in honor of William Amsinck, Consul Hamburg. Bronze proof   Size 30

2505 ALBERT WALLENSTEIN NATUS PRAGUAE in BOHEMIA, 1583. Obit. 1638. Bust; rev. Inscription. Beautiful bronze.   Size 28

2506 MEDAL of "Prof. D. Tonk, Dr. RITT, Dec. 1831." Fine proof.   Size 24

2507 BAPTISMAL Medal; Jubilee Medal (NUN ISTS ENTSCHIEDEN WO SIND WIR. 1800-1801;) SCHOLE MELDORFICAE Medal. (view of the edifice): and Jesuit Medal. Extremely fine lot. Size 20.   4 pieces

2508 MEDAL of Handel; Jeton of Dr. Luther; Jubilee of 1860, etc. etc. Extremely interesting lot. Bronze and tin, various sizes.   10 pieces

## SCHWARZBURG.

### Silver.

2509 GUNTHER. Count in 1544; crown; Gunther on horseback, under the horse a child; rev. arms, two supporters with standards. Extremely rare.

2510 CHRISTIAN WILLIAM; two-third Crown, 1676. Bust in mail and wig; rev. arms—comb in one compartment. Nearly uncirculated. Very rare.

2511 —— Another, Two-third Crown; same Count, but a variety.

2512 CHRISTIAN GUNTHER, 1758 to 1794. LXXX. FINE FEINE MARCKE. 1764.

2513 LOUIS GUNTHER, 1767 to 1790; Crown, 1786. Bust; rev. arms, two wild men for supporters. Uncirculated. Rare.

2514 FREDERICK GUNTHER, 1864. Thaler. Uncirculated. Brilliant.

2515 SMALL Coins, one early Bracteate.      11 pieces

## WALDECK.

### Silver.

2516 CHRISTIAN and WOLRATH, brothers, Counts. 1608. Arms of Waldeck; rev. Imperial Arms. Ex. fine. Dime size. Rare.      2 pieces

2517 GEORGE, Frederick, John and Wolrath. 1654; obv. a tree; rev. IV. Marien Gro. and II. M. Gro. Fine      2 pieces

2518 CHARLES AUGUSTUS FREDERICK. 1728 to 1763. Twelve Einen Reichs Thaler. 1752. Fine and very rare.

2519 FREDERICK. Count from 1763 to 1811. Uncirculated Crown. (X. Eine Feine Mark), 1816. Rare and valuable. (Wellen. 4332).

*Coins of Wurtemburg.—Silver.*

2520 GEORGE HENRY. 1813 to 1824. Crown. 1824; obv. palm tree, "Cresit Palma Subpondere." Uncirculated. Very rare.

2521 SMALL Coins, quarter, one-sixth Thaler and smaller.
8 pieces

## WURTEMBURG.

### Silver.

2522 ULRICH, Duke, 1503 to 1520. Duke on horseback. date (1507) under the horse; rev. coat-of-arms. Fine and very rare Crown. (Not in Wellenheim).

2523 ULRICH II., 1534 to 1550. Medal Crown of 1537. VL. DVX . WIRT . ET . TECK . CO . MO . BELL D. G. Bust with broad-brimmed hat; rev. coat-of-arms. Uncirculated. Wellenheim, 3262. Called rare.

2524 —— Duplicate. Rare crown.

2525 CHRISTORF. 1550 to 1568. Rare coin, dime size.

2526 JULIUS FREDERICK. (60 ? 1823). Half Thaler. Stag lying down; rev. arms; not in Wellenheim. Fine and rare.

2527 JOHN FREDERICK. 1608 to 1628. Crown of 1621. Bust; rev. coat-of-arms under a crown; Well. 3283. Rare.

2528 —— Crown of 1624, set in heavy cable of four chains with loop. Extremely fine and rare.

2529 —— Klippe Thaler (square). 1625. Bust; rev. I.H.S. Very fine, rare.

2530 —— Crown of 1626. Bust in the Roman habit; rev. coat-of-arms. Very fine and rare.

2531 FREDERICK CHARLES, Administrator, 1677 to 1693. Splendid uncirculated medal of beautiful work, burnished field, bust within a border, known on gems as *etruscan;* rev. Hercules slaying the Hydra. DVRA PLACENT FORTIBVS. Wellenheim, 3308. Marked rare.

## Coins of Austria.—Silver.

2532 EBERHARD LOUIS, 1677 to 1733. Thick heavy medal. gilt, mailed bust in wig; rev. arms from a cloud holding a banner with eagle displayed. PRO. DEO. ET. IMPERIO. Ex. fine and rare.  Size 33

2533 —— Half Thaler. 1733. Very fine, rare.

2534 CHARLES (RUDOLPH). 1737 to 1742. "Land Munz. 15 Krs." Uncirculated. Rare.

2535 CHARLES CHRISTIAN. Rix Dollar of 1785. Bust; rev. coat-of-arms, (in one quarter a bust). Uncirculated. Very rare.

2536 WILLIAM, King from 1816. Medal by Voight. Laureated bust; rev. Germania seated between two boys with cornucopia and fasces. 30 Oct., 1841. Uncirculated.  Size 20

2537 —— Duplicate.

2538 —— Double Thaler. Rev. Charles of Wurtz and Olga, of Russia. Their busts *jugata*. Ex. fine, rare.

2539 CHARLES, King, Double Thaler (medal). Bust; rev. Cathedral of Ulm. Ex. fine.

2540 —— Thaler. Rev. angel standing on guns and flags. Fine proof. No date.

2541 —— Same. Uncirculated.

2542 —— Others. Fine.  2 pieces

2543 SMALL Coins. Many very old and fine.  13 pieces

---

### AUSTRIA.

*Silver.*

2544 CHARLEMAGNE. 800 to 814. Penny. CARLVS REX. FR. In the middle a cross; rev. METVLLO. In the middle his monogram, $\mathrm{K^R_{\Lambda}V_LS}$. Fine and rare.

2545 LOUIS I. 814 to 840. Penny. HLVDOVVICVS IMP. In the middle cross and balls; rev. RISTIANA RELIGIO. Church with cross on the top. Madai I. p. 58. Ex. fine and rare.

## Coins of Austria.—Silver.

OTHO I. 936 to 973. Penny. O-D-D-O, in the angles of a cross; rev. a church. A good, sound coin not fairly struck. Very rare.

OTHO III. 938 to 1002. O-D-D-O, in the angles of a cross; rev. a church. Very fine and rare.

—— Duplicate. Equally fine.

CONRAD III. 1137 to 1152. Penny. Crowned King seated, holding a mund and cross; rev. a church with steeple; on each side a tower. Ex. fine and rare. Well. 6416.

BERTRAND, Patriarch of Aquelia, 1334 to 1350. Obv. image of the Virgin, BERTR. ARDVS. P.; rev. eagle, AQVIL. ENS. Well. 9455. Fine and rare.

GREGORY. 1275. The Patriarch seated, holding a banner and cross, GREGO. RIV. PA.; rev. eagle. AQVIL. EGIA. Dime size. Well preserved and very rare.

ANTONY PANCIERA. (Aquileja). Penny. 1402 to 1412; Uncirculated. Rare.

WENCESLAUS I. (Bohemia). 1230 to 1253. Small coins (Scherfs); W. and Lion. Rare. 3 pieces

—— Penny; bust, in front, dagger; rev. bust, full face. Uncirculated. Very rare.

WENCESLAUS II., 1278 to 1305. WENCESLAVS SECVNDVS. In the middle a crown; rev. lion. Groat. Fine.

WLADISLAUS II., 1471 to 1516; with the exception of difference in name, like last; Groat. (Marked by Wellenheim, R. R.) Fine, rare.

—— Penny, dated 1510. Ex. fine and rare.

FERDINAND I. 1526 to 1564. Groat, same type.

SIGISMUND (Tyrol). 1439 to 1496. Crown. The Duke standing; rev. a Knight galloping, (Turnier-Ritter); around, a circle of shields. Date (1486), under the horse. Extremely fine.

—— Duplicate, same in all respects.

These are coins of the Teutonic Order of Knights, and are rare.

154     *Coins of Austria.—Silver.*

2561 SIGISMUND (Tyrol.) Half-dollar. 1484. Crowned bust; rev. *Turnier-Ritter.* Madai, 1372; Well., 9198. Fine and very rare.

2562 MAXIMILLIAN I. 1493 to 1519. Double Crown, 1509. Obv. the King on horseback, the horse covered with blazonry with plumes on his head; rev. crowned shield within a semi-circle of 7 shields; a full circle of 19 shields and outer circle of inscription surrounding all. Uncirculated. Slightly concave. Beautiful and rare. Madai, 2386. Wellenheim, 6790.     Size 36.

2563 —— ¼ Dollar, bust; rev. cross, a shield in each angle; and 1 smaller, different type. Fine.     2 pieces

2564 CHARLES V. 1519 to 1558. Gulden, 1551. Rare.

2565 JOHN AUSTEN. (Son of Chas. V.) 1571. Small coin, penny size. Ex. fine.

2566 FERDINAND I. 1564. Crown, without date. The Arch Duke standing with sceptre and sword; rev. coat-of-arms. Ex. fine. Rare.

2567 —— Crown. 1563. Crowned bust to r. in field, arms of Germany; rev. double-headed eagle and shield. Very fine, and pronounced very rare.

2568 —— Half-crown. Similar. Fine.

2569 —— Broad Crown. 1557. Well preserved.

2570 —— Brilliant, nearly proof, Crown. 1616. Beautiful.

2571 —— Small Coins. Fine lot.     5 pieces

2572 RUDOLPH II. 1576 to 1612. Triple Dollar, struck for the Tyrol. 1604. Laureated bust, high ruff; rev. coat-of-arms. Rare. Very fine.

2573 —— Crown. Same date. Rev. double-headed eagle; on each wing a sceptre. Extremely fine and rare.     Size 28

2574 —— Duplicate, except date. 1593.

2575 —— Medal. 1599. Rev. 7 shields, initials of 7 provinces. Thick. Said to be very rare.     Size 18

2576 —— Small Coins. Rare lot.     7 pieces

2577 MAXIMILLIAN. Charles and Ferdinand, Arch Duke Austria and Regents of Spain; their busts crowned. 90. (1590?) Fine and doubtless rare crown. Not in Wellenheim.

## Coins of Austria.—Silver. 155

2578 SIGISMUND BATHORI, Prince of Transylvania, 1581 to 1598, Remarkable Crown of 1595; Figure in mail, shown to the hips, holding sceptre and sword; rev. arms, claws of a bear, supported by two angels. Extremely fine and rare. Wellenheim, 1387.

2579 MATTHIAS. 1612 to 1620. Medal Coin on his coronation, 1612; rev. crown with rays from sun and moon; in twisted border, loop removed. Fine. Size 20

2580 —— Crown on his coronation. 1612. Ex. fine. Rare.

2581 —— Crown, 1618, uncirculated, beautiful. Rare.

2582 —— Half-crown. Fine.

2582* —— Broad Crown. 1620. Extra fine.

2583 FERDINAND II. 1619 to 1637. Broad crown, 1824. The Arch Duke standing with sword, sceptre, and mund; rev. double-headed eagle and lion of Bohemia. Extremely fine.

2584 —— Half-crown, equally fine; same type.

2585 —— One-third Crown, same mintage.

2586 —— Medalets on his coronation. 1619. Fine. 2 pieces

2587 —— Small Coins. Good lot. 5 pieces

2588 FERDINAND III. 1637 to 1657. Medalet on his coronation. Extra fine.

2589 —— Crown. Laureated bust, rich robes; rev. double eagle. Broad and extremely fine.

2590 FERDINAND IV. Coronation Medalet. Brilliant. Size 10

2591 MAXIMILLIAN. (Brother of Rudolph II.) for the Tyrol. Count, from 1612 to 1620. Obv. bust royally draped, head bare, 16—16; rev. coat-of-arms. Brilliant uncirculated Crown. Very rare.

2592 —— Equally splendid Crown of 1618. See Madai, 3411; or Wellenheim, 9286.

2593 LEOPOLD. (Son of Charles V.) Count of Tyrol from 1623 to 1632. Double Crown without date; crowned busts of Leopold, Arch Duke, and Claudia, Arch Duchess. (Medeci.) Rev. crowned eagle. Not entirely uncirculated. Excessively rare.

This is not in Wellenheim's Catalogue, but a similar one, dated 1868, is described and marked "R. R."

2594 LEOPOLD. (Son of Charles V). Crown of 1622. Good. Rare.

2595 STEPHEN BOTSKAY, (Siebenbürg.) 1604 to 1608. Groat; and 1 of Gabriel Bethlen. Rare.   2 pieces

2596 GABRIEL BETHLEN, (Hungary.) 1620 to 1628. Crown of 1621. Bust with sceptre, head bare; rev. coat-of-arms under crown. TRANS PRINCEPS. ET SICVLOR. COM. Wellenheim, 809. Madai, 1611. Broad, fine Coin, and rare.

2597 —— Crown of 1628. (Siebenbürg). Bust in cap and plume; sceptre; rev. coat-of-arms N. B.—Madai, 1612, or Wellenheim, 1447. Very fine and very rare.

2598 GEORGE RAKOEL II., (Siebenbürg). 1649 to 1660. Crown of 1659. Bust in embroidered robes, fur cap and feathers; in his hand a sceptre; GEORGIVS RAKO. D. G. PT; rev. PAR REG. HUN. DOM ET SIC. COM. .1658. Coat-of-arms and crown. Extremely fine. Rare. Well., 1496.

2599 —— Crown of 1659. Only different in the abbreviations and date. Uncirculated. Beautiful.

2600 —— Crown of 1660. (His last year.) Similar. Equally fine. Rare.

2601 MICHAEL APAFI. (Siebenbürg.) 1660 to 1690. Broad Crown of 1672; bust in the dress of his predecessor. MICH. * APFI * DG. PR. * TR. Rev. double-headed eagle, nearly covered by a shield, with sun and moon shining—a smaller shield, with sword and helmet over the first; S-B., and other symbols in the field of the Coin. Well., 1520, marked "R. R." Broad and nearly uncirculated.

2602 —— Small Coin. Similar. Fine and rare   Size 16.

2603 MEDAL of Alt Bunzlau, Bohemia; Virgin and Child, rays around; rev. inscription in ten lines. Very fine.
   Size 28

2604 SIGISMUND FRANCIS. Tyrol. 1662 to 1665. Grossus. (Size 12.) Very fine, rare.

2605 HUNGARIAN ⅜ Crown. 1706. Very fine.

## Coins of Austria.—Silver.

2606 MEDALETS and Coins, Hungarian and others; some coronation of the Arch Dukes of Austria—valuable lot. 13 pieces.
2607 —— Similar, of larger size, larger t an Groats; all old. Rare lot. 7 pieces
2608 FERDINAND CHARLES, Arch Duke, Aus. Duke of Burg. Count of Tyrol. 1662. Beautiful uncirculated Double Crown; bust bare head; rev. crowned eagle displayed. Very rare.
2609 LEOPOLD I. 1658 to 1705. Uncirculated Double Crown; evidently executed by the same hand as last. Bust of Leopold in the same style, but laureated; rev. like last. Rare.
2610 —— Crown. Obv. same; rev. coat-of-arms, 1668. Very fine.
2611 —— Crown of 1692; laureated bust, thick mouth; rev. double eagle and shield. Broad, ex. fine and rare.
2612 —— ¼ Crown, different type. Fine. 3 pieces
2613 —— ⅙ Thaler, 3 and 1 Groshen. Very fine. 3 pieces
2614 —— ⅙ Thaler, 3, 2, and 1 Groshen. Fine. 8 pieces
2615 JOSEPH I. 1705 and 1711. (As King of Hungary, crowned in 1687). Young bust; Coronation Medal. Thick; pierced. Size 18
2615* —— Square Medal Dollar. (Klippe.) Eclipse of the sun and four favorable events associated, occurring in 1706. A beautiful piece. Not in Wellenheim.
2616 —— Splendid uncirculated Crown of the same year; raised milled rim and edge; *guilloche* border. Very rare.
2617 CHARLES VI. 1711 to 1740. Uncirculated Crown, 1731. Equal to last.
2618 —— ¼ Crown, head in a square; rev. arms in a square; very broad. Uncirculated.
2619 —— ¼ Crown. Thick Coin. Fine.
2620 —— Mortuary Medal. (1740.) Fine proof. Size 20
2621 CHARLES VII. (Emperor in opposition to Maria Theresa, supported by Frederick the Great.) Beautiful proof Crown, 1745. Excessively rare.

2622 CHARLES VII., etc. Medalet. VNIONETO, etc. Pierced. Fine. Size 12
2623 MARIA THERESE, 1740 to 1780. 30 Krs coin of 1742. Young bust in square compartment; rev. arms in same. Uncirculated. Rare.
2624 —— ¼ Crown, same year. Thick Coin; ex. fine.
2625 —— Small Coins, Hungary and Austria. Fine.
2 pieces
2626 —— Medal by *Du Vivier*. Obv. bust in the Roman style; rev. a tower "Status Fornacesii." Proof. Slightly scratched. Size 20
2627 —— Medal of the NVMISMA ACADIMIAE SCIENTARVM ET LITERAR BRVXELL. Very fine. Thick. Size 20
2628 —— Crown of 1780, brilliant; uncirculated.
2629 JOSEPH II. 1765 to 1790. Uncirculated Crown of 1782. Coat-of-arms; rev. St. Maria and Jesus.
2630 —— ½ Thaler. (Mantua.) 1783, very fine; with one of 1788 (Flanders.) 2 pieces
2631 —— 20 Krs uncirculated, and 30 do. of M. Theresa.
2 pieces
2632 LEOPOLD II. 1790 to 1792. Coronation Medalets.
Size 15. 2 pieces
2633 FRANCIS II. 1792 to 1806. Coronation Medalets and Coins; very fine lot. 3 pieces
2634 CORONATION Medalets (1 Mortuary of Joseph II.) and Coins of Joseph I., 1705; Charles VI., 1711; Francis I., 1745; Joseph II., 1764, etc. Fine and valuable lot. 20 pieces.
2635 FRANCIS I. (new dynasty). 1804 to 1835. Crown of 1815. Fine.
2636 —— ½ Crown of 1826. Uncirculated.
2637 FERDINAND I. (took his seat in 1835.) Coronation Medal as King of Bohemia, 1835. Beautiful. Size 12
2638 —— Thick Medalet; HOMAGIUM PRAESTITUTUM CIBINI, 1837; Coat-of-arms of Siebenbürg. Extra fine. Well., 8681. Size 13
2639 —— 20 Krs. and 5 Krs. Uncirculated. 2 pieces

Coins and Medals of Austria, etc.—Copper. 159

2640 FRANCIS JOSEPH I. (present Emperor), Thaler of 1858.
½ Thaler, same date. 2 pieces
2641 —— Marriage Medal, with Elizabeth of Bavaria, and ½
Thaler. 2 pieces
2642 —— Thaler of 1870. Nearly proof.
2643 —— for Hungary; set Florins; 20, 10, and 5 Krs.
Uncirculated. 4 pieces
2644 —— "Lira." Uncirculated (for Italy), 1853, and 20
Krs. Austria. Equally fine. 3 pieces
2645 HUNGARIAN and Austrian Coins. Some very old.
15 pieces.

*Copper Coins and Medals—(Austria, Bohemia, and Hungary.)*

2646 OLD and remarkable Coins, 14th to 16th centuries.
10 pieces
2647 OLD Coins of Hungary; uncirculated. Valuable.
4 pieces
2648 OTHERS of Hungary, to 1849. Fine lot. 10 pieces.
2649 BVDA CAPTA 1686.—PRO LIBERTATE 1704.
—Maria Theresa, Prague, 1743.—Conquest of Neuheusel from the Turks, 1663.—And Medal of Charles
V. and Ferdinand I., 1781. (Busts of both.) Extremely
fine and interesting lot. 5 pieces
2650 MARIA THERESA. Fine coins, no duplicates. 10 pieces
2651 JOSEPH I., Charles VI., Francis I., M. Theresa, etc.
Selected and *very* fine. No duplicates. 12 pieces
2652 THIRTY, fifteen, and six Kreutzer pieces of 1807. Bright.
3 pieces
2653 RUDOLPH II.; Mortuary medal; one of the three allied
Sovereigns against France 1814, and silver-plated
Jetton, O. GIEB. MIR. BROD. MICH. HUNGERT.
3 pieces
2654 AUSTRIAN Coins. Miscellaneous. 15 do.
2655 —— Similar lot. Aus. and Tyrol. 20 do.
2656 —— Similar 10 do.

2657 DUTCH MEDALETS, by Looz. WIE ARGUS AUF. DER HUT.—STETS MIT. DEM. GLUCK IM. BUND.—RASCH! UND DAS SPIEL GUT.—Fine figures on principal side of each. Proof. Size 16. 3 pcs
2658 MALTESE CROSS; and Kossuth Buttons united by loop. Fine. 2 pieces
2659 MEDALS struck at the beginning of M. Theresa's reign, 1742 and 1744, having the character of Pasquinades. Queen carrying a doll; rev. four kings seated—before them a map, SAX. BOHEM. BAV., etc. A Queen drawing on a pair of breeches, VOVS AVES PERDS; rev. a Queen nude, three figures on each side, J'AI GAGNE. Silver-plated. Ex. fine. Size 24. 2 pieces
2660 —— Duplicates. 3 do.
2661 LEOPOLD I. To commemorate victories over the Turks, etc. Original medals. Size 24. 3 pieces

2662 MEDAL of John Guttenberg, in two pieces, splendid proof; and old, and extremely fine medals in tin; one of the latter, original of Charles V., Duke of Loth., on his death, 1690. An unusually fine lot. Size 25. 6 pcs
2663 TIN MEDALS. Among them a beautiful proof of Kossuth and Bem. Av. size 25. 7 pieces
2664 MEDALS in wrappers, with a full description in Dutch, newly added to this collection, some as late as 1872, generally relating to the war. Tin. Size 24. 5 pieces
2665 SIGISMUND. 1404–1437. Bust to the middle in rich costume; rev. relics. "The Lance and Nail of the Lord." "From the Manger and Cross of the Lord," etc. Very fine and rare. Tin. Size 26
2666 ERNEST BOGESLAUS. Old tin medal, with quant old bronze plaques, or medals without reverses. About size 35. 3 pieces
2667 THE EMPEROR OF GERMANY and King of Spain, Charles V. A fine medal of his time. The Emperor with sceptre; rev. eagle between the pillars of Hercules. Bronze. Size 35

*Silver Medals.—Religious.*

2668 RUDOLPH II. Old medal in brass, gilt. See Wellenheim, 6939. Size 14
2669 BRONZE Medals. Size 25. 5 pieces
2670 TIN Medal of "Mauritio Saxo. Gall., Maresch. Gen. S. Curl et Sem." Two varieties. Size 35
2671 JOHANN ERZHERZOG VON ŒSTERREICH. Bust; rev. in the cavo-relievo manner, with beautiful oak wreath and border of beads, a double-headed eagle. Fine bronze proof by Lange. Size 32
2672 FERDINAND I., Emp. Aus., Lombardy and Venice, 1837. Coronation medal by Roth. Splendid bronze proof. Size 25
2673 SCHOOL MEDAL, by Lorenz. Splendid proof. Size 25
2674 FRANCIS JOSEPH I., present Emperor. Two beautiful medals, one of 1873. Tin. Size 25
2675 MEDALS and Medalets. 10 pieces
2676 " GAMBRINUS," Beer Token. (Will,buy a drink). C. H. POSTHSCHE BRAURIE-LAHR ; rev. *"* Gut fur Einen Schoppen bier." Klippes and old coins. Rare lot. 12 pieces

## SILVER MEDALS.

*Religious.*

2677 JESUS bearing the Cross. Old Dutch Medal, base silver. Size 23
2678 SCRIPTURE Texts illustrated. Jonah and the Whale on one side; rev. Jesus, etc. Good silver. Size 24
2679 OVAL MEDAL, loop at each end ; Noah's Ark, the dove returning, a hand from the roof receiving the olive branch. Size 28x24
2680 THE TEMPTATION OF EVE IN EDEN; rev, Crucifixion. Gilt. Ins. in two circles. Very old medal. Size 26
2681 CHASED MEDAL, with loop and filigree border. Prov. 12 and Prov. 19; very elaborate ; fine figures. Size 32
2682 CAST MEDAL. Christ surrounded by Roman soldiers, sinking under the Cross, 1565 ; the figures in high relief; tooled and field burnished. Perfect. Size 30

2683 JOHN HUSS. Dollar Medal; obv. bust of Huss; on his head a cap; rev. his martyrdom at the stake. JO HVS. ANNO. A CHRIST NATO, 1415. Very fine and rare.

2684 REFORMATION MEDAL; struck to commemorate the first centennial jubilee, 1617. MARTINVS LVTHERVS THEOLOGIE; rev. lighted candle; the "bushel" lifted by Luther's hand. ECCLESIA NORICA JVBILANS. Extremely fine, rare. Size 20

2685 MARTIN LUTHER; dollar Medal. JVBILAM SEC-VNDVM; obv. bust of Dr. Luther; rev. bust of the Martyr Huss.—Same as obv. of 2683. Extremely fine and rare. Size 28

2686 JUBILEE OF THE REFORMATION. Second Festival, June 25, 1730. Beautiful proof medalet. Size 12

2687 —— Third Festival. June 25, 1830; rev. Luther standing. Uncirculated. Size 14

2688 —— The Sun in splendor. A Bible open. DAS NEVE TESTAM JES. CHR. DEVTSCH DVRCI D MART LVTHER, 27 Aug., 1842; rev. Arms of Hildebrand and ins. 1542. Ex. fine and rare medal by *Looz*. Size 22

2689 —— "Zwingle," "Jeuner." Zurich, 1519. l. f. Very fine. Size 14

2690 GRYLLUS Medal. Double head on obv., and rev. Pope, Devil—Monk, fool—or words to that effect. Cast and skillfully tooled. Brilliant, thick medal. Size 22

2691 —— Double head on one side; rev. EFFE MINATI DOMINA BVNTVR EIS 1544. Beautiful and rare. Size 20

2692 BASTISMAL; rev. Birth of Christ. Very fine. Size 23

2693 MOSAIC Medal. The two tables of the law on a heart; in rays, the Hebrew name of God; rev. three trees in pots. German ins. Pierced, but fine. Size 22

2694 —— The two tables and cross on an altar; rev. inscription. Fine proof. Size 16

2695 ARKITE Medal. Noah's Ark. The Patriarch offering sacrifice after the flood. Size 14

Silver Medals.—Marriage and Amatory. 163

2696 DUTCH Medal. Jesus seated; before Him a standing group. Long ins. Very fine. Size 16

2697 —— "Im Perando Orando Laborando Consistit." Two arms issuing from a globe, gloved hand on an open book—sword, spade, etc; rev. Hebrew name of God. An inscription in Dutch. Rare. Extremely fine. Size 27

2698 SYMBOLIC Medal. Crucifix, anchor, lamb, shield, serpent, Stork feeding her young, and monument supporting an even balance; rev. St. George and Dragon. Without date. Uncirculated. Beautiful. Size 26

2699 —— Sun; in centre JHS. A heart crossed by olive branches, upheld by two hands issuing from clouds; below, two doves; GOTT UNSER HERTZ, etc.; rev. man presenting to a female a burning heart—Symbols around. Old medal, cast and chased. In fine preservation. Heavy. Size 31

2700 —— Another medal of similar style and composition. On reverse a Roman Fasces and axe. L'UNION NOUS SOUTIENT. Has been gilt. Fine. Size 26

*Marriage and Amatory Medals.*

2701 ERED. ERNEST (Orange) and Wilhelmina. Prussia. Married 1791. Very fine. Size 20

2702 WEDDING Scene 1624; rev. two doves swinging on one bough. Loop removed. Size 20

2703 FRIDERICI CHRISTIANI Reg. Pol. etc. And Antoniæ Bavariæ. 1747. Proof. Size 20

2704 JOSEPH A. A. and Princess Phillippe of Spain. Beautiful proof. Size 18

2705 FERDINAND and BEATRICE of? 1771 and one of Charles of Sicily and Amalia of Poland. Size 16. 2 pieces

2706 "AUF EWIG." Serpent ring; rev. two doves on a tree. DEIN. Very fine. Size 22

2707 "VINCENT AMOR SILVA;" and a Dutch medal with picture of a lady fastening a connubial yoke on her lord. Fine medals. Average size 19. 2 pieces

2708 "Prudentia, Amore, Experentia. Friendship Medalet. "David and Jonathan." On two shields.
2709 Large medal without rev., and medalet. 2 pieces
2710 "Umsonst." Cock and hen; rev. Cupid. Fine. Size 15
2711 —— Similar. Copper.

## Commemorative Medals.

2712 Charles V., Duke of Lorraine, Bust in mail, full wig; rev. Phœnix. In ex. OB WELSI. 1690. Extremely fine. Size 26

He was nephew to the Emperor Charles V. He entered the service of Leopold I., and was a great friend to Prince Eugene of Savoy.

2713 Charles III. of Spain. Bust in same style; rev. bee-hive. Madrid, 1706. Beautiful. Size 30
2714 "Terror Turcarum, 1687," to commemorate the victories of Lepanto, Corinth, Castle Tornese, Castle Novo, etc. Two figures of Fame supporting shields, with busts, etc. Fine proof, Medal. Size 30
2715 Medal of this period (1688), to commemorate the infamous league between Solyman, Louis XIV., Mezomorto, James II. and the Devil. "Contra Christiansmum." Aptly illustrated. Well preserved and rare. Size 24
2716 Louisa Augusta Wilhelmina Amelia, of Prussia. Bust. Above, crown; rev. death 1810. Proof. Size 24
2717 Blucher. Wellington. Their busts *vis a vis* within a wreath of laurel; magnificent proof *by Looz*. Size 24
2718 Series *by Looz;* single heads in the same style, of Blucher von Wahlstadt, Wellington, Barclay de Tolli, Schwarzenberg, and Gneisenau; rev. coats-of-arms. Executed in a truly superb style. Fine proofs. Size 18
5 pieces
2719 Schiller. Bare bust; rev. ins. within laurel wreath. Brilliant proof. Size 18
2720 Hufeland. His bust; rev. figures of angels standing beside a woman and two children on the ground; behind them a monument. 1833. *By Brandt.* Proof. Size 27

2721 " OVENS Malling ad Publica munera vocato D 27 Jan. 1777. Grate ceves D 27 Jan. 1827. Bust; rev. SALVS PVBLICA. Hygeia standing. Fine proof. Koenig. Size 32

2722 ANDREAS Petrus Greane Af Bernstorf, etc.; rev. altar in a wood; before it a harp and open book. 1787. Looz. Fine. Size 27

2723 MEDALETS, generally without busts. A fine lot. Worthy of a separate description. From size 10 to 16. 8 pieces

2724 FREE LOVE TOKEN. A hand full of money. KOM. STV-MIR-ALSO; rev. young woman's head, front face; before the face an open hand. SO KOMME ICH DIR SO. Very rare. Size 16

 This would not appear to be "Free love" in the sense that it costs nothing. Aulus Gellisu relates an anecdote of Demosthenes, to the effect that he paid a visit to the charming Lais, and prudently desiring to know how expensive the entertainment would be, when informed that she demanded ten thousand drachma, declined, saying that he would not purchase repentance at so dear a price.

2725 LUD. JOSEPH Oppenheimer; bust; rev. the Guillotine; a medal box; within, 16 pictures in water colors, beginning with the cradle and ending with an execution. Fine. Size 24

## Miscellaneous Medals.

2726 MEDAL of "Industrie," Augusburg, 1852 (prize medal.) Fine proof. Size 35

2727 " GLUCK un freude, etc. Fortune standing. By Looz. Ex. fine. Size 23

2728 PRIZE medal. " D. JOSE BALTA." View of a bridge, PUNTA BALTA 1869. Very fine. Size 24

2729 MARINE medal. Luneville. 1801. Francis II. and the French Republic, etc. Another on the same occasion. By Looz. Size 20. 2 pieces

2730 PRIZE Medal; "Fidelity, Happiness;" another; obv. two partridges; rev. fox. Size 20. 2 pieces

2731 MEDALS by Looz. Time on the wing; on his head an hour-glass. DIE ZEIT ENFLEHT. Rev. a globe;

DRVM MVTZE SIE. Same obv.; rev. "Doch Meine freindschaft nicht." Fine proofs. Size 22.
2 pieces
2732 FREDERICK THE GREAT. War Medal. Victory of Chottusite, 1742. Size 21
2733 MASONIC Shield, charged with symbols on a Maltese Cross, gilt, 23 x 21.
2734 MISCELLANEOUS Medalets and Tokens. Av. size 12.
8 pieces
2735 SIMILAR lot small Token and Coins. 10 pieces

## GOLD COINS.

### Miscellaneous.

2736 BRACTEATE (Bohemia), probably 13th century. Lion holding trefoil or flower. Rare to excess, and as fine as when struck. Size 22
2737 ANTIQUE Half-stater; rude head; rev. winged horse. No inscription. Very fine, rare.
> This is not a Coin of Corinth, as the type would indicate; it appears to be barbarian.

2738 ANTIQUE Aureus of Honorius, son of Theodosius Magnus, A.D. 395. Fine.
2739 CHARLES IV., grandson of Henry VII. He ascended the imperial throne in 1347; founded the university of Prague, and died in 1378. CAROLVS DE ROM. IMP. HOISP RIX. On both sides coat-of-arms. Size of gold Angel of England of the same period. Fine and excessively rare.
2740 SIGISMUND I. Ducat. Arms of German Empire; rev. Christ standing. Very fine and rare.
2741 ALBERT, Duke of Saxony. Same type as last. Ducat. Nearly uncirculated. Rare.
2742 Ducat. WESAL. Arms of Osnaburg. Two pieces. One counterstamped with double-headed eagle. Without date. Fine.
2 pieces
2743 FREDERICK? Emperor of Germany. Ducat. Rev. the Virgin and Jesus. No date. Extra fine.

Gold Coins.—Miscellaneous.

2744 MAXIMILLIAN I. Ducat. Rev. Jesus standing. Extra fine.
2745 LUBEC. Fine Ducat. St. John standing.
2746 WILLIAM? GVILL DVX. COMES HOL. Armed man standing; rev. coat-of-arms. FLORINI DE HOLAND. Ducat size. Fine, rare.
2747 HOLLANDIE. 1733. I. S. Bundle of arrows tied in the middle, the ends spread like a fan. Very fine half Ducat.
2748 REP. SOLODORENIS. Rev. "St. Ursus, Martyr." 1706. The martyr standing with sword and banner. Rare Ducat.
2749 EPISCOPAL Ducat of Franconia, with bust of Adam Frederick, Duke, 1774. Very fine.
2750 GEO. FRED. CHARLES. Margrave Brandenburg, 1727; rev. a swan and tree. CANDOR ILLAESVS Ducat. Proof. Rare.
2751 EMPEROR CHARLES VI. Ducat. 1730. Very fine.
2752 EPISCOPAL Ducat of Augustus, consecrated 1770. Very handsome reverse. Fine.
2753 CRISTORF 1st, Grand Duke of Baden, 1527. Ducat, without date. Very rare.
2754 EPISCOPAL Ducat of John II. 1733. St. Willibaldus standing. Very fine, rare.
2755 FREDERICK III. 1457 to 1493. The Emperor standing crowned. Fine and rare Ducat.
2756 EPISCOPAL. VRBEM CHRISTE TVAM SERVA. Arms of Germany. Fine Ducat.
2757 REFORMATION Medal Ducat. 31 Oct., 1717 (the second centenary). Monument surmounted by an Agnus Dei. Regensburg. Fine and rare.
2758 MEDAL Ducat. (No date, handsome coat-of-arms.) L. F. D. G. A. & E. M. E. B. Rev. female seated, CONCORDIA. Fine proof.
2759 CHARLES THEODORE. Bust; rev. EX AVRO ISARAE, 1780. Ducat. Fine proof.
2760 ESZTERHAZY. (Pr. Nicholas.) 1770. Splendid proof Ducat; bust; rev. coat-of-arms. Very rare.

## Gold Coins.—Miscellaneous.

2761 CHAS. FREDERICK, Grand Duke of Baden. 1807. Fine Ducat; rev. river god seated.

2762 FRANKFORT Ducat. 1796. View of the city and cathedral. Fine.

2763 BASE gold Ducat, silver alloy. Uncertain value.

2764 FREDERICK, King of Sweden. 1748. Uncirculated ½ Ducat.

2765 BREMEN ¼ Ducat. (1 Schwaren.) 1781. Uncirculated.

2766 POLAND. ½ Ducat of Fred. Aug. 1702. Fine and *rare*.

2767 "DUCATUS civit Bisunt, A. D. 1655"; rev. CAROLVS V., IMPERATOR. Emperor standing. A beautiful ½ Ducat.

2768 HALF Ducats of Lubec and Frankfort. Fine. 2 pieces.

2768* —— Same of Ratisbon and Holland. (1677). Fine. 2 pieces.

2769 SAME of Sweden (Frederick). 1731 and 173-. Very fine. 2 pieces

2770 ANOTHER. Same. Fred. Adolphus. 1710 and 19. Very fine. 2 pieces

2771 SAME of Emp. Chas. V. and Leopold I. 1792. "

2772 GEORGE II., King of England and Hanover (½ Thaler), Frederick III. and Denmark, (111 Mark). Ex. fine. 2 pieces

2773 QUARTER Ducats. Fred. Count of Mansfield, 1670; and one with DAVID—JONAT on two shields. Rare. 2 pieces

2774 SAME. Papal and Prussian. "

2775 SAME. Waldeck and Nuremberg. Very fine. "

2776 MINUTE gold coins, round and square. Nuremberg, etc. 3 pieces

2777 MEDALETS (Sweden). Fred. and wife, and Frederick alone. Fine. 2 pieces

2778 RUSSIAN Coins. Rubles of Elizabeth, 1756. Very fine. 2 pieces

2779 SAME. Katherine and Ancient. Fine. "

2780 QUARTER Ducats, with other coins of same value. "1 Dreiling," "2 Pfenning," and "1 Kreutzer." Fine and desirable for a coll. 6 pieces

## Gold Coins.—Miscellaneous.

2781 SIMILAR lot. Brandenbury, Russia, Bremen, etc. Fine. 6 pieces
2782 SMALL coins. (Av. ½ Thaler value.) "
2783 SAME. Japanese and German. "
2784 LEOPOLD I., Christian V., and George William, Duke of Brunswick, 1690. Beautiful ¼ and ⅛ Ducat. 3 pieces
2785 CHARLES, Landgrave, Hesse; rev. stork; and Frederick I., Sweden. Uncirculated ¼ ducats. 2 pieces
2786 WALDECK and Sweden. Very fine ¼ and ⅛ Ducat. 2 pieces
2787 JEROME NAPOLEON. Westphalia. 5 Francs. Very fine. Rare.
2788 DOLLARS. Mexico. (1825 and 1855); the last uncirculated. 2 pieces
2789 —— Costa Rica (1 Peso). Two varieties. 1855–66. 2 pieces
2790 —— New Granada and Central America. "
2791 —— Guatemala and Chili. 1859–61. "
2792 —— Portugal and Bogota. "
2793 —— Central America. 1 counterstamped. "
2794 —— U. S., 1849, and one with American and Turkish characters. 2 pieces
2795 FIVE Francs Napoleon III. and Victor Emanuel. "
2796 DOUBLE Dollars. Mexico, 1851, and Bolivia, 1855. (½ Pistoles). Fine and rare. 2 pieces
2797 SAME. Newfoundland. (Victoria, 1865.) Very fine.
2798 SAME. Isabella, Spain, 1865. Rare.
2799 INGOT stamped 20 D. Cut in halves. Val. 10d. ?
2800 DOUBLE Fred. d'Or ($7.80). Fred. William, Prussia. 1737.
2801 DOUBLE Moidore ($9.50). "Petrus II.," Brazil, 1851.
2802 CARRERA. "Fundater Guatemala." 5 Pesos (5 Dolls.) 1869. Uncirculated. Rare.
2803 ITALY. 20 Lire (4 Dolls.) 1848. Very fine.
2804 —— Same. Pius IX. 1869. Uncirculated.
2805 —— 2½ Scudi (2½ D.) Pius IX. 1859. Uncirculated.
2806 RUSSIA. 3 Rubles. 1838.
2807 —— 3 Rubles. 1869. Uncirculated.

170 *Silver Coins of German Cities, etc.*

2808 PRUSSIA. Kaiser William. 1871. "20 M." (5 Dol.) Uncirculated.
2809 —— The same. "10 M" (2½ Dol.) Uncirculated.
2810 BADEN. 1872. Fred. G. Duke. "10 M" (2½ Dolls.) Uncirculated.
2811 BAVARIA. 1872. Louis II., King. "10 M" (2½ Dolls.) Uncirculated.
2812 SAXONY. 1873. John V., King. "10 M" (2½ Dolls.) Uncirculated.
2813 WURTEMBERG. 1873. Charles, King. "10 M" (2½ Dolls.) Uncirculated.
2814 HAMBURG. 1873. Free City. "10 M" (2½ Dolls.) Uncirculated.
2815 HESSE. 1873. Louis III., King. "10 M" (2½ Dolls.) Uncirculated.
2816 BADEN. 1830. Louis G., Duke. 5 Thalers. Uncirculated.
2817 BAVARIA. 1854. Max. II., King. 2½ Dolls. Uncirculated. Very fine.
2818 —— 1830. Louis I., King. 2½ Dolls. Uncirculated. Very fine.
2819 —— No date. Max. Joseph, King. 1 gold Gulden. Value 2½ Dolls. Very fine.
2820 ONE Gold Pfenning. "Scheide Munz," 1818; and 2½ Thalers, Hanover. $1.63 each. 2 pieces
2821 JAPAN, Cobany. (5.00); and Quarter do. "

---

## SILVER COINS OF THE DUCHIES, PRINCIPALITIES, AND SEQUESTRATED CITIES OF GERMANY.

*[Catalogued in Alphabetical Order.]*

2822 AACHEN (Aix la Chapelle). Crown of Maximilian II. 1568. MO . REGIÆ . SEDIS . VRBIS . AQVIS CRANI. The Emperor seated, with sceptre and mund; rev. double eagle. Well preserved and very rare.
2823 —— MONETA . VRB . AQVIS . ANNO . DOMINI MILESIMINO, in two circles inclosing cross; rev. the

## Silver Coins of German Cities, etc.

Emperor seated, holding mund and model of church. S KAROL . MA . IPERATO. Very rare, old and fine groat without date. (See Well. 8182), with others equally interesting and valuable. 4 pieces

AACHEN (Aix la Chapelle). Coronation medal coin, 1752, and others. 5 pieces

ALTORF. Jubilee Reformation, Klippe (1723, 29th June). Beautiful proof, and very rare. Size 19

ANDERNACH (City). Keys crossed; rev. St. Michael. App. IV. 251; Well. 8198. Very rare coin. Fine. Size 15

ANDREASBERG, Anno 1667. St. Andrew; rev. John Frederick, Duke; arms, 5 crests; beautiful crown. Nearly proof. Very rare. Size 29

—— Small coin. Same date (24) G.

AREMBERG (Duchy). Uncirculated crown of Louis Engelbert, 1785. Bust, and fine coat-of-arms. "XEINE MARCK." Rare.

—— Another very fine crown. Same in all respects.

—— Same, with thaler of different type; rev. eagle displayed standing on a rock. Rare. 2 pieces

AUERSBERG. Splendid proof crown of Prince William, 1805. Bust, and beautiful coat-of-arms. Rare.

AUGSBURG. (Arms, fir cone). Nearly uncirculated. (½ crown) of the Emperor Charles V., 1527, with his figure to the middle. App. IV., 289. Rare.

—— Crown, with St. Ulrich, 1625. Uncirculated, rare. Size 28

See Madai, No. 2,151.

—— Crown, 1625, with view of the city. Broad and fine.

—— Same, 1626, angels supporting arms above the city. Fine.

—— ¼ crown, same date. Very fine.

—— Dollar of Alexander Sigismund, Bishop. 1694. Bust; rev. two shields under a crown. Very fine, and said to be especially rare.

—— Dollar of 1644, formed into a box; in the box a number of pictures.

2840 AUGSBURG. Beautiful uncirculated crown 1743, under Charles VII., with his laureated bust. (Madai, 4761.)
2841 —— Similar crown under Francis I., 1765. Fine.
2842 —— Medalet of the city, 1752. Fine laureated bust; rev. 2 shields united under the arms of Augsburg. *Proof*. Appd. IV. 335.
2843 —— Small coins. 4 pieces
2844 BAMBERG (City and Bishopric). Small coins of Anton, Bishop from 1440 to 1459. A(nton), B(amberg). Very rare. 2 pieces
2845 —— St. Henricus and St. Kunigund supporting a cathedral with 4 towers above the arms of Bamberg; rev. bust of John George, bishop, 1623—1633. Very fine broad and rare crown. Madai, 774.
2846 —— Double Crown of Francis Louis, Bishop. 1786. "Merces Laborum." An angel holding aloft a civic crown, and pouring coins from a cornucopia. Fine, but base metal.
2847 —— Episcopal Groat; rev. St. Henry with sceptre and mund, 1698 and others, old and rare. 6 pieces
2848 —— Money of Philip, Val., Bishop. 1653–1672. LXEINE FEINE MARK, etc. Av. size 18. 5 pieces
2849 BACHARACH. Groat of Frederick, Duke. Ex. fine. 2 pieces
2850 BARBY, Count. 1613. Groats. 2 pieces
2851 BATENBURG. William Bronchorst, Baron, under the Emperor Charles V. (1550), marked in Well., R. R. Broad Crown.
2852 BATTHYANI, Prince Charles. 1764. Crown. Bust, hair in a queue; around his neck chain of the Order of the Golden Fleece; rev. arms, order chain and crown on ermine, etc. Fine.
2853 —— Half Crown. Same type. Madai, 5844. Fine.
2854 —— Crown of 1768, by Todai. Extra fine. (Madai, 4149), and one with rev. of 2852. 2 pieces
2855 —— Beautiful Uncirculated Crown of Prince Louis, 1788. Bust in the Roman style; rev. coat-of-arms as before.
2856 —— Half Crown. Same type.

Silver Coins of German Cities, etc.    173

2857 BERLIN (City). Groat of Joachim and Albert. 1510. JOAC. Z. ALB. On rev. BERLINENSIS. Excessively rare. Nearly uncirculated.

2858 —— Medalet. BETE UN ARBEITE; rev. SO WIRD DICH GOTT SEEG NEN. Proof.    Size 15

2859 BENTHEIM. Maurice, Prince of Bentheim and Tecklenberg. Rude but extremely fine and rare Crown. (1650). Bust; rev. arms, crest, a peacock with tail spread. Madai, 1672.

2860 —— XII. Marien Gros, (Half Thaler). 1672. Fine and rare.

2861 —— Ernest William, Count. Quarter Thalers and small coins; many varieties. (1662).    10 pieces

2862 —— I. Adolphus. 1676. Thaler. "XXIV. Marien Gros." Fine silver. In Wellenheim. Marked rare.

2863 BERG. (Duchy). Groat of "Wilhelm Comes." 1389 to 1408; rev. church. Thick fine coin resembling the French Groat of the period. Very rare.

2864 —— Groat of same date and type, and Half Groats to 1513.    6 pieces

2865 —— Small Coins.    4 do.

2866 —— Crown of William III., Count 15–17; rev. coat-of-arms. Very rare.

2867 —— Crown without date. "Sanctus Oswaldus Rex. Nunius No. D. Hefdel." Fine, rare.

2868 —— Duplicate of last.

2869 —— Thaler of Max. Joseph, 1805.

2870 BIBERACH (City). Groat. Poor, rare.

2871 BESANCON (City). MONETA CIVIT IMBER BISVNTINÆ, Double Eagle; rev. COROLVS QVINT ROM. IMPERATOR. 1659. The Emperor standing. Fine and very rare crown.

2872 —— Small Coins with Arms of the City, open hand and bust of Charles V.    3 pieces

2873 BEESKOW (City). Bracteate.

2874 BONN (BVNNE), University. Coin without date, and token. 1699. Fine and rare.    2 pieces

2875 BRANDENBURG. (Bayreuth and Anspach). George Anspach. 1532 and 1534. Uncirculated Groats. 2 pcs
2876 —— Klippe and small coins. All rare. 4 pieces
2877 —— Small coins. Base silver. 10 do.
2878 —— Christian Ernest. 1711 and '12, 12 and 6 Einen Thal. One fine. 2 pieces
2879 —— Christian. (Bayreuth). 1622. Uncirculated Double Groat.
2880 —— Frederick, Albert, and Christian brothers, Margraves. 1627. Their busts; rev. coat-of-arms. Fine crown.
2881 —— Medal Crown of "Christ, Car. Tutrix, Reg. Brand Onold." Female bust; rev. two coats-of-arms crowned. Splendid proof. 1727. A very beautiful piece.
2882 —— Charles William Frederick. Medal Crown. Mortuary. (Died 1757). Uncirculated.
2883 —— Alexander Margrave. 1765. Medal Crown. The Mar. on horseback; rev. on military trophies, a shield surmounted by an eagle crowned. SECVRITATI PVBLICÆ. Uncirculated.
2884 —— Alexander. Crown of 1777. Bust; rev. coat-of-arms with fifteen crests. Uncirculated.
2885 —— George Frederick and Alexander. Their busts face to face; under the first, 1567, the last, 1769; rev. monument. Medal crown. Fine and rare.
2886 —— Medal of Alexander, with a view of the Bruckberg Porcelain Factory, 1767. Uncirculated. Very rare. Size 20
2887 BREMEN. Denarius of Siegfried I. 1178–1184. The Archbishop seated; rev. Arms of Bremen (Key). Wellenheim, 5023. Marked R.R. 2 pieces
2888 —— Solidus of Henry I. 1307. Obv. arms, "Moneta Bremenensis;" rev. St. Peter seated, in one hand key, the other, sword. HENRICVS DEI GRATIA. Fine and very rare.
2889 —— Duplicate. Fine.
2890 —— Double Groat of John Rode. 1496 to 1511. St. Peter on a Throne. JOH. S. DEI. G. ARG. EPI BRE; rev. key in a circle with tressure. Ins. "Mo-

## Silver Coins of German Cities, etc.   175

neta," etc., and date, 1499. Excessively rare. Marked R.R.R. in the books. Very fine.

2891 BREMEN Solidus of Christoph. 1511–1558. A coin much in the style of the last, except name of the Archbishop. ESTOF. D. G., etc. (He was also King of Brunswick). In good preservation.  Size 18

2892 —— Duplicate; nearly as fine.

2893 —— Solidus of George I., (also King of Brunswick). 1558 to 1566. Arms; rev. St. George and Dragon. Well preserved.  Size 18

2894 —— Crown of same. 1562. Bust in fur cape and cap; rev. arms surmounted by horse running. Fine crown and very rare. (Well. 5030).

2895 —— Coins of Frederick, Archbishop of. 1635–1645. Called "Three Schilling Stuck." XVI. on the coin. Old bust. Well. 5094.  4 pieces

2896 —— Crown. 1617. Mathias, Emperor. Fine.

2897 —— Two-third Crown. 1673. Charles XI., (Sweden). Fine, rare.

2898 —— Selection of small coins, old and curious. 10 pieces

2899 ——     Do. of Groats and Half Groats.  10 do.

2900 ——     Do. Half Groats and smaller.  12 do.

2901 —— Uncommonly fine Crown, under the Emperor Ferdinand III., 1657. Two lions supporting the arms of Bremen; rev. imperial arms. Madai, 4788.  Size 29

2902 —— Quarter Crown and "XII. Grot," Ferdinand III. Fine.  2 pieces

2903 —— Fine broad Crown, dated 1660, at the beginning of the Emperor Leopold's reign.  Size 29

2904 —— Half-thalers (24 Grot), of same. Fine.  3 pieces.

2905 —— XII. Grot (¼ Thalers.) Same.  2 do.

2906 —— VI. do. Leopold and Ferdinand. Fine. 6 do.

2907 —— Splendid proof Crown, under Charles VI. 1723. One of the most beautiful Dollars in the collection. Rare.  Size 28.

2908 —— Fine Crown of same. 1743.

2909 —— Thaler; two varieties, and 1 Half-thaler (1748–'49, and 53) of Francis I. All uncirculated.  3 pieces

2910 BREMEN. Medal in honor of Burgomaster Dr. John Smith bust; rev. town hall, 1846. Fine thick piece.   Size 32
2911 —— Medal in honor of Dr. John Henry Bernh, D.D. By Wilkens, 1832. Brilliant proof.   Size 30
2912 —— Medal Thaler (EIN THALER GOLD.) Arms of Bremen, "Jubelfier der befriung Deutschlands 1863." Brilliant proof.
2913 —— Medal Thaler, to commemorate the opening of the new Bourse. View of the edifice. 1864; rev. inscription. Brilliant proof.
2914 —— Medal Thaler, on the occasion of the "Zwlites Deutches Bundes-Schiessen in Bremen, 1865." Brilliant proof.
2915 —— Medal Thaler. "Zur ermnerung an den erkampften Frieden 10 May, 1871." Brilliant proof.
2916 —— Six Groat and 12 Groat, 1840. Uncirculated.   2 pieces
2917 BRESLAU. John Turzo, 1506—1520. "Breiter Groschen." (See Well. 6884.) Rare.   2 pieces
2918 —— Dollar of 1544. ECCE VICIT LEO DE TRIBU JUDA. Madai, 2172; Well. 6439. Well preserved. Rare.
2919 —— Coin of Fran. Louis. (1683 to 1702.) Bust; rev. arms. 1683. Fine.   Size 20
2920 BREZENHEIM. (Principality). Crown of Charles Augustus, 1790. Bust; rev. arms, two ostriches for supporters. Uncirculated. Rare.
2921 —— Small Coins. Quarter-thaler and base Coin. Fine.   2 pieces
2922 BRUNSWICK (City). Broad Crown of Ferdinand II., 1624. Arms of the city; rev. imperial arms. Nearly uncirculated.
2923 —— Crown of 1632. Same reverse. Still finer.
2924 —— ¾ Crown. 1675. Lion between two towers; rev. bust of Rudolph Augustus. (Luneburg). Fine.
2925 —— Early Coins, bracteate; Charles V. "1 1 1 1 Gute Pfenning"; and others. Fine and rare lot.   6 pieces

## Silver Coins of German Cities, etc.

2926 BRUNSWICK (City.)  Quarter-thaler, (Virgin and child.) 1534 and 1556.  2 pieces

2927 BINGEN and Brannan; (One siege Coin.) Rare. 3 pieces

2928 CALCAR (KALKAR.) Old Groats. Adolphus, Count. Knight standing; rev. cross. Fine.  3 pieces

2929 CLEVE; ADOLPH 1408—1437. ADOLPHVS DVX. MONT; the duke on a throne wearing a cap; rev. MONET, etc. "Albus," marked "R. R." Good Example. See Wellenheim, 7821.

2930 —— John I. 1448 to 1481. Groat; rev. long cross, fleur de lis in angles. Well., 7883. Fine and rare.

2931 —— William, Duke, 1539 to 1592. GVILIIELMVS. D. G. IN DEO SPES MEA; bust in a cap; rev. coat-of-arms. Well., 8075. Crown.

2932 —— Mathias, Duke. Double Groat. Good.

2933 —— Billon Money.  2 pieces

2934 COBENZL. Medal of Prince Charles. (Belgium.) Bust; rev. within an order chain, a book of statutes, open. Beautiful proof.  Size 2½

2935 COBURG and Coblentz, (cities.) Small Coins. 4 pieces.

2936 COLMAR. Groats. Arms (sceptre with star of eight-points); rev. imperial arms. 1660—1669. 2 pieces

2937 COLOGNE (Coln). City. Arnulph, King, 887 to 899. Penny; Ao Lo.—1 1 1 1 and cross; rev. short cross, "Colonia." Excessively rare.

2938 —— Otho I. (the Great), 936 to 973. Penny ODDO. Fine and very rare.

2939 —— (Bishopric.) Pilligrin, Arch, 1022 to 1035; bust; rev. PILI; as it came it from the die, uneven. Excessively rare penny.

2940 —— Herman, 1035 — 1056; Arch. seated, RADVS; rev. church; penny. Well. 7861. Rare.

2941 —— Hildolphus, 1076—1079. Penny. The Archbishop seated. HIT. ARC. HEICOPV. Rev. EA-COTONIA. EPAICI. Well., 7867. Fine and rare.

2942 —— Another of Hildolphus. Equally fine.

12

2943 COLOGNE (Coln). City. Adolph. 1193—1205 A. D. EPIS. The Archbishop seated; rev. church with steeple and tower at each side; as it was struck; Wellenheim " R. R." Denarius.

2944 —— Engelbert. 1216—1225. ENC. TIZ. Archbishop seated; rev. church. Very fine penny.

2945 —— Bracteates of this period. 8 pieces

2946 —— Pennies and Half-pennies, similar to those described. Rare lot. 9 pieces

2947 —— Sede vacante Groat; the Virgin seated. JASP-MELCH. BALTH; rev. arms (3 Crowns.) Ex. fine and rare. No date (1261) Varieties. 2 pieces

2948 —— Frederick III. 1370-1411. Groat. St. Peter seated. FRIDICVS AREPVS COLON; rev. arms. MONETA, etc. Very rare, fine.

2949 —— Theodore II., 1414-1462. Groat; St. Peter seated. A. DN. TEOD. IC. Fine, rare.

2950 —— Coins of the City and Bishopric; Groat, Albus, Solidus, Obolus, and other denominations. All good coins. 10 pieces

2951 —— Coins of Max Hen. Max, Fred. Leopold I., and Charles VI. Fine and rare lot. 4 pieces

2952 —— Miscellaneous base coins. 6 pieces

2953 —— Token; Augsburg Confession Memorial, 1730. Arms of the city; rev. cup, copper plug. Size 14

2954 —— Elector's Medalet; the Elec. on horseback; rev. two swords and cross. Beautiful proof. Size 12

2955 —— Jubilee Medal; within wreath of oak and vine, JUBEL HOCHZEIT FEIER ZU KOLN, 1798; rev. an altar placed between rows of trees; on it a Roman lamp burning; hands clasping a caduceus above; in Ex. GLUCKLICH. Psal. 127. Proof. Size 30

2956 —— Adolphus (Schaumberg) Archbishop, 1547-'49. Crown, 1549. See Well., 7,963. Fine and rare.

2957 —— Salentin. Arche, 1567-77. Crown, St. Peter standing, date 1568; rev. Arms, ARG TVICI. Ordinary. See Well., 7,966. Rare.

Silver Coins of German Cities, etc.

2958 COLOGNE (Coln). City. Another Crown of Bishop Salentin, 1569. St. Peter walking to r.; rev. Coat-of-arms; (Well. 7,968.) Rare.
2959 —— Maximillian II., 1569. Uncirculated Crown.
2960 —— Duplicate. Fair condition.
2961 —— Max. Henry (Bavaria) Archbishop, 1650 to '88. Fine bust; head bare; rev. arms crowned, 1662. Fine and rare crown.
2962 —— Sede Vacante Crown, 1688. St. Peter; rev. The three kings. BALTHASAR, CASPAR, MELCHIOR, paying homage to Jesus in the arms of the Virgin. Fine and rare.
2963 —— Sede Vacante; crown of the same type of different execution, and very fine, 1761.
2964 —— Joseph Clemens, Bishop, 1693 and 1694. ⅔ Crown. Different style. Fine.                                        2 pieces
2965 —— Leopold I., Emp. (Germany), ⅔ Crown, 1700.
2966 —— Clement Augustus; rev. view of mines, 1749; date in long letters, ⅔ Crown.
2967 CONSTANZ. Penny of Hugo. "Græf," 1496–1520. Rare.
2968 —— Groats of Maximillian I. and Ferdinand II. Fine.                                        2 pieces
2969 —— Do. of the City. Fine.                          2 pieces
2970 —— Groats and Half-groats.                        3 pieces
2971 —— Medal of Cardinal Francis. Burnished. Size 23
2972 —— " small do.            Size 18
2973 CORVEY (Abbey); Bracteate, 1111 Pfennings, and 11 Marien gros. Only date 1656; rare.   3 pieces
2974 —— 11 Mar. Gros, 1653. Large A and lily, D. G. EL. ET CON. ABB. CORB. Very fine and rare.
2975 —— Broad Crown of Christopher " El. et. con. Abbas Corbei, S. R. I. P., 1686. Coat-of-arms; rev. St. Vitus with eagle, lamb, and palm. Uncirculated, (valuable).                                Size 32
2976 —— ⅔ Crown of St. Christopher; has his bust. Fine and rare.                                 Size 24
2977 —— Small Coin.                                    2 pieces

2978 CASTRIN (City.) 111 Groshen of John, Margrave of Brandenburg, 1545. Bust, good.

2979 CYRITZ. (City.) Bracteate.

2980 DARMSTADT, Martin Luther; Memorial of the Reformation Jubilee, 1817, Oct. 31. Bust of Dr. Luther; rev. ins. Uncirculated. Size 12

2981 —— Similar, to commemorate "Zum Andenken, der Golden Hochzeit," 1827. Louis and Louisa, Gr. Duke and Duchess of Hesse.

2982 DORTMUND (City,) King Rudolph I, 1273-91. King seated with mund and cross staff; DOL; rev. head in a triangle—over it, cross. CIVI. D. Solidus. Fine, rare.

2983 —— Duplicate. Equally good.

2984 —— VI. Pfennings; TREMONIENSIS; some with countermarks; good examples. 4 pieces

2985 —— Twelfth and twenty-fourth Thalers. Uncirculated. 2 pieces

2986 —— Varieties, small coins. 6 pieces

2987 —— Ferdinand II., 1638. Bust; rev. Eagle within two circles, with "Moneta nova civitat Imper Tremoniensis," in larger circle; "Domine da pacem," in smaller. Ducat or dollar. Rare. Well preserved.

2988 —— Crown of Charles VII., 1742. Fine and rare.

2989 —— Leopold and Ferdinand ¼ Crowns. 2 pieces

2990 DRESDEN. Large Klippinger, crown-size, 1662. Square pyramidal column, with shields at top and base; hand from a cloud on each side, crowning the summit; beneath the Hebrew name of Jehovah. On each side pillars twined; on them two doves and a flame; rev. ins. in Dutch. Uncirculated. Rare.

2991 —— Medal of John George III., Elector of Saxony; beautiful bust, JEHOVA VEXILLVM MEVM; rev. view of the City on the River Elba. Uncirculated. Size 26

2992 DULKEN (City). Groat, CIVIT DVLKENSI, in small circle around; motto of France, "Sit No," etc. Small cross; rev. edifice within a border of fleur-de-lis.

## Silver Coins of German Cities, etc. 181

CIVIS TVRONVS, thirteenth cent. Fine and very rare.

2993 DUREN (City). Groat William VII., Duke, 1339–1361. Very fine and rare.    2 pieces
2934 —— Groat, similar to 2992. Equally fine and rare.
2995 —— Small coins.    3 pieces
2996 DUSSELDORF. (City). Small coins. Fine.    2 do.
2997 DIETRICHSTEIN. Crown of Sigismund, Louis Count. 1638. Bust; rev. double eagle, on its breast FIII; below, family arms, LIBER BARO. IN. HOLLEN-BVRG, etc. Madai, 1681. Well. 9519. Uncirculated. Rare.
2998 —— Splendid uncirculated Crown of Ferdinand I. 1695. Madai, 1648. Well. 9527. Rare.
2999 EGGENBERG (Principality). Beautiful Crown of John Christian, and John Seyfried, 1658; the two brothers face to face; rev. beautiful coat-of-arms and crown. Madai, 4156. Well. 9538.
3000 EICHSTADT. Episcopal Dollar of John Eucharius, 1694. Arms with four crests; rev. St. Wilibald standing. Very fine. See for similar dollar, Well. 2440; Madai, 802.
3001 —— Twenty Marks (Half Crown) John Anton II. 1755. Bust in Episcopal robes; rev. arms. Uncirculated.
3002 —— Sede Vacante (or vacancy of the See). 1757. Convention Dollar, by Œxlein. See Madai, 5276. Wellenheim, 2448. Fine. Rare.
3003 —— John Anton III. 1781–1790. Convention Dollar of 1783. Bust; rev. coat-of-arms. See Well. 2455. Fine.
3004 —— Duplicate. Fine.
3005 —— Convention Gulden, same date. (20 EINE, F. M.) Uncirculated. See Well. 2456.
3006 —— Duplicate. Fine.
3007 —— Small coins.    4 pieces
3008 —— Sede Vacante, 1790. Double Convention Crown. very broad. Episcopal chair or throne vacant; rev.

182  *Silver Coins of German Cities, etc.*

tree supporting fifteen shields, WILLIBALOSBVRG, Splendid proof. Well. 2457.

3009 EICHSTADT. Duplicate. Very fine.

3010 —— Josephus, (of Stubenberg). Convention Gulden. 1790. XX EINE FEINE MARCK. Bust and coat-of-arms. VASCVLIS AVLAE, etc. Well. 2458.

3011 EINBECK (City). Groschen, or IV. GUTE PFS. 1568 . MO . NO . EINBECK. G. under a Crown. Fine.

3012 —— Groats; rev. Virgin and child, 1669, and imperial symbol. Uncirculated. 2 pieces

3013 —— VI. Marien Groschen, 1669. Large ornamented letter E. Fine and rare.

3014 —— Same of 1673, and small coins. 4 pieces

3015 EISENACH, in Grand Duchy of Weimar, where Dr. Luther was confined. Medal in commemoration of events in Luther's life, EISENACH IN LEID UND FREUD. View of city, castle, and church; various quotations from the Bible—one on the edge. On one shield an open Bible; on another DOCT. MARTINVS LVTHER VON EISLEBEN; extremely fine and valuable Medal. Nearly proof. Size 28

3016 EISLEBEN, birthplace of Luther. Broad Crown with Dr. Martin Luther's bust, full face; "1661" on his breast; rev. view of four edifices with spires; in front, a row of trees; in ex. shield; inscription in quaint German characters, MART. LUTHER, etc. In extremely fine preservation, and very rare. Size 30

3017 —— Small coin, with name of city; an artisan seated at his work, driving a stamp—pronounced R. R. Size 14

3018 ELBING (City). Groschen under Gustavus Adolphus, (Sweden). 1659. MON. NO. ELB.; and another. Rare. 2 pieces

3019 ELWANGEN; Episcopal Dollar of Anton, 1765. Convention piece, described in Madai, 5435. Wellenheim, 3402. Bust in ermine, on the breast, cross, etc. Very fine, rare.

3020 —— Half Dollar (Gulden), same type and date. Fine.

*Silver Coins of German Cities, etc.*

3021 EMDEN. Dollar, under Ferdinand II. Coat-of-arms of the city; rev. coat-of-arms of Germany; not in Wellenheim. Good, rare.

3022 —— Thaler, Leopold I., Emp., (Two-third Crown). 1688. Very fine.

3023 —— Quarter do., and two (Stuver).   2 pieces

3024 —— Thaler (Forty Stuver). MONETA NOVA AR. LOS. CIVITAT EMBD. Lion; rev. "*Rittersman*." Soldier standing, at his feet a shield, CONFIDENS DNO. NON. MOVETVR. Uncirculated. See Wellenheim, 4534, R. R.

3025 EMERICH, (City). X Heller. 1568. Fine and rare.

3026 ESSEN. Small Coins. Arms, two fishes. Rare.   5 pieces

3027 ESSLINGEN. Luther Medal in commemoration of the Jubilee, 1717. Bust of Dr. Luther within two circles of inscription; rev. view of the State-house—blazing sun and double circle as before. Extremely fine and rare.   Size 20

3028 ERFURT, arms, a wheel. Collection of small coins, all rare.   8 pieces

3029 —— Groats 1624 and 12 Einen Thalers; on both sides wheel. Very fine, rare.   4 pieces

3030 —— Crown of 1617. MONETA. ARGENTA. CIVITATIS EREFORD. Rev. DATE CAESARIS CAESARI QVADE DEO. Fine and rare.

3031 —— Medal in honor of Frederick Charles Joseph. 1777. Bust; rev. city. Fine.   Size 32

3032 ERPACH. Arms of Erpach; rev. double-headed eagle. FERDINANDVS II., etc. 1623. Crown, described in Wellenheim, 3925, and Madai, 1684, as rare. A fine example. Nearly uncirculated.

3033 ESTERHAZY. Fine Crown of Nicholas Joseph, 1770. Bust and coat-of-arms (Convention Dollar). See Wellenheim, 1316.

3034 FRANKFORT-ON-THE-MAIN. A collection of early Coins. 2 ALBVS, Denari, etc., with later examples of the coins of the city. Fine and not easily got together.   8 pieces

184     *Silver Coins of German Cities, etc.*

3035 FRANKFORT-ON-THE-MAIN. Uncirculated Coins, recent date; 6, 3, and 1 Krs. Brilliant.   11 pieces

3036 —— Medal or Coin in memory of the Reformation festival, in 1617; VERBVM DOMINI—an angel with the Bible; rev. inscription in nine lines. See Wellenheim, 4286. Not fine, rare.   Size 16

3037 —— Crown of 1637. Cross bearing the arms of the free city; rev. arms of Germany and title of Ferdinand II. Fine and rare.

3038 —— 1774. 1 Heller, fine silver. Proof. See Well., 1308.   Size 14

3038* —— Medalets, (no date,) to incite industry.   Size 15

3039 —— Convention Crown 1776. (X Marks.) DEO ET CAESARE. 3 figures beneath the All-seeing Eye; rev. inscription within laurel crown. Very fine. Nearly proof. Well., 4309, called rare.

3040 —— Jubilee Medal, third centennial festival of the Reformation, 1817. Pierced.   Size 17

3041 —— Similar. Same date.   Size 15

3042 —— Double Thaler. View of the free city. 1840. Nearly proof.

3043 —— Thaler 1848, on the election of the Arch Duke John, as Vicar of Germany. Very fine. Nearly proof. Rare.

3044 —— Duplicate.

3045 —— Thaler in commemoration of the birth of GOETHE —centennial anniversary, 1849. Fine, rare.

3046 —— Thaler in memory of Schiller's birth — the first centenary, 1849. Fine, rare.

3047 —— Double Thaler of 1862. Female bust crowned with wreath of oak leaves. Very fine.

3048 —— Thaler. Same type.

3049 —— Target Festival Thaler. 1862. Very fine.

3050 —— Thaler of the free city, struck in 1863. View of the house in which the princes met in convention. Uncirculated. Rare.

3051 —— Norman confederation. Gulden.

## Silver Coins of German Cities, etc.

3052 FRANKFORT-ON-THE-ODER. Copper Bracteate; two shields, helmet and hen. Wellenheim, 6610. 2 pieces

3053 —— Jubilee Medal to commemorate the foundation of the Academy; the second centennial festival, 1706. See Wellenheim, 6612. Rare, beautiful. Thick. Size 15

3054 FREIBURG (City). Bracteate, and small coin. Head of a monstrous bird or dragon. 3 pieces

3055 —— Crown 1568. CIVITAS FRIBVRGENS. Monstrous head; rev. bust of Ferdinand I. Well., 3698. Rare, fine.

3056 FRIEDBURG (City). Under John Eitel Diede. (See Well., 3938.) Gulden, 1675; obv. St. George and Dragon; rev. double eagle. Rare. Size 24

3057 —— Convention Gulden, 1766. "Moneta Castri." Coin of the castle of Friedburg. See Well., 3946. Rare. Nearly proof.

3058 —— Convention Crown of 1804. MON NOV CASTRI IMP FRIEDBERG; St. George on horseback transfixing the dragon; rev. FRANC H. D. G. R. I. S. A. CONSERVATOR CASTRI. Double eagle. See long description in Wellenheim, who calls it rare. Extremely fine. Nearly proof.

3059 FREUDENBURG 1803. 2 small coins; lion couchant. ZVR FREUDE DER IUCEND. Fine. 2 pieces.

3060 FUGGER. Max., Count under Ferd. II., 1622. Crown. See Wellenheim, 2482. Broad and fine. (Arms, 2 fleur de lis.)

3061 —— Small Coin.

3062 —— Quarter-crown. Poor.

3063 FULDA. (Bishopric.) Medallion Crown of Placidus, bishop? etc.; bust in robes with cross on his breast, on his head a cap; rev. oval shield with two helmets and cross. PIETATE ET CONSTANTIA. 1688. Madai, 961; Well., 3958. Slightly rubbed, yet fine and rare. Size 30

3064 —— Small Coins, early date. 5 pieces

3065 —— Adolphus. Curious Coin. 1728. Rare.

186      *Silver Coins of German Cities, etc.*

3066 FULDA. Sede Vacante (vacancy of the See.) 1788 Superb Medal Crown; obv. a bishop seated under a canopy or in the holy gate; rev. arms of Fulda (square cross) within a circle of the shields of 14 canons. Proof.

3067 —— Medal Coin (60 eine feine mark) in memory of Henry VIII., Bishop of Fulda, etc., etc., 1788. Size 18

3068 —— Adalbert III. 1788 to 1802. Convention Crown, 1795. Bust; rev. PRO DEO ET PATRIA. Very fine. Well., 3986.

3069 —— Same; Crown, 1795; in place of bust, a coat-of-arms; rev. same as last. Fine proof. See Well., 3987.

3070 —— Same; Crown of 1796, with bust. Extra fine.

3071 —— Duplicate.

3072 —— Half-crown or Convention Gulden 1796. Extra fine. Well. 3989.

3073 FURSTENBURG. Prince Joseph William Ernest, 1729. Splendid Medal Crown, "Ausbente Thaler," bust; rev. view of mines. Madai, 1654. Well., 3713. Size 28

3074 —— Same; Crown of 1762. Bust; rev. shield, etc. Extremely fine.

3075 —— Small base coins.                         2 pieces

3076 FREISINGEN. Bishop Conrad; Crown, 1790.

3077 GIMBORN; small coin (24 Ein Thaler), Louis, Count of Walmoden; his monogram. Rare.

3078 GLUCKSTADT. (City). 1666. "XVI Ereich's Thaler;" rev. bust of Frederick. Ex. fine. Well. 5001.

3079 —— Bracteates, large G.                      2 pieces

3080 GLATZ, Count John. Fine gilded crown, 1542; MONETA COMITATVS GLACENS, lion; rev. two shields; on one, bull's head, front face. See Well. 6964 for crown of 1540. Fine and rare.

3081 —— With unclassified coins.                  5 pieces

3082 GOTTINGEN and Gluckstadt.                    2 pieces

3083 —— Others; one of Christian III., Denmark.   3 pieces

3084 GOSLAR. Solidus, Henry, Kaiser 1056—1106. Bust, full face, crown, HEIN; rev. the Apostles Simon and Judas—IVDA. See Well. 4547. Fine and very rare.

3085 GOSLAR. Another; thin and never in circulation. Same type.
3086 —— Others. Same type. 3 pieces
3087 —— Broad groat. Lion and eagle; rev. the Apostles Simon and Judas. Very rare.
3088 —— Groat. Eagle; rev. Virgin and child. Uncirculated. Rare.
3089 —— Small coins with the arms and title of Goslar; eagle displayed, GOSLAR—a great variety, such as 2 and 4 pfennings, marien groschen (with the Virgin Mary), etc., etc. Fine lot. 7 pieces
3090 —— Similar lot. 8 pieces
3091 —— IIII Gute Groschen 1674. Nearly uncirculated.
3092 —— Crown (15)96, the Virgin and child; below, on shield, the Goslar eagle; rev. the double eagle of Germany, under Rudolph II. Madai, 2233. Well., 4552. Fine and rare.
3093 —— Crown 1622, under Ferdinand II. Same type as last. *Very* fine and broad.
3094 —— Splendid uncirculated crown of 1705 under Joseph I. DEI ET MARIAE FILIUS SPES NOSTRA IESUS: on a label crossing the field RESP—GOSL. Not in Wellenheim. Very rare, and one of the best executed coins in the collection. Very broad.
3095 —— Another of equal beauty, 1723. ⅔ crown. Entirely uncirculated.
3096 GREVESMOLEN (City). Groschen. Rare. 3 pieces
3097 GUSTROW and GARTZ. City and Count of. Groschen and half groschen. Fine and rare. 2 pieces
3098 GURK. Francis XAVIER, Bishop and Prince of Gurk and Count of Salm; splendid uncirculated crown of 1801. Bust; rev. coat-of-arms, IN TE DOMINE SPERAVI. *By Donner.* In Appel Thal. Sam. 332. Well. 9951. Rare.
3099 HAGENAU, Groschen of the city. 1551. Fine.
3100 HALDENSTEIN (Barony). Arms; rev. cross. 2 pieces

188     Silver Coins of German Cities, etc.

3101 HALBERSTADT. Crown of Albert, Margrave of Brandenburg and Cardinal, 1540. Coat-of-arms; rev. St Stephen, SANCT STEF PROTO MARTIR. Wel 7202. Well preserved and rare.
3102 —— Thaler of 1629; MONETA NOUA HALBEI STAU; coat-of-arms and St. Stephen. Very fine.
3103 —— Andreas Thaler, under Henry Julius of Brunswick, 1605. St. Andrew, HONESTUM PRO PATRIA. Uncirculated. Rare.
3104 —— Crown of the city, 1691. Coat-of-arms, with helmet and plume; rev. St. Stephen (I. C.) Beautifu uncirculated pieces.                    Size 2
3105 —— Duplicate, nearly as fine.
3106 —— Early coins, bracteates, etc.        6 piece
3107 HALLE (Schwabia). Small coins, pennies and smalle with the sign of Halle—outstretched hand—and cross Fine and very rare.                3 piece
3108 —— Another, similar lot.                "
3109 —— Similar, with "Friedmunz" 1714.       "
3110 —— Crown of Halle, under Charles V. 1545; tw shields, hand and cross, and arms and title of the Em peror. Madai, 2239, Well. 3409. Fine and rare.
3111 —— Reformation Jubilee, 1717, second centennial NVLLAS HIC METVIT VNDAS, Noah's ark; rev bust of Dr. Martin Luther. Entirely uncirculate medalet.                                Size 1
3112 —— On the inauguration of the Academy in 1694 Pelican and young. Thick medalet. Beautiful proof
                                            Size 1
3113 —— Half-crown under the Emperor Francis I., 1746 His bust, laureated. *By Werner.* Fine.
3114 —— Extremely fine crown of Halle under Joseph II *By Œxlein.* Uncirculated, rare.
       Not in Wellenheim.

3115 HAMELN (City). (The arms resemble halves of the lette O placed back to back. The coins of this city gene rally have a church or cathedral with two towers an cross on a pointed gable). A fine collection of earl coins, silver and billon.                  8 piece

## Silver Coins of German Cities, etc.

3116 HAMEL N (City). VI. Marien Groschen. 1668. Fine.
3117 HAMM (City). Small coin. 1729.
3118 HAMBURG (City). Arms, (gates with three towers). Bracteates. 4 pieces
3119 —— Solidus. MONETA HAMBVRG; rev. BENE-DICTVS. DEVS; cross with arrow heads in the angles. Fine and rare.
3120 —— Quarter Crown of the city under Rudolph II. (16)86. Similar (thin), (16)97. Both fine and rare. 2 pieces
3121 —— "II. Schill. current, Hamburg," under Charles VI. 1727, four do., under Francis II., 1797, and others. All fine uncirculated coins. 10 pieces
3122 —— Another lot not as good. 8 pieces
3123 —— School Medal, BRABEON SCHOLE, etc.; rev. laurel crown on a mountain top; student kneeling, in his hand a flower; (Emblem of Hope). Fine. Size 19
3124 —— Another; rev. arm from a cloud with sword and Bible, BELLI PACISQVE MINISTRAE. Uncirculated. Size 22
3125 —— Crown under Ferdinand II. 1621. See Madai 2245. Wellenheim, 1503. As it came from the die. Rare.
3126 —— Another, same date. Uncirculated.
3127 —— Medal of the City with inscription on both sides, not understood. Size 24
3128 HANAU; PHILIP MAURICE, Count. 1614. Quarter Crown. Bust within double circle of inscription; rev. arms. Madai, 5849. Well., 4004. Rare, in good condition.
3129 —— John Reinhart I. 1610. Count, under Ferd. II. Quarter crown. Well. 4020.
3130 —— Same (XII. Stuck). 1625.
3131 —— Small coins. 4 pieces
3132 —— Crown of Katharine Belgica. 1622. Under Ferdinand II. Fine. See Well., 4000.
3133 —— Duplicate, but without date. Finer than last. Rare.
3134 —— Thaler of Frederick Casimer. 1675. Bust of the Count; rev. arms. Fine.

190    *Silver Coins of German Cities, etc.*

3135 HANAU, etc. Duplicate, without date. Rubbed.
3136 —— Thaler of Philip Reinhart. 1693. Very fine.
3137 —— Do. 1694. Equally fine.
3138 HANOVER. (Kingdom.) Arms, gate with two towers. Lion and flower with three leaves. Collection of the earliest small coins from 1538. Rare lot.    6 pieces
3139 —— Beautiful coins from 1535, with trefoil, and Virgin and Jesus; XII. Marien Groschen, with the gate, etc. Rare lot.    3 pieces
3140 —— XII. Marien Groschen 1669; rev. gate, trefoil and lion. Very fine. Rare.
3141 —— Others. One fine.    2 pieces
3142 —— Crown of the City under Ferd. II. 1625. Extremely fine.
3143 —— Shooting Festival Thaler. 1872. Brilliant proof
3144 HAZFELD. Three Gute Krs. 1684. Rare.
3145 HELLIGENSTADT. Small coin. Rare.
3146 HUTSFORD. Small coin. St. Andrew's cross on square cross. Rare.
3147 HEIDELBERG. Medal Crown of 1686—the third jubilee of the University, (founded in 1386). Three figures seated in a gothic edifice; rev. long inscription. Extremely fine and rare. See Madai, 2372. Well. 3722.
3148 —— Medal Crown of 1699. Arms of Heidelberg, IN PACE ET AEQUITATE; rev. St. Anthony with crosier and open book. Beautiful uncirculated piece. Rare.    Size 30
3149 —— Jubilee of the University—Fourth centenary. LAETA SAECULI V. AVSPICIA. Pallas seated; rev. bust of Charles Theodore, INSTAVRATOR. Extremely fine, rare. Wellenheim describes one in copper. No. 3725.    Size 23
3150 —— Medal in honor of Charles Theodore, El. Palatine. Bust, view of the city. Fine proof.
3151 —— Two-third Crown, under Francis I; rev. 1761. Uncirculated.    Size 24

## Silver Coins of German Cities, etc.

3152 HEILBRONN. Jubilee of the Reformation, 1717—second centenary. Double Groschen; on one side, within an edifice, a spring with lilies growing. See Wellenheim, 3421. Uncirculated and beautiful. Rare.

3153 HILDESHEIM (City and Bishopric). Bracteate and early coins. Small size. 10 pieces

3154 —— Another selection, larger and finer coins 5 pieces.

3155 —— VI. Marien Groschen, 1673, and XII. do., 1676 Virgin and arms of Hild. See Well. 1605. Rare. 2 pieces

3156 —— Jodocus Edmund, 1694 and others, some not in Wellenheim. Fine and rare lot. Twelve and six Marien Groschen. 6 pieces

3157 —— Twenty-four Marien Groschen, 1690. VI. do., and One-third Reich's Thaler. All fine. 3 pieces

3158 —— Fred. William Bishop. 1764. XX. Eine feine marks. (Thaler). Bust good.

3159 —— XXIII. Marien Groschen, City of Hildesheim. 1763. Nearly proof. Rare.

3160 —— Superb Triple Dollar, under Rudolph II. Arms of Hild, on a shield covering the imperial eagle; DA PACEM DOMINE IN DIEBVS NOSTRIS HILDESHEIM; rev. Rudolph on horseback, his head laureated. Not in Wellenheim. Rare. Size 39

3161 HOHENLOHE. Wolfgang Julius, Prince of Neuenstein. Splendid uncirculated Crown of 1697. Bust with shield; rev. cavalier galloping over prostrate enemies. SO FAHRT EIN BECHT EDLER SINN. See Madai, 1723. Well. 3428. Marked rare.

3162 —— Duplicate. Burnished, but really a fine crown and rare.

3163 —— Convention Piece (sixty marks), of Neuenstein. 1783.

3164 —— Louis, Fred. Charles, Pr. of Oeringen. Very fine crown of 1770. (Convention Dollar), by *Oexlein*. See Well., 3433; Madai, 6791. Scarce.

3165 —— Convention Dollar or Crown of same Prince. 1785. See Well., 3437. Ex. fine, rare.

192    *Silver Coins of German Cities, etc.*

3166 HOHENLOHE. Another of 1797. Same Prince. Equally fine and rare crown; altogether different design. Not in Well.

3167 —— Small Coin of this Prince. 1804. Rare.

3168 —— John Frederick, of Langenburg. Beautiful crown of 1695. Coat-of-arms; rev. cavalier. Rare.

3169 —— Christian Fred. Charles, of Kirchberg. Convention Crown of 1781. Bust; rev. coat-of-arms. See Well., 3439. Very fine. Marked rare.

3170 —— Half Dollar, same type. Rare.

3171 —— Convention Gulden, by *Oexlein*, of Charles Albert, of Schillingsfurt. 1770. See Well., 3449. Rare type.

3172 —— Coins of the ¼ Dollar size, to match some of the foregoing. Fine.                                3 pieces

3173 —— Under Ferdinand II., 1623. A fine Crown. Rare.

3174 HOHNSTEIN. Dollar of Ernest III. (15)85. Count. Coat-of-arms; rev. St. Andrew DO IN LORA E CLETTENB. Rare.

3175 —— 12 Marien Groschen of Fred. Ulrich of Brunswick. Arms; rev. Wild man. See Well., 4622.

3176 —— Small coins.                                2 pieces

3177 HOLZAPPEL (in Anhalt). Beautiful Dollar of Charles Lewis, of Schaumberg; view of mines; above, blazing sun. AN GOTTES SEGEN, etc., 1774. Uncirculated. Rare.

3178 —— Gulden. Same type. Well., 5,374.

3179 HORN. Crown of Philip V., Baron of Montmorenci, and Count of Horn. (1568.) See Well., 8,902. Two shields with two helmets; rev. St. Martin dividing his cloak with a beggar sitting on the ground—St. M. on horseback. *Fine*, and very rare.

3180 —— Another, in good preservation.

3181 —— Half-crown of this rare type. Fine. Marked R. R. by Well., 8,905.

3182 —— Half-thaler of Phil. de Mont. Rare.

3183 HOYA. Groschen 16–19. Arms, two claws; rev. sign of the Empire. MENSCHEN. Uncirculated, and very rare.

3184 —— Same, with coins of double size.            3 pieces

## Silver Coins of German Cities, etc.

3185 HOXTER AND HOERDE. "Moneta Nova Hoxe," 1551 and Mon. Nov. Hoe. Pennies and groats. Fine and rare lot. 6 pieces

3186 HENNBERG. (arms a hen). Small thin coins. 2 pieces

3187 —— ⅔ Stuck of 16–92 (Thaler size.) Coat-of-arms and hen. FELIX FODINARUM ILME NAVIENSIVM REPARATIO, with a countermark. Well., 6,288. Good.

3188 —— Crown of 16–96; arms on two shields, supported by two miners. "Moneta Nova Ducum Saxoniæ"; rev. hen standing. "Crescit Et Hoc Tuto Gaudet Tutissima Septo." Extremely fine, rare.

3189 ISNY (City). Groat without date. "Moneta Nova Civitas Isnia." Eagle displayed, on his breast, a horse shoe; rev. star of six points; above, eagle. Fine and very rare.

3190 —— Same, except small star of five points in the angles of the large one. Equally fine and rare.

3191 —— Groschen of 1595, under Charles V., has his name. Fine and rare.

3192 JENA. Denarius. King seated; rev. view of an edifice. (cathedral?) Fine one of 1616; view of the university; and one Bracteate. 3 pieces

3193 JEVER. (in Oldenburg) Maria Count, in 1517–1575. Coat-of-arms and helmet. "MARIA C D. V. FR. T JEVER. RV. OS. V. VV; rev. Daniel in the lion's den (15) 67; crown: in excellent preservation, and very rare.

3194 —— Duplicate in all respects. See Well., 4,953.

3195 —— Early coins. A great variety, displaying the cross in many forms—"1 and 2 Jever Stuiver," and others. Interesting lot. 7 pieces.

3196 —— Thick Coin of Frederick Augustus (of Anhalt) from 1746 to 1793. "12 Jever Groot," 1764. See Well., 4959. *Rare.* About thickness of a dollar. Size 12

3197 —— Duplicate. Same in all respects.

3198 —— 4 Groots and 1 Groot. Same Count. 2 pieces

3199 —— Others. Same. 2 pieces

13

194        *Silver Coins of German Cities, etc.*

3200 JEVER. Reichs Thaler of Fred. Aug. Sophie, 1798.  See Well., 4,960. Very fine.
3201 —— Duplicate. Same in all respects.
3202 —— Half-thaler. Same.
3203 —— "1 Grote," 1798. Same.  2 pieces
3204 JULICH. MON NO DVCIS CLIVI JVLIZ. (Cleves and Julich.) Varieties.  3 pieces
3205 —— Similar.  3 pieces
3206 —— "Albus," 1678. Philip William, Count, etc Fine and rare.
3207 KAUFBEUERN. Crown of 1542. Arms of Kauf; rev Bust of the Emperor Charles V. KAROLUS V., etc A rare Crown, and well preserved.
3208 —— Medalet issued to commemorate the first Jubilee festival of the Augsburg Confession 25 June, 1630; teachers and children with the Bible, etc. Ex. fine, rare.  Size 14
3209 —— Small Coin. Base.
3209a KLAGENFURT. (City) Beautiful little Coin, 1681. Rare.
3209b KNYPHAUSEN. Groat of Count Bentinck, 1807. Rare.
3210 KONIGSTEIN. Groat of Eberhard VIII., 1544. Pierced. See Well., 3,793.
3211 —— Another, similar.
3212 KEMPTEN, 1545. Crown of Charles V. (CAROLVS V.) Very fine; but little circulated. Very rare.
3213 —— Bracteate and Small Coins. Rare.  4 pieces
3214 KREMNITZ. St. George Crown. The saint piercing the dragon, S. GEORGIUS EQUTUM PATRONUS; rev. Christ with seven companions in a ship, IN TEMPESTATE SECURITAS. Loop. Extra fine and rare.  Size 30
3215 —— Similar. Only three persons in ship.
3216 LANDAU. Obsidional of the city 1713. Oblong, with shield at each corner; CAES IMP. ES. LANDAU Monogram in centre. 20x14. Very rare.
3217 LANDSHUT. Bracteates.  2 pieces
3218 LEITMERITZ. Little Medalet of Bishop Wenc's, Leopold Size 7

3219 LEININGEN. 'George William, Prince, 1691. XV. Krs. Rare.
3220 —— Two others—(Arms, three eagles). Fine. 2 pcs.
3221 LEICHTENSTEIN (Principality). Dollar of Joseph Wenzel. 1758. Madai, 5483.
3222 —— Half-Dollar. 1729. Joh. Jos., Ad., etc. Appel III. 3387. Rare.
3223 LEUCHTENBERG. John, Landgrave, 1522. Double Groschen. Three shields; rev. DEVS TIBI SOLI GLORIA. Well. 2580. Good and rare.
3224 —— Double Groschen of George, Landgrave. 1534. Under Carolus V. Well. 2583. Fine and rare.
3225 —— Crown of 1547, under the Emperor Charles V. St. George standing. Almost uncirculated. Very rare.
3226 —— Small coins, 1525, with some unclassified. Fine lot. 5 pieces
3227 LEIPZIG. Medal in honor of Churf and George Duke of Saxony 1631. The city enclosed by a wall; above, a canopy supported by angels, long ins.; rev. Mercury and Apollo, and advancing towards them an angel and child, in the child's path a snake. Beautiful proof. Size 32
3228 —— Medal to commemorate the Third Centennial Jubilee Festival in honor of the Foundation of the University, Anno 1409. GRANDIOR ÆTATE. View of the city; in foreground tree. Extremely fine Size 30
3229 LIMBURG. Bracteate of William I., and unclassified coins—twelve Ein Thals., XX. Ein Marks, etc. 6 pcs
3230 LIEGNITZ. Double Groschen of Frederick I., Duke. (1488). Saint holding a church; and two small coins. 3 pieces
3231 LINDAU. A beautiful bracteate. Linden tree, and fine border. Very rare.
3232 —— Medalet to commemorate the Peace of Westphalia. JUBILA. PRIMA 1748. With the Arms of Lindan (Linden tree). Fine proof. Size 12
3233 LOBKOWITZ. Twenty Krs. 1794. Fine. Rare.

196 *Silver Coins of German Cities, etc.*

3234 LOWENSTEIN-WERTHHEIM; Medalet of Max. Charles' (1711–1718), on the birth of Prince Leopold, 1717. See Appel III. 1722. Fine. Size 14

3235 —— Quarter Crown, Prince Charles, 1767. Arms within a square. Fine, rare.

3236 —— Similar, not a duplicate. Poor.

3237 —— Constantine, Prince, 1769. Bust; rev. allegorical design; in ex. EX. VOTO CIVIT WERTHEIMEN. A Klippe described by Wellenheim, 3737. Extra fine, rare. Size 19

3238 —— Charles Louis. Convention Crown, 1769. Bust; rev. coat-of-arms, lions supporting. Good.

3239 —— Same. Crown. Bust; rev. tressure of five shields and crown. DEUS PROVIDENT. Madai, 6829. Well. 3747.

3240 —— Small Coins. 4 pieces

3241 LUBECK. Denarius. MONETA LVBICENSIS, Double Eagle; rev. cross. CIVITAS IMPERIAL. Well. 5146. Appel IV. 1966. Fine, rare.

3242 —— Same in all respects.

3243 —— Other denarii of this rare type. Fine. 3 pieces.

3244 —— Pennies, Half do., and Drellings. Rare. 6 do.

3245 —— Repetition of last. 5 do.

3246 —— Denarius—on both sides double eagle; fifteenth century. Extra fine and rare.

3247 —— Duplicate. Equally fine.

3248 —— Double Groat. King seated, "Moneta Lubicc;" rev. John the Baptist standing. JOHANIS BABTISTA. No date. Not in Wellenheim. Uncirculated. Very rare.

3249 —— Double Groat, 1522. John Baptist standing; rev. shield on a cross; CRVX. FVGAT OMME MALVM. See for similar, Well. 5149. Fine and extra rare.

3250 —— Coins of same size. (16 and 24 Ein Thaler). 1652, 1654 and 1670. Fine. 3 pieces

3251 —— Small lot. 3 do.

3252 —— Others, different. 2 do.

LUBECK. Groat (double groschen). On both sides double eagle. Well., 5,148. Fine, rare.

—— Same; rev. cross; in the angles, lilies. Good and *very* rare.

—— Groat and 12th thaler.  2 pieces

—— Double Groat. Figure seated holding a child with the head of a bear; rev. arms, on a cross; CRVX FVGAT OMNE MALVM. Said to be *very* rare. Very good.  Size 17

—— Groat " Civitas Impercalis," 1624, and small coins.
5 pieces

—— Crown, 1549. Double eagle. .MON, etc.; rev. St. John with lamb and cross. " Civitatis Imperialis." Madai, 4,985. Well., 5,159. Very little circulated. Rare.

—— Another, 1559. Same type. Fine, rare.

—— Half Crown. Same type counterstamped, dated 1549. Very fine. See Well., 5,155. They are marked R R.

—— Crown of the City under Charles V. Extremely fine bust of the Emperor; rev. mailed knight kneeling, with shield and drawn sword, date, 1537; mint mark, a large fly, " Bramsen thaler." (Gadfly Dollar). One of the finest and rarest Crowns in the catalogue.

—— Thaler of 1549, with arms of Hamburg, Luneburg, and Wismar. According to Wellenheim, even more rare than last. Very good.

—— Half Crown of Rudolph II., 1581, has figure St. John. Very good and rare.

—— Quarter Crown. Same type. ¼ do. of Ferd. II., 1622. Both fine.  2 pieces

—— " 1 Shilling Lubisch," 1789, etc., do.  2 pieces

—— Proof Crown, 1797, " 32 Schillinge, Lubisch Courant Geld." Rare.

—— Double Crown, without date (about 1600) with arms of the Burgomaster of Lubeck. Obv. double eagle, ADVERSVS HOSTES NVLLA, etc; rev. St. John standing, full length, MEDIOCRITAS IN

198   *Silver Coins of German Cities, etc.*

OMNI RE EST OPTINA.+ Entirely uncirculated and brilliant. See Madai, 2,272. Well., 5,165.

Size 38

3268 LUBECK. Triple Crown. Same date or period. Christ on the cross between two thieves—soldiers in the foreground—Jerusalem in the distance; rev. the creation of man; the giving the two tables to Moses; the crucifixion, DER IESVS HILFFET ALLEIN AVS NODT MOSES, etc. Extremely fine and rare.

Size 38

3269 LUNEBURG. Pennies of the oldest type. On both sides a lion. Not in Well. Very rare. 2 pieces

3270 —— Solidus. LVNEBERG. Lion; rev. cross and lion. As fine as when struck. Rare. For similar see Well., 4,692.

3271 —— Groats. Gate with three turrets, rev. St. John; and one with cross and lilies, DA PACEM, etc. Good coins and rare. 3 pieces

3272 —— Silver Ducat, 1546. Arms of the city, MON NO CIVITATIS LUNEBVRG; rev. half-moon. VISITAVIT NOS ORIENS EX ALTO. Thaler size. Fine and rare.

3273 —— Crown 1546. Mint mark, Swan to right. Same type as last. Nearly uncirculated. Rare.

3274 —— Similar Crown of 1548. Swan to left; the face of the half-moon also reversed.

3275 —— Double Crown. Arms, DA PACEM, etc.; rev. St. John, and to the left half-moon, ECCE AGNVS DEI, etc. Madai, 2,276. Well., 4,643. Very fine and rare.

3276 —— Crown of the city, under Ferdinand II., 1622. Strictly proof and brilliant. Very rare.

3277 —— Duplicate Crown in all but date, (1627) only finer.

3278 —— ⅔ Crown, 1702. Good.

3279 MAGDEBURG. Very old Ecclesiastical coins, bust of St. Maurice, with banner and cross. Ex. fine. Size 19. 2 pieces

3280 —— Same, with towers of a church. 2 pieces

## Silver Coins of German Cities, etc.

3281 MAGDEBURG. Same, with St. Maurice holding palm and double cross. Ex. fine and rare. 2 pieces
3282 —— Repetition of two last. 4 pieces
3283 —— Denarius and Bracteate of the City. 2 pieces
3284 —— Groats of the City, 1621. Woman on a wall between two towers. 3 pieces
3285 —— Groats, pennies, etc. 5 pieces
3286 —— 24 Einen thalers, 1675. 2 pieces
3287 —— Reformation Jubilee, Klippe, 1617. 15x15.
3288 —— Third thaler and ½ Ort. Rare. 2 pieces
3289 —— Episcopal Crown of Albert, Cardinal, 1537 (brother of Joachim I.,) bust; rev. coat-of-arms. Madai, 3,239. Well., 7,258. Good.
3290 —— Crown of the City, 1571. View of the State House, with Margaret on the wall holding aloft a Crown; rev. Double eagle. MAX II. Madai, 2,278. Well., 7,306. Ex. fine, rare.
3291 —— Episcopal Crown, 1603. St. Maurice with shield and banner. Very good, rare.
3292 —— Episcopal Crown of Christian William, Bishop. 1605. St. Maurice standing as before, SANCTVS MAVRITIVS; rev. coat-of-arms, MONE ARCHIE-PISCOPATVS MAGDEBVRG. Entirely uncirculated and brilliant. Very rare.
3293 —— Jubilee Crown of the Reformation, 1617. Busts of John Huss and Martin Luther to the middle, long inscription in two circles; rev. shield on double eagle. MON NO REIP MAGDB. Broad crown nearly uncirculated. See Madai, 2279, Well., 7310; by both pronounced R. R. Size 30
3294 —— Episcopal of Christian William, 1624. Bust; rev. coat-of-arms. Madai, 3250; Well., 7269. Fine and rare.
3295 —— Episcopal (sede Impedita). Arms and St. Maurice. Madai, 3254; Well., 7288.
3296 —— Coronation Crown of Augustus, King of Saxony, 1638. MAGDEBVRGVM RESTAVRATVM, etc. Very fine broad crown. See Well., 7290; Madai, 3256.

200  *Silver Coins of German Cities, etc.*

3297 MAGDEBURG. Thaler. Medal in honor of Anna Maria, Duchess of Saxony, etc., born, etc.; rev. Jacob wrestling with the angel. Not in Well. Very rare, also fine.

3298 —— Crown of the city, 1673. View of the city; rev. arms of Magdeburg and Lippe. Very fine and rare. Madai, 2282.

3299 —— ⅔ Crown (Thaler) of the city, 1674. Magde on the State House; rev. inscription VERB DOMINI MANET, etc. Well., 7319. Fine and rare.

3300 —— Duplicate. Same in all respects.

3301 —— Medal of Fred. William, 1681. His bust above the city, upheld by two hands from a cloud; rev. an eagle with sceptre and cornucopia descending upon a woman with uplifted hands, PARTHENOP HOMAG, 1681. Fine proof. See Madai, 626. Size 31

3302 MANNHEIM. "Nov Albus Manheim"; rev. bust of Carl Theodore; dime size. Fine and rare.

3303 —— Huldiget Carl Theod., 29 Apl., 1794, medalet; and another, view of edifice. Size 12. 2 pieces

3304 —— Marriage of C. Phil. Theod. and M. Eliza Augustus, 17th January, 1742; another, confirmation medal of Chas. Theod., 1744. Very beautiful. Size 12 and 18. 2 pieces

3305 —— Gulden of Manheim under Frederick, Grand Duke of Baden, 1863. Uncirculated.

3306 MANSFIELD (Count). Bracteate. Arms.

3307 —— Small coins, old pennies, groschen, etc. 6 pieces

3308 —— Double groschen. "

3309 —— Crown of Hoyer, Gebhard, Albert, and Philip, Counts, 1539. Arms; rev. St. George and Dragon. MON ARG COMI DE MANS. Well preserved, rare.

3310 —— Crown of John George, Peter Ernest, and Christorf. (1577). Double coats-of-arms and St. George. Very fine, rare.

3311 —— Crown of Peter Ernest, Christorf, and John Hoyer. About same date; in good preservation. Not in Well. Rare.

## Silver Coins of German Cities, etc.

MANSFIELD (Count). ¼ Crown of John George, Peter Ernst, John Albert, John Hoyer, (or Hojer), brothers, counts. (15)79. Very rare. Not in Wellenheim.

—— Henry II. (Count and Lord), (15)95. Handsome coat-of-arms; rev. St. George and Dragon. Splendid crown. Very rare.

—— Bruno, William, Gebhard and Volrat, brothers, Counts, 1611. Same type. Fine and rare crown.

—— Frederick Christorf. Ins. in 8 lines within a circle; rev. St. George, GEDVLT IN VNSCHVLDT, etc. Very fine and rare crown, (1631). Madai, 1805; Well., 7365.

—— Henry. Count in 1774. Fine crown.
—— Same. Splendid uncirculated ½ do.

MARSBERG. City. Small coin. 2 pieces

MAYENCE. Bracteate. Two busts, one above the other; to r. of one, a cross, the other a star. [This star, enclosed as it came to be by a circle or ring, is the wheel so conspicuous on the coat-of-arms of Mayence]. Probably of the 12th century. Entirely perfect. Size 29

—— Bracteate of Conrad, Count of Wittesbach, 1162. CVNRA. Extra fine and rare. Size 17

—— Bracteate, half solidus, and small coins. 6 pieces

—— Small coins, about 1650.

—— 1 Albus. II. do & 12 Krs., 1694. 3 pieces

—— Double Groschen of Adolph II. (of Nassau), Archbishop from 1467 to 1475. St. Peter seated, and coat-of-arms. See Well., 4090. Fine. 2 pieces.

—— Wolfgang, Archbishop, 1582—1601 — on his election. A gilt medal (base), with bust of a very fat man, full face; rev. coat-of-arms with three helmets, and in the field a wheel. Very curious and rare. Size 22

—— Fine Medal of Anselm of Ingelheim, 1694. Bust of the Archbishop; rev. arms of Mayence. Thick heavy medal. Size 32

202   *Silver Coins of German Cities, etc.*

3327 MAYENCE. Medalet on the death of Lothair Francis, in 1729. Uncirculated. Size 16

3328 —— Do., without date. Elector on horseback. Very pretty. Size 12

3329 —— Do. of Emeric Joseph, 1774.

3330 —— Crown of Fred. Charles Joseph, (Convention piece.) 17—94; below bust, I. F. S.; rev. ZEHEN EINE, etc. See Well., 4147. Uncirculated. Rare.

3331 METZ. Denarius of Herman, Bishop, 1073—1090. Bust to left, HER; rev. hand and cross. METS—NS. Well., 1609, where it is marked "R. R."

3332 —— Duplicate; both as they were struck.

3333 —— Denarius of Gerard, 1180—1201. See Well., 1611. Fine and R. R.

3334 —— Money of Theodore, 1365—1384; rev. St. Stephen; and other coins. 3 pieces

3335 —— Grossus Theodore, Archbishop. Rev. S. STEPHA. PROTH—the martyr, kneeling between two shields. Rare. Well., 1621.

3336 —— Another. Rev. the bishop standing. Extra fine and rare groat.

3337 —— Groat of the City, 1660. (VI. G.)

3338 —— Crown of the City. 1631. Double eagle; rev. St. Stephen standing. Good.

3339 —— Crown of 1643. Coat-of-arms; rev. bust of St. Stephen. Very fine and rare.

3340 MEININGEN. (City.) Medalet of Charles and Louisa. C. and L. united under a crown; rev. inscription. Fine proof. Size 15

3341 MINDEN. (Bishopric.) "1 Halb. ort." of Christian of Brunswick. 1627. (Size 17.) With a number of earlier dates and some later, making a valuable lot, thrown together to avoid tediousness. 10 pieces

3342 —— Similar lot. Extra good. 6 pieces

3343 —— Thaler of 1633 of Christian.

3344 —— Klippe of the City. 1634. Obsidional. Very rare. Square. Size 10

3345 MONTFORT. (City.) Crown of Hugo and John, Counts in 1621, under Ferdinand II.; on both sides, coat-of-arms. Not in Well. Rare, fine.

3346 —— Anton. Thaler. (60 G.) 1691. Fine bust and coat-of-arms. Fine and rare. Madai, 4306.

3347 —— Francis Xavier, Dollar 1759. Two varieties. Madai, 4310. 2 pieces

3348 —— Small Coins. 6 pieces

3349 MUHLHAUSEN, in Thuringia. Shield; rev. cross. Early Groat, etc. Very old and fine Coins. 3 pieces

3350 —— 12 Ein Thaler, and smaller. 4 do.

3351 —— Small Coins. 6 do.

3352 —— Crown of the "Civitas Imperialis Mulshusinæ. 1767," under Joseph II. Madai, 7498. Well., 7377. Fine.

3353 MUNSTER (in Westphalia). Gerard, Bishop. 1263–1277. Denarius; title and cross; rev. head of SANCTVS PAVLVS. Very fine and rare. See Wellenheim, 7615.

3354 —— Denarii of Bishops Conrad, Louis, Poto, etc.—all before the 14th century; head of St. Paul on the rev., and on the principal side a half-length figure holding church model; seated figure with crosier and books; church with three towers, etc., etc. Rare. 6 pieces

3355 —— Similar of succeeding bishops. Rare. 5 do.

3356 —— 12 and 24 Einen Thalers. Rare. 10 do.

3357 —— Crown without date. Baptism of Christ; DIT. IS. MIN. LEVIE. SON. etc.; rev. the devil tempting Christ, PACK DI SATHAN, etc. See Madai, 2360. Well., 7679. Extremely fine and rare.

3358 —— Medal of John Van Leyden, King of the Ana. Baptists. 1534. His bust to the middle with sceptre and scroll, on his head a cap, round his neck a heavy chain; JOHAN VAN LEIDEN, EIN KONINCE DER WEDERDOPER ZU MONSTER; below bust, WAR HAFTICH CONTER; rev. arms—globe pierced by two swords; above, cross and crown; GOTTES MACHT IST MIN RACHT ANNO MDXXXVI. Cast and burnished. Very fine and rare. Size 27

3359 MUNSTER. Crown of John of Leyden; his bust to right, Similar inscription; rev. inscription in eleven lines. Extremely fine and acknowledged to be of the highest rarity. Size 32

3360 —— Ana Babtist Crown. 1534. Without bust; inscription in two circles; within JHO MVNSTER; rev. DAT WORT IS FLEISCH GE WORDEN VN WANET, IN VNS. Ex fine and broad. (Size 31.) Rare. Wellenheim, 7683.

3361 —— Double Crown of this date and type. Uncirculated. Not in Well. Ex. rare.

3362 —— Double Crown of the same type. Circulated, though fine.

3363 —— Crown. Birth of Christ, four figures and animals in a stable, inscription in Dutch; rev. the four kings presenting gifts. Well preserved and remarkable coin, without date. A work of the same period as preceding.

3364 —— Another Crown of the same religious character. Same period. Quotations from the Bible and illustrations. Well preserved.

3365 —— Episcopal Crown of 1535; Francis of Waldeck. St. Peter and St. Paul standing. Fine, rare. See Wellenheim, 7626. Madai, 834.

3366 —— Crown of same bishop, 1541. Busts of St. Peter and St. Paul. Fine and rare. Not in Wellenheim.

3367 —— Crown of the Monastery. St. Paul, Patron. 1638. View of the city of Munster with St. Paul standing; under Ferdinand, Duke and Elector of Baden. See Madai, 838; Well. 7628. Very fine.

3368 —— Another Crown of Ferdinand. 1539. (Episcopal). Very fine.

3369 —— Duplicate. Fine.

3370 —— Crown of the City. (1648). View of the town; above MONAST WESTPH; rev. a crown, three doves descending with olive branches, PAX. OPTIMA RERVM. Proof. Not in Well. Very rare.

## Silver Coins of German Cities, etc. 205

3371 MUNSTER. Extra broad double Crown. 1648. MON. WEST, etc.; rev. two hands with olives and cornucopiæ. Similar to last. Fine and rare. Size 34
3372 —— Double Groschen of this date. 2 pieces
3373 —— Klippe Dollar. (Square). 1660. See Madai, 2290; Well. 7690. Extra fine and rare.
3374 —— Duplicate equally fine. L. B. A. 1820, neatly engraved on back.
3375 —— Dollar (or one and a half), of the City and Monastery of West. 1661. St. Paul above the city; rev. handsome coat-of-arms with five crests; quotation from the 143d psalm. Struck after the siege of the city. Uncirculated. Nearly proof. Very rare.
3376 —— Extra fine and broad Crown or Medal of 1678. (Not in Well.) Ins. in ten lines; rev. coat-of-arms as before. Uncirculated. Size 32
3377 —— Sede Vacante Crown. 1638. Under the Emperor Leopold I. His bust, with fine bust of St. Paul. Proof. One of the finest pieces in the collection. See Madai, 844; Well. 7639.
3378 —— Sede Vacante Crown of 1706. Helmeted coat-of-arms and church, with three steeples. Uncirculated. Gilt. Madai, 847; Well. 7617.
3379 —— Mortuary Crown (same date). Arms; rev. ins. FRED–CHRISTIAN, etc. Uncirculated. Not in Well. Rare.
3380 —— Centenary Medal. Sun rising on the city, 1648. View of the same under a meridian sun in 1748. Proof. Rare. Size 20
3381 —— Sede Vacante Medal. 1761. St. Paul and Charles the Great. (See Well. 7654). Very fine. Size 16
3382 —— One-third Dollar and smaller. Fine. 3 pieces
3383 —— Sede Vacante Crown. 1801. On a shield, a bust of St. Paul; rev. Charlemagne standing. Uncirculated. Splendid. Rare.
3384 NEISSE. Letter N. and 3 lillies. Small base coin.
3385 NEUBURG. (Monastery or cloister of): King standing, holding a church model and banner, with five birds

206   *Silver Coins of German Cities, etc.*

thereon. S-L.; rev. coat-of-arms, and bishop's mitre. AP-ZC. Small coins well preserved and extremely rare.

3386 NEUBURG. Another, nearly same.

3387 NEUMARK, Count Otto II. Groschen without date; two shields, below, O; rev. large helmet. Appel IV., 2243; Well. 2616. Very good.

3388 NEUSS. Bracteate. Small, rare.

3389 —— Crown of the City, 1539. Double Eagle. NVSSIA SAN. ECCL. COL. FIDELIS FILIA; rev. St. Quirinus standing, banner and two shields. Madai, 2291. RRRR.

3390 —— Crown of 1569, with different reverse. Good, rare.

3391 NORDLINGEN (City). Groat of 1527, with bust of Charles V. Good and very rare.

3392 —— Double Groschen. Same.

3393 NORDHEIM or NORTHEIM (City). Groat. MO. CIVIT. NORTHE, large N. on cross. Fine and very rare.

3394 —— Same, and half groat.   2 pieces

3395 —— Same. View of the State House, in the gate a leopard. Appel, 2304; Well. 4651, R.R.

3396 —— Small Coins.   3 pieces

3397 NORDHAUSEN. Eagle, NORTHAVSEN. Double groat, Groat, and Half-groat.   4 pieces

3398 —— Crown of the City. 1660. NORTHVSÆ. Under Leopold I. Ex. fine, has been gilt. Not in Well.

3399 —— Medal. 1764. Joseph II. HIS. QVOQVE DIVA FAVEBIT. Shield and helmet; rev. JR. and ins. in a small ring, within circle of nine shields. Very fine. Wellenheim, 7391. Rare.   Size 30

3400 NURENBERG (or NUREMBERG). A collection of the small coins of the old city. Fine.   10 pieces

3401 —— Crown. "Pflegamter-thaler." 1580. Gilt and partially enameled as to the shields. Arms of the city in a circle of sixteen shields; rev. inscription and seven shields, DVRET IN ÆVVM, etc. Very fine and rare. See Well. 2792; Madai, 5543.

## Silver Coins of German Cities, etc.

NURENBERG. Double Crown. 1627. MONETA NOUA ARGENT REIPUB NORIBERGENSIS. Angel holding the city arms on two shields; rev. Ferdinand II. on a prancing horse. Magnificent. Very rare. Not in Well.; Madai, 2304.

—— Klippinger, 1650. "Vollzúg des Frieden," the 16th June; rev. MAGNAS FERTE DEO GRATES. See Well., 2,824. Fine.                    Size 20

—— Klippe. Same occasion. Boy riding a hobby horse; rev. VIVAT FERD. Well., 2,825. Fine and rare.                                   Size 14

—— Dollar of 1694, the city under rays. Hebrew name of God. Uncirculated. Madai, 5,072.

—— Same, 1742; rev. bust of Charles VII. Uncirculated. Madai, 2,316. Well., 2,873.

—— Convention Dollar of 1765. "Domine Conserva Nos In Pace." Under the Emperor Francis I.; a female sacrificing. Fine, rare.

—— Dollar of 1795. FRANZ DER ZWEITE DEUTSCHER KAISER; rev. X EINE, etc. Uncirculated. Rare.

—— Half-thaler. Loop removed.

—— Love Token. Two fowls.            Size 10

OBER-STEINBACH (city). Jubilee Medalet in honor of Martin Luther and the Reformation. MARTINVS LVTHERVS THEOLOGIAE DOCTOR. Second centennial, 1717. Very fine         Size 15

OELS AND OHLEN, (Cities). Small coins.  2 pieces

OETTINGEN. (Principality.) Double groschen of Count Joachim, 1516; rev. Martyrdom of St. Sebastian. Fair. Very rare.

—— Groschen. Same date and type; but with full length figure of St. Sebastian. Very rare.

—— Double Groat of Wolfgang, Martin, and Louis 1521. See Well., 2,940. Rare.

—— Another.

—— Groschen of Charles Louis, under Ferdinand II., (1548).                                 2 pieces

3418 OETTINGEN. (Principality.) Crown of Carl, Wolfgang, Ludiwig, and Martin. 1546. See Madai, 1,823. Wellenheim, 2,951. Fine and rare.

3419 —— Louis Eberhard, Count, 1623; splendid crown; besides the beaded ring, a beautiful chain border on both sides; arms of Oettingen, (OTING) and double eagle, under Ferdinand II. See Madai, 4,314. Well., 2,953. Rare.

3420 —— Albert Ernest, Count, 1657. Gulden (60), A. E. in monogram; rev. dog standing. VIAGILANTIA ET FIDELITATE. Two types. 2 pieces

3421 —— John Alois I., 1759. Obv. bust; rev. coat-of-arms, dogs supporting. Splendid convention crown. Well., 2,959. Rare.

3422 OLMUIZ (Bishop's See), Francis, Bishop, 1618; bust in cap; rev. 3 shields, "Prince Episcopus Olmuce," (1)618, groschen. Good, rare.

3423 —— Double Groschen of Charles, Prince of Lichtenstein and bishop of Ohnutz. Fine, rare.

3424 —— Groschen. Fine. 2 pieces

3425 —— Charles of Lothringen, bishop, 1701. Fine Crown of that date. Madai, 853. Well., 12,187.

3426 —— The same. Crown of 1704; arms on a cross. Fine.

3427 —— Wolfgang. Uncirculated Crown of 1727. Rare.

3428 —— Thaddaus, Prince, etc., 1779; rev. hand pouring coins through the open roof of a cottage. Size 16

3429 OPPELN (city). Groschen of Charles, Pr. of Leichtenstein. Fine and rare.

3430 OST. Friesland (East Frisia). Early coins. Small. 4 pieces

3431 —— Eno I., 1466–1491. Fine groschen. Coat-of-arms; rev. St. Andrew's cross on a rose; NO. C. FRI, etc. Rare.

3432 —— Edzard, 1565. Arms; above, crown and lily. EDZ. CO FRI. ORI. Motto, DA PACE. DIEBUS NOS. Eagle with head of a king and body of a fish. ½ dollar size. Well preserved. Rare.

Ost. Crown of Edzard, under Ferd. II., 1564; bust of
Ferd. Fine and rare.
—— Crown of the same, with his brother John, 1570.
DA PACE DOM, etc. Extremely fine. Nearly un-
circulated. Rare.
—— Same, 1584. Equally fine.

> They all have the reverse, as 3,432.

—— Remarkable Crown of Eno III., 1614; bust; rev.
arms of the Empire. Fine and rare. Madai, 1,848.
Well., 4,705, R. R.
—— Christian Eberhard, 1665–1708. Fine. ⅔ Crown.
Rare.
—— George Albert, 1708–1734, ⅙ Crown, 1730. Good.
—— Marriage Medal. Eberhardina, Sophia, with
Prince of East Frisia; a gardener trimming a grape
vine. Rare.                                   Size 18
—— Old coins, ¼ and ½ dollar size.         4 pieces
Osnabruck, Osnaburg. Solidus of Gerhardt, 1186—
1217. Bishop seated with staff and book; rev. wheel.
Well., 1652.                                  2 pieces
—— Same, with other small coins.              10 "
—— Francis William, Prince of Wartenberg, bishop,
1625—1634. Crown with his bust; rev. coat-of-arms,
1631. Madai, 3356; Well., 1662. Well preserved,
rare.
—— Sede Vacante, 1698. Splendid crown or medal.
Obv. St. Peter with keys and book; above, the arms of
Osnaburg; rev. a cathedral—sun rising. Madai, 861;
Well., 4677.
—— Sede Vacante, 1715. Similar crown. On this,
however, St. Charles is standing before the church.
Madai, 863; Well., 4679.
—— Sede Vacante, 1761. Busts of St. Peter and St.
Charles, surrounded by shields of Canon—sengrailed
edge. Extremely beautiful proof medal with slight
scratches.                                    Size 32
—— Small coins, VI Groschen, etc.           4 pieces

210 *Silver Coins of German Cities, etc.*

3447 PAAR. John Wenzeslaus, Prince, 1771. Fine crown. Madai, 6799.

3448 PADERBORN. Theoderic Adolph, Bishop, 1655. St. Liborius standing; one counterstamped P. Rare double groschen. See Wellenheim in loc. 2 pieces

3449 —— Small Episcopal coins. 3 pieces

3450 —— Similar. "

3451 —— Sede Vacante, 1683. Extremely fine and rare medal crown; busts of St. Liborius and Charles the Great. Madai, 873; Well., 7721.

3452 —— Herman Werner, 1685. Fine and broad crown; shields with 5 crests; rev. St. Anthony of Padua. Madai, 874, and Well., 7729.

3453 —— Sede Vacante, 1719. Cathedral; above, St. Liborius; rev. insignia and inscription. Madai, 877; Well. 7734. Fine and rare crown.

3454 —— William Anton, Bishop, 1767. Coat-of-arms; rev. St. Liborius on a cloud, "St. Liborius, Patron, Paderborn, etc." Madai, 6427; Wellenheim, 7744. Extremely rare (RR), and fine convention crown.

3455 —— ½ Crown (24 Marien Grosch). Same.

3456 —— Frederick William (of Westphalia), bishop, 1786. Convention Gulden. Entirely uncirculated, brilliant. Well., 7753.

3457 PAPPENHEIM, Christian Ernest, Count, 1721. Coin of the *Granzbesuchung*. Well., 2966. Size 15

3458 PASSAU (Bishop's See). Groat of Bishop Wigileus Froskel, 1510—1519. Fine and rare.

3459 —— Groat of Ernest of Bavaria. Rare.

3460 —— Fine crown of John Philip, bishop. PATAVIENS (Passau). 16—97. Madai, 3371; Well., 2998. Rare.

3461 —— Extremely fine crown of Leopold Ernest, bishop of Passau, 1779. Not in Wellenheim.

3462 —— Duplicate. Equally fine.

3463 PETTAU, (City in Stiermark). Klippe, 1673. Uncirculated. Size 10

Silver Coins of German Cities, etc. 211

3464 POLLING, (Monastery). Francis Topsl, Abbot from 1744 to '96. Bust and inscription; very fine medal. See Madai, 1,794. Size 30

3465 POMMERANIA (Province). Prince Francis, 1622. Winged lion; rev. DS. Schilling and double schilling. 2 pieces

3466 —— Charles XI. Stuck (½ crown), 1674. Bust, coat-of-arms. Fine.

3467 —— Same. Crown, 1690; rev. coat-of-arms, men in arms supporting. See Madai, 6157; Well., 6801. Good; rare.

3468 —— Adolph Frederick, 1763. ⅓ crown. Bust, NACH Dem LEIPZIGER FVSS VON, 1690. Madai, 5251; Well., 6805. Fine and rare.

3469 —— Small coins. 3 pieces

3470 PRESSBURG. Coronation medal of Francis I. and Ferd. V., 28th Sept., 1830. Two heads. Proof. Size 14

3471 QUEDLINBURG Monastery: Dorothea of Saxony, Abbess, 1610—17. Groschen, 1616. DOROTHEÆ MON. Arms and symbol of Empire. Appel. I. 413; Well. 1400. Uncirculated. Rare.

3472 —— Dorothea, Sophia. 1622. Double groschen. Good; rare.

3473 —— Anna Dorothea (Saxe Weimar), 1685—1704 (the last Abbess). Splendid medal. Bust, long ins. in two circles; rev. view of the monastery, sun in the sign *Cancer*, ARDVA DIFFICILI ADSCENSV. Madai, 974; Well., 7418. Size 30

3474 —— Medalet of the same; same bust; rev. monastery in the distance; the sun going down in splendor. ABITU DECORATUR AMOENO. As fine as last and equally rare. Size 16

3475 —— Small Token. Rare.

3476 RATZBURG Episcopal Coins, Augustus of Brunswick. 1610—1636. Groschen. 3 pieces

3477 —— Medalet on his death. Size 17

3478 RAVENSBURG. City. Small coins. City gate. Rare.

## 212 Silver Coins of German Cities, etc.

3479 RECKHEIM. (Barony.) MON. LIB. BARONATVS IMP. RECHEIME, under Emperor Charles V Double eagle with his title. Fine Crown without date Madai, 1958. Well., 9084.

3480 RECKLINGHAUSEN. (City.) Groschen. Good, rare.

3481 REICHSTADT. (City.) Groschen of John, Christian, and George. Very fine, rare.

3482 RIL. (City.) Double Groschen. MON MVRILLE. Theodore of Mons. Rare.

3483 REGENSBURG. (Ratisbon.) Episcopal coins with some of the City (RATISPON.) Arms, two keys crossed. Fine lot. 10 pieces

3484 —— Medal of the City. MO. REIP. RATIS. Arms of the city and double eagle on two shields; rev. inscription and date, 1586, finely executed border. Entirely uncirculated and very rare. See Well., 3061. Half-dollar size.

3485 —— Reformation Klippe. 1617. A little beauty. Size 12.

3486 —— Medal, 1641, *of the Reichstag.* Bust of Ferd. III., laureated; rev. arms of the electors on 7 shields arranged in a circle. Well., 3075. Extremely fine and rare. Half-dollar size.

3487 —— Beautiful Medalet of Francis I., with view of the city. Half-dime size.

3488 —— Medal of 1705. Genius of the city sacrificing; rev. same presenting the arms of the city to St. Joseph. PATRONA, etc., the figures in a boat. Well preserved and very rare. Size 26

3489 —— Convention Crown, with bust of Charles VII., 1759, by Looz. Uncirculated. Rare.

3490 —— Duplicate. Very fine.

3491 —— Sede Vacante, 1787. St. Joseph in a boat; around, circle of the shields of 15 canons; rev. inscription. Beautiful medal dollar.

3492 —— Duplicate. Fine.

3493 —— Shooting dollar of 1788; rev. cross-bows, spears, and banners. Proof. Well., 3112. Rare.

REGENSBURG. Crown of 1809, to commemorate the confederation of the Rhine. Uncirculated. Rare.
REINSTEIN and Reitberg. Small coins. 3 pieces
ROSTOCK. City. MONE NOVA ROSTOCHTEN. Griffon; rev. cross. Denarius. *Very rare.*
—— II Schilling and XVI. Eine Reich Thaler, etc. 5 pieces
—— Coin, Quarter-dollar size. Griffon and cross. Rare.
—— Crown of (1)610, under Rudolph II. Uncirculated. Extra rare.
SALM. Convention coin of Prince Frederick III. Bust; rev. arms, crowned. 10 Krs. Very fine.
SALZUNGER. (City.) Reformation Jubilee piece. Bible on altar; rev. inscription. 1817. Uncirculated Rare. Size 12.
SALZBURG. Small coins. Three shields; rev. plain. 2 pieces
—— Small square coin and others. 6 do.
—— Leonard V., archbishop. 1495 — 1519. Obv. LEONARDVS ARCHI SALZ. two shields 1500. Rev. SANCT RVDBERDVS, the saint standing. Double Groschen. Has been gilt. Very fine and rare.
—— Dollar. 1522. Mathaus V., Cardinal. Bust in cap; rev. St. Rupert and St. Virgilius full length. S. RVDBERTVS ET S. VIRGILIUS EPIS SALZBV, in excellent preservation and very rare. See Well., 10,224.
—— Small coin, double Groschen of same. 1532.
—— Crown of Wolfgang Theodore, Cardinal 1587 —1612; rev. St. Rupert seated. Fine. Well., 10,374. Rare.
—— Thaler Klippe, without date. St. Rupert; below, coat-of-arms; rev. a tower of three stories surmounted by a pyramid. Extremely fine and rare.
—— Maximillian Gandolph. Cardinal, 1668 — 1687. Double Groschen and XX. (Quarter-dollar size; base.) Rare. 2 pieces

3510 SALZBURG. John Ernest. 1687—1709. Small. 2 pieces
3511 —— Francis Anton. 1709—1727. Dime size. Uncirculated. Rare.
3512 —— Crown of same. 1725. Rev. arms of the Archbishop. Very fine and rare.
3513 —— Sigismund, bishop, 1753—1771; fine Crown, with his bust, (called in Well. a medal); rev. St. Rupert seated. NAT GERM PRIMAS. 1757. Very rare. Madai, 7255.
3514 —— Crown of same. 1758. Mary and babe; rev. St. Rupert standing. Ex. fine. Madai, 3287. Rare.
3515 —— Crown of same. 1761. Nearly uncirculated.
3516 —— Splendid uncirculated Crown of Leopold Anton, 1729. Obv. arms, and Mary and Jesus; rev. St. Rupert seated, by his side a shield. Madai, 3,228. Well., 10,794. Rare.
3517 —— ⅛ Crown, same; and another. 2 pieces
3518 —— Uncirculated Crown of Ferdinand, (Austria) 1805; another of 1803, nearly as fine. Called by Wellenheim, medals. Rare. 2 pieces
3519 SAYN-WITTGENSTEIN; Coins of John, Count, 1634–57. Cited by Wellenheim as R. 3 pieces about dime size.
3520 —— Gustavus, Count, 1676. ⅔ Crown, bust; rev. coat-of-arms; TANDEM FORTVNA OBSTETRICE. Fine and rare.
3521 —— Same, counterstamped. Well., 7,781. Rare.
3522 —— "16 Gute Grosch, 1677; rev. a stag running, (⅔.) Rare.
3523 —— Small coins. 2 pieces
3524 SCHLESIEN (in Silesia.) Klippe without date (very old). 111 TALER OV MONETA. ARGENTEA SILESIÆ. Eagle, in one corner stamped M: thick piece about 1 inch square.
3525 —— Early coins of various princes and cities, as Fred. II., 1543; Sylvius Frederick, 1675; George, Louis, and Christian, Dukes Silesia, etc., etc. Some older.
10 pieces

3526 SCHLESIEN (in Silesia). George Christian and George Rudolph, Dukes. Fine crown of the brothers (1)608; their busts half length, facing; rev. shield with three helmets, eagle, etc. Madai, 1,562. Well., 6,999. Rare.

3527 —— Same. A crown of the next year, slightly different. Equally fine. See Well., 7,000. Rare.

3528 —— Same, crown dated 1619; bust of the brothers; rev. similar to 3,526.

3529 —— Splendid Crown of George, Louis, and Christian, 1656; the three brothers full face, shown to the hips; rev. very handsome coat-of-arms and crests. Size 30. Very rare.

3530 —— Half Crown same type. Equally fine.

3531 —— Equally fine Crown of George alone, Duke of Silesia; bust and arms as before.

3532 —— Crown of Henry Wenceslaus and Charles Fredericks, Dukes, etc., their busts face to face, underneath, 1620; rev. coat-of-arms. DVC. SIL MONS. ET. OLS. CO. GLA. Wellenheim says R. R. In good preservation.

3533 —— George William. A medal or coin on his death, 1675; bust and ins. PIASTE AE, etc. See Well., 7,012, marked R.—more than ½ Crown in weight.

3534 —— Wolfgang Christian, on his death, 1672. A fine coin or medal. Size of one last described. Very fine.

3535 —— 24 Krs., under Ferdinand II., 1622.

3536 —— Beautiful Medal of George, Marquis of Brandenburg. Size 14

3537 SCHLICK. Count Stephen, from 1526; double Crown; bust in hat; ins. in two circles. DOMINVS STEPHANVS SLICE, etc., etc.; rev. coat-of-arms—image of Pan above shield. A rare medal, injured by burning.

3538 —— Crown of same. St. Jaochim (S. J.) standing, with staff and shield; rev. Bohemian Lion. LVDOVICVS PRIM, etc. Madai, 1,870, Well., 12,011. Fine and rare.

3539 SCHLICK. Henry. Uncirculated Crown, 1642, HEINRIC. SCHLICK COMES A PASSAN. St. Anne standing; below, shield. S. ANNA; rev. FERDINAND III., double eagle, etc. Madai, 4,373, Well., 12,030. Rare.

3540 —— Small coin.

3541 SCHWARZENBERG. Splendid broad Crown (size 30) of Ferdinand, Prince, with Maria Anna, his wife; their busts jugata, 1696. Madai, 1,665. Well., 12,069. Rare.

3542 —— Similar Crown. Not a duplicate, same date. Equally fine and rare.

3543 —— John, Prince of Schwarzberg, 1783. Bust; rev. arms in chain of the Order of the Golden Fleece. Fine and rare.

3544 —— Same. 20 krs. Uncirculated. Rare.

3545 —— Small Coin.

3546 SCHWEIDNITZ (City) Groschen, 1526 SWIDNI; rev. eagle. "Ludovicus," etc. Very good, rare.

3547 SOEST. (City), Solidus, without date. Cathedral, the gable surmounted by a fleur de lis; rev. saint with crook and book. Very rare. 2 pieces

3548 —— 1 Albus, 1681, key and griffons. 2 pieces

3549 SOLMS (Count of,) MONETA. AR. COMES SOLMS, of Matthias, Rudolph, Ernest, and Philip. Fine lot groschen. 5 pieces

3550 —— Token. L. S. in monogram, long-billed bird standing. Uncirculated. Size 12

3551 —— Convention Crown of Solms-Laubach; bust of Otto in low hat; rev. pyramid with inscription thereon. Very fine. Madai, 6,874. Wellenheim, 4,252.

3552 —— Medal Crown of Christian Augustus, 1738; his bust; rev. bust of his wife, Elizabeth Amalia. Fine proof impression, slightly circulated. Madai, 4,391.

3553 SPEYER. (Bishopric) Convention Crown, 1770, of Augustus Philip Charles; rev. Minerva and attendants, DEO. O. M. AVSPICE. Madai, 6,444. Well., 3,149. Very fine and rare.

3554 —— Half-crown. Same type. Fine.

3555 SPRINZENSTEIN. Medal crown of John Ernricus, count, 1717. Fine. Madai, 1909 ; Well., 11,099.

3556 STADE. (City in Bremen.) CIVITAS STADENSIS. Coin, groat size ; 1614. City arms, (key, griffons supporting.) Rev. MATTHIAS, etc. Double eagle. Fine and rare.

3557 —— Similar. Equally fine. Rare.

3558 —— Groat, 1620. Same type. Ex. fine.

3559 —— Similar. Very fine.

3560 —— Medalet of 1739 ; rev. St. Anthony of Padua, with staff and pig. Extremely fine and rare. Not in Wellenheim. Size 14

3561 —— Medal, with view of the city ; in ex. STADE ; rev. ANNO 1712, DV. VII. Septemb. FRIDE- RICO IV. REGE DANIÆ CAPTA. Probably very rare. Half-crown size. Not in Well.

3562 STENDAL (City.) A Bracteate. Very fine and rare.

3563 STETTIN (Duchy.) Bracteate and small coin, known by the Griffon with large wings. The few that are described by Wellenheim, are pronounced rare. 6 pcs

3564 —— Groschen. MON NOV STET. 1519. Lion on cross ; rev. griffon. RVDOLFVS DVX STET. Not in Well. Very fine and rare.

3565 —— Similar. D. S. in monogram. Very fine and rare.

3566 —— Others. Uncirculated. Ex fine and rare. 3 pcs

3567 —— Twelve ein Thaler, Charles XI., Sweden, and others. Rare. 3 picces

3568 —— Splendid uncirculated Crown of Philip Julius, duke, 1620. His bust ; rev. handsome coat-of-arms, in nine compartments, PATIENT. PALMAM. FATA, FEREN. FE.

This and following are among the finest and rarest Crowns in the Catalogue.

3569 —— Bogislaus, Duke, etc., 1633. Bust ; rev. coat-of-arms. E. P. CAM. CO. GVTZK. TER. LEOB. ET BVR DVM. Another splendid uncirculated crown.

3570 STETTIN (Duchy). Half-crown, 1677. Fred. William of Prussia. View of the city.

3571 STOLBERG. Dollar of Ludovicus, count, 1547; cross with shield in the angles; rev. eagle, CAROLVS V. Madai, 4398; Well., 7435. Fine and rare.

3571*—— Similar, dated 1549. Equally fine.

3572 —— Wolfgang, with Louis, Henry, Albert George, and Christoph, counts and brothers. Coat-of-arms; rev. a stag. (15) 7–5. Very fine. Nearly uncirculated. Not in Well.

3573 —— Christoph, Frederick, and Justius Christian, brothers, 1719; their busts conjoined; rev. two hands clasping; the sun in splendor. Madai, 1927. Uncirculated, and very broad crown. Rare.

3574 —— Duplicate. Very fine.

3575 —— Two-third Crown, 1738. Same; coat-of-arms and stag.

3576 —— 24 Marien Groschen. Same date and value.

3577 —— Jubilee Medal, 1760. Christian Ernest; bust and altar; GOTT SEY GEBENEDEVT. FVRDIESE SELTNE ZEIT. Madai, 4422; Well., 7450. Nearly proof. Dollar size.

3578 —— One-third Crown, on the second centenary of the Reformation, 1717. "Das wort sie sollin," etc.; reverse, a stag.

3579 —— Two-third Crown. Augsburg Confession Memorial, 1630. Inscription; rev. stag; "Gott seegne," etc. Very fine and rare.

3580 —— Jubilee of the Reformation Medal, under William and Joseph, counts, 1817; rev. Bible and lighted torch. Proof. Well., 7467. Size 22

3581 —— Similar. Same type; smaller. Size 18

3582 —— Two-third Crown; one-sixth do., twelve Einethalers, twenty-four Eine-thalers. 4 pieces

3583 —— Collection of early Coins of Stolberg. A very fine and rare lot. Small size. 10 pieces

*Silver Coins of German Cities, etc.* 219

3584 STRASBURG (bishopric and city). Small coins without date, penny, bracteate and others of the city; arms and titles. Very rare. 5 pieces

3585 —— Dollar Klippe, under John George, Marquis of Brandenburg, 1592. Three shields within border; rev. plain. Ex. fine and rare. See Madai, 900; Well., 1832.

3586 —— Jubilee Klippe, 1617; first centenary. Fine and rare.

3587 —— Charles of Lorraine, Cardinal of Strasburg. (Argentoratensis.) Fine bust, 1605; rev. shield and cardinal's hat. ALSAS LANGRA. One-third Dollar. Called by Madai rare. Very fine.

3588 —— Duplicate; poor, and another. 2 pieces

3589 —— Testoon of same cardinal. Uncirculated, without date. Rare.

3590 —— Quarter Dollar of the city; lily and cross. "Deo Gloria in Excelsis." Varieties. Fine and very rare. 2 pieces

3591 —— Smaller coins of the city. 7 pieces

3592 —— Crown. Lions with lilies supporting the arms of the city; rev. a lily, "Solius virtutis Flos Perpetuus." Extra fine. Madai, 2334; Well, 1807.

3593 —— Crown. Numus. Reip. Argen.; rev. similar to last, with a different motto. Equally fine and rare.

3594 —— LX. K (60 krs.) Same type. Fine.

3595 STUTTGART. Klippe, view of the city; rev. PROSIT SIT NEUE JAHR. Appel, 3,507; Well., 3,532.

3596 —— Medalet; two busts. Charles and Frederick Charles. PRIMI SAEC. GYMNASII ILLVST. STVTTC, 1786. Extremely fine. Size 16

3597 TEUTONIC ORDER. (Deutchen Ordens) Early coins: Arms on lozenge-shape shields within scalloped border. 2 pieces

The Order of German Knights was founded in Jerusalem during the third crusade, A. D. 1190. The earliest coins of the Province of Prussia were issued by the grand masters of this order, and were called SCHELLINGS, GROATS, and SCHOTS. The legend was MONETA DOMINORVM PRVSSIE. After 1220 the commander was called High Master (Hoch-meister), and his residence was changed from Culm to Marienburg, where it remained until 1525, Albert of Brandenburg, being the last High Master. From 1527 Mergertheim, in Wurtemberg, was the seat of the Teutonic Knights until Napoleon abolished the order in 1809.

3598 TEUTONIC ORDER. Denarius. MAGISTER GENER-ALIS Shield with the eagle and cross of the order; rev. DOM INORVM PRVSSIE; cross on a shield. Well., 6,628. Very fine and rare.

3599 —— Schelling of Henry Dusener, 1345 to 1351. MAGS HEINRICVS. Eagle on a cross; rev. MONETA DNORVM PRV. Cross of the order on a shield. Well., 6,631. Fine and rare.

3600 —— Schelling or "Cross-groat" of Wunrich, 1351–82. Similar, but MAGIST WVNRICVS PRIMVS. Ex. fine. Well., 6,633. Rare.

3601 —— Schelling or "Kreuze groschen" of Conrad III., 1393–1407. MAGIST CONRADVS TERC. Shield with cross and eagle as before; rev. MONETA DNORVM PRVCI. Shield and cross. Extra fine and rare. Well., 6,636.

3602 —— Schelling of Ulrich 1,407–10. MAG VLRICVS, etc. Very fine. See Well., 6,640.

3603 —— Schelling of Michael, of Sternberg. H. M., 1414–1422. MICH. Same type, except that the cross on the rev. quarters the coin. Fine and very rare. See Well., 6,641.

3604 —— Same of Henry Russ. H. M., 1470.

3605 —— Same of Martin, 1477–1489, MAGIST MAR-TINVS. Eagle and cross; rev. MONETA, etc. Shield and short cross. Very fine. Well., 6,651. Rare.

3606 —— Similar coins. "Cross groats" of this period; Fine and valuable. 3 pieces

3607 —— Schot or cross groschen of the last Hoch-meister, 1525. (The seat of the order after this date was Mergentheim, in Wurtemberg). Albert of Brandenburg. ALBERTVS D. G. MAGISTIR. C. Eagle within circle; rev. SALVA NOS DOMINA, 1513. Appel I. 188; Well., 6,656. Very fine and rare.

## Silver Coins of German Cities, etc.

3608 TEUTONIC ORDER. Small coins; indifferent. 3 pieces

> In 1466 Poland acquired jurisdiction over the eastern part of Prussia, and the Teutonic Knights became vassals to that kingdom. The following pieces were coined during that period; but I cannot give an accurate description of them, finding no assistance from any work within my reach.

3609 —— Double Groschen of Walram, 1341–49. Size of English or Bohemian groat. Bust, full face, WAL-RAM, ARCH. COLONIE; rev. small cross within two circles of inscription, MONETA. TVVCIEN. (Julich). Fine.

3610 —— Groat as before. St. ? seated. On each side shield with arms of the order; rev. similar to last. Fine and rare.

3611 —— Groat, shields with emblems of the Teutonic Order. Fine.

All that follow were coined by the High Masters at Mergentheim.

3612 —— Maximillian, Arch Duke of Austria, "High Master" of the Order. His figure full length, in regalia and armor. Emblems to right and left; his titles ending with A. D. M. 1.; rev. mounted knight within a circle of shields, 1603. Extremely fine crown. Rare.

3613 —— Crown of the same date and type, from a different die. Equally fine. Madai, 925; Well., 3,466.

3614 —— Crown of the same, 1613. A marked variety; splendid. Madai, 926.

3615 —— Double crown, same type. The H. M. and knight on horseback, 1614. Madai, 925; Well., 3464. Very fine and rare.

3616 —— Double crown, 1614; same as last. Carefully burnished for a cabinet; has the splendor of a proof.

3617 —— Brilliant uncirculated crown, 16–15. Obv. bust of Maximillian (H. M.); rev. arms of the order. Madai 3,410; Well., 3,469. Very rare.

3618 —— Half-crown of same. Max., 1616. Fine.

3619 TEUTONIC ORDER. John Eustachius, G. M., 1625–27; beautiful crown of 1625. Order, arms, titles, etc.; rev. St. Mary standing, with young Jesus. ORD IN TE. See Madai, 929; Well., 3,484; marked by the latter R. R.

3620 —— Clement Augustus, H. M., 732–61 ½ thaler, 1755. Uncirculated. Rare.

3621 —— Charles Alexander. Convention crown of 1776. Bust, with title and cross of the order; rev. coat-of-arms and crown, supported by two eagles, each wearing a double cross suspended from the neck by a chain, Uncirculated. Well., 3,501. Rare.

3622 TANN (City). Small coin.

3623 TESCHEN. 3 Groschen of Adam Wenzel, 1607; bust and coat-of-arms; uncirculated.

3624 —— Small coins. 2 pieces

3625 —— Medal Dollar, IN MEMORIANI PACIS TESCHINSENSIS, 1779; uncirculated; rare.

3626 THOREN (Thorn), Province of Limburg; coined by the Abbess Margaretha, 1531–77; crown of 15-63, MARGARE · D · BREDROD; rev. DENARIVS NOVVS. Madai, 976; Well., 9106; marked R. Well preserved.

3627 —— Crown of same Abbess; 1570; MO LIB IMPERIALIS FVNDAT IN THORN; rev. double eagle, Maximilian II., etc. Madai, 978; Well., 9108. Well preserved and rare.

3628 —— Duplicate of last; equally good crown.

3629 TRAUTSON (Count), Paul Sixtus, 1620; bust in robes and chain of the Order of the Golden Fleece, PAVLVS SIXTVS, etc.; rev. arms within the chain of the Order of the Fleece, AVREI VEI, etc.; uncirculated and brilliant crown; see Well., 11,110. Very rare.

3630 —— Crown of same, 16–20; slight variety; uncirculated and brilliant.

3631 —— Crown of same, 16–20; still different; equally fine. Rare.

## Silver Coins of German Cities, etc. 223

3632 TRAUTSON (Count). Crown of same date, a variety. Fine.

    In Wellenheim the differences in these crowns are carefully noted and described.

3633 TREVES (Trier), Bishopric. Solidus, bracteates, and coins with a stamp on only one side; to the time of Baldwin, A.D. 1307.    6 pieces

3634 —— Later coins, small; to the time of John Hugo, 1675. Some extremely rare.    6 pieces

3635 —— Similar from (and including) John Hugo, Carl and Casper, to Francis George, 1750.    6 pieces

3636 —— Others; rare, but poor.    3 pieces

3637 —— Groats; a fine lot. St. Peter seated, PETER MENTGER, etc., etc. Valuable lot.    5 pieces

3638 —— John Hugo, 1705; ¼ Thaler. Fine.

3639 ULM (City); Reformation Jubilee medal; first centenary, 1617; MEMORIAM * JVBILAE * EVANGELICI * ; within palms, an open Bible; rev. arms of Ulm and inscription; fine and rare. Not in Wellenheim.    Size 16

3640 —— Crown of the city, MONETA–NOVA VLMINENSIS, 1620, under Ferdinand II.; city arms and double eagle. Uncirculated and brilliant. Rare.

3641 —— Duplicate; very fine.

3642 —— Medal of the city, 1622; view of the town and cathedral; above, VLMA; rev. 8 medallion shields; on one, ½ length figure without arms; above, full face or mask, PRO–PATRIA–FERRE–PARATI; uncirculated, nearly proof. Madai, 2348; Well., 3546—described as rare.    Size 24

3643 —— Medal; obv. same as last; rev. the 8 shields differently arranged, upheld by an angel; silver gilt, 1667. Not in Wellenheim. Same size.

3644 —— Siege piece (Klippe) of 1704; DA PACEM, etc. Madai, 5142; Wellenheim, 3551. ½ crown. Rare.

3645 ULM (City). Medals, 1704. Bust of Marshal Charles, etc., in mail, wearing the chain of the Order of the Golden Fleece; rev. the city personified by a turreted female with shield, OB. CIV. SERV., giving her right hand to a figure in mail, Minerva crowning him, ADSERTORI LIBERTATIS; in ex. VLMA GALL EREPT, 13 Sept., 1704; edge lettered. A fine uncirculated medal. Size 26

3646 —— Medalet, same date, BOIIS ARTE CAPTA, D. 8 Sept., 1702; YSDEM ET GALLIS MARTE EREPTA, 10th Sept., 1704. Proof. Size 16

3647 —— Small coins. 2 pieces

3648 URACH, one side plain, a horn (jagdhorn), and the letter H; pfenning without date. Rare.

3649 VIENNA (Wein) city; Klippe, 1529; a triplet of leaves repeated 4 times. Fine and rare. Size 12

3650 —— Medal of the city. A memorial of the war against the Turks, 1683. Size 17

3651 —— Medal dollar (Salvator thaler), with the head of Christ; rev. the city; SVB VMBRA—ALARVM TVARVM; below, in a cartouche, MVNVS VIENNES. Fine impression and not circulated, but slightly notched on edge. Rare.

3652 —— Crown of 1781. Episcopal of Cardinal Christopher. Bust; rev. arms and cardinal's hat. Fine and very rare. Not in Wellenheim.

3653 —— Beautiful uncirculated thaler of 1868. "III Deutsches bundes schiessen wein, 1868," double eagle and crown; rev. a female hanging shield of Prussia on a tree; below, SEIDAN. NIR WOLLEN SEIN, etc.

3654 WALKENREID Abbey, 1657; CL. under a crown, and one of 1688. Bust of Fred., Duke of Saxony; groschen and double groschen. Not in Wellenheim. Very rare. 2 pieces

3655 WALLENSTEIN, Duke Albert (of Friedland), groschen, 1627-8-9 and '31; bust of the Duke and different reverses. Described by Wellenheim and Appel. in full. Rare. 5 pieces

3656 WALTERHOUSEN (City). Beautiful medalet. "In Memoriam Saecularem Noveler Constitutæ Formæ Scholastic du Lucræ"; edifice and shield. Size 15
3657 WALLMODEN, Count Louis of Gimborn; "XX Eine Feine Mark." ½ crown, 1802; beautiful coat-of-arms. Rare.
3658 WERDEN Abbey; MON–NO–REV–DOM–CON; within the circle, LXX; below, IIII; rev. ABB–IN–WED ET HEL; within "VIII"; base. Very rare. Well., 8133.
3659 —— Duplicate.
3660 —— (or Donauworth, not Abbey of). Uncirculated, but stained crown of Charles V., (15)43; his bust, with sceptre and crown, double eagle with "W" on small shield covering his breast. Rare. (See Well., 2425).
3661 —— Half-crown, same. Rubbed.
3662 —— Beautiful proof medal of Werden, 1704. Bust of Louis William, of Baden; rev. HOSTE–CAESO–EVGATO–CASTRIS DIREPTIS; a fortified town, Neptune lying before it holding aloft a crown. See Well., 13,151. Size 24
3662* WEISSENBERG (City), ⅛ dollar. Rare.
3663 WIED; Count Frederick Alex.; his bust; rev. view of a port; ⅓ crown, medal style. Beautiful uncirculated piece.
3664 —— A variety of his coins from 1745. 4 pieces
3665 WERLE (City in Gustrow, Mecklenburg); bracteate, solidus, and half solidus. Fine and rare lot. 4 pieces
3666 —— Solidus, MONETA GUSTROWE, cross; rev. CIVIT DNI DWERLE; see Well., 5426. Fine and rare.
3667 WESEL (City). Coins resembling a Bohemian groat, MONETA WESEL, cross; rev. arms on shield and ins. Two varieties, fine and rare. Not in Well.
2 pieces
3668 WESTPHALIA, Kingdom under Jerome Bonaparte, "Two Francs," by Tiolier. Bust laureated, edge lettered; barely circulated. Very fine and rare. 1808.

## Silver Coins of German Cities, etc.

3669 WESTPHALIA. ½ Franc. Same type and date. Uncirculated. Rare.

3670 —— Medal Coin of 1811, convention piece. Bust; rev. GLUCK AUE GLAUSTH ALIM AUGUST. Ex. fine and rare.

3671 —— Base coins. $\frac{1}{6}$, $\frac{1}{12}$ Thaler, 20 cents, etc.   6 pieces

3672 WISMAR (in Mecklenberg). Solidus; obv. * MONETA WYSMAR, cross fleurie, in centre, star; rev. full face, or mask, CIVITAS MAGROP. (See Well., 5293). Very fine and *excessively* rare.

3673 —— Solidus; same legend, different type. Equally fine and rare.

3674 —— Pennies, with long and short cross.   2 pieces

3675 —— 24 Einen-thalers, 1652, etc. Very fine.   2 do.

3676 —— Same.   2 do.

3677 —— Brilliant uncirculated Crown of 1622, under Ferdinand II.; obv. St. Lawrence standing; rev. double eagle. Very rare.

3678 —— Half-crown, same or similar type, 1672. Well., 5298.

3679 —— Quarter-crown   do.

3680 WIEDENBRUCK (City.) Arms of Osnaburg. (Wheel.) Rare denarius.

3681 WITTENBERG (City). Small coin. Solidus. Rare.

3682 —— Medal to commemorate the plague, soon after Luther's death, 1551. Half-dollar medal; on one side Moses and the Israelites before their tents, serpent on a cross, text from the Bible; rev. crucifixion of Christ, another text. A medal of the time, cast and tooled. Very rare.

3683 —— Another Plague Medal; crown, very broad, called "Pest-thaler," from a die; very beautiful; inscription on both sides in two circles, cross, serpent twining, Num. 21; rev. crucifixion, two Roman soldiers. Uncirculated.   Size 30

3684 —— Same, beautiful, nearly proof crown Medal. Both sides crowded with figures, serpent in the wilderness and crucifixion as before. Very rare.

## Silver Coins of German Cities, etc.

3685 WITTENBERG (City). Same, equally interesting and rare crown. Nearly as fine.
   A description of these medals may be found in Madai, No. 2369.

3686 WINDISCHGRATZ. Half-crown of Prince Joseph Nicholas, 1777; bust and coat-of-arms. See Wellenheim, 11,238. Fine and rare.

3687 WORMS (city). Reforination Jubilee Klippe, 16–W–17; on a shield, key. Rare.

3688 —— Extremely fine uncirculated crown to commemorate the same evangelical jubilee. LVMEN EVANGELI, Bible and candle; rev. NOMEN DOMINI, light on a tower. Madai, 2356; Well., 4274. Very rare.

3689 WOLGAT (City.) Small coin. Rare.

3690 WURZBURG (or Wurtzburg). Episcopal coin of Otho, bishop, 1207–123–; bust; rev. church; Wellenheim, 3159. Fine and rare denarius.

3691 —— Half-denarius of Berthold, bishop, 1267–1282. Well., 3160. Rare.

3692 —— Others, not classified. Old and rare.      6 pieces

3693 —— Melchior, bishop, 1544–1558; fine crown, 1554. Saint Killian standing, shield on breast, sword and staff, with large head, MELCHIO WIRCHBVR; rev. CAROLVS V., double eagle. Fine and very rare. Madai,905; Well., 3165.

3694 —— John Phillip, 1642–1673; St. Killian standing, etc. Groschen and double groschen.      2 pieces

3695 —— Others; some older than last, others later. 6 do.

3696 —— John Philip, bishop from 1699 to 1719. Splendid uncirculated crown medal, 1702; bust; rev. fir tree, below, shield; SEMPER IDEM. Madai, 918; Well., 3195. Rare.

3697 —— Mortuary medalet of same. Size 16 and 18. Rare and fine.      2 pieces

3698 —— Anselm Francis, 1746–1749. Groschen. Fine.

3699 —— Charles Phillip, 1749 to 1751. Groschen. Rare.

3700 —— Unclassified. Small.      2 pieces

3701 WURZBURG. Francis Louis, 1779–1795. Splendid uncirculated medal crown, 1791; bust; rev. emblematical picture, MERCES LABORUM. Appel, 637; Well., 3230. Rare.
3702 —— Same. Crown of 1794; rev. PRO PATRIA. Well., 3234. Very fine.
3703 —— Same. Bamberg convention dollar, 1795; coat-of-arms; rev. X MARK. Fine.
3704 —— George Charles, 1795–1801, (coined from church silver.) Crown of 1795; bust; rev. PRO PATRIA. Fine. Well., 3238.
3705 —— Same, from another die, different coat-of-arms. Nearly proof crown.
3706 —— Same. Half-crown, 1795; rev. St. Killian between two allegorical figures. Very fine and rare.
3707 YSENBERG. A single coin; dime size.

## MISCELLANEOUS SILVER COINS.

3708 BRACTEATES of the 13th century, size 14; Emperors' heads, arms, etc., etc.    12 pieces
3709 —— Similar.    12 do.
3710 —— Similar, but smaller; size 10.    10 do.
3711 —— Similar lot.    11 do.
3712 —— Remarkably large and fine.    2 do.
3713 DENARII; Halle, Worms, etc. Fine and rare lot. 14 do.
3714 —— Some smaller, and struck only on one side. A rare lot.    10 pieces
3715 Groats and old episcopal coins, groat size; unclassified. Remarkably fine.    10 pieces
3716 GERMAN Coins, 12 Einen-thalers.    Size 10
3717 KLIPPE and two of Hildesheim. Rare.    3 pieces
3718 BASE silver coins.    25 do.
3719 —— Similar.    25 do.
3720 —— do.    25 do.
3721 —— do.    25 do.
3722 —— do.    25 do.

Copper Coins of German Cities, etc.      229

3723 BASE Silver coins.                       25 pieces
3724 JAPANESE Itzben and 4 Quarter do.        5 do.
3725 EMANUEL Pinto, 4 tari, 1768.
3726 ANDREAS Gritti; doge, Venice. 1523–29.   Quarter-crown.
3727 GIOACCHIM Napoleon (Murat). 2 lira, 1813.
3728 UNCLASSIFIED, average franc value.       6 pieces
3729 GOSLAR. Thick dollar of the 15th century. (Size 18.) St. Simon and Judas standing. Uncirculated, and probably very rare and valuable. Full weight.

## COPPER COINS AND TOKENS OF SEQUESTRATED GERMAN CITIES, PRINCIPALITIES, ETC.

*Alphabetically Arranged.*

3730 AHLEN. Tokens, VI—1.                     2 pieces
3731 AIX LA CHAPELLE (Achen) coins.           18 do.
3732 ALTENBURG, (city). Medal in honor of a minister. Size 20
3733 ALTONA. Tin medal in honor of Conrad Von Blucher, 1845, by Lorens. Fine proof. Size 24
3734 ANHOLT and Annaberg.                     3 pieces
3735 ANSPACH. Of the thirty-years' war, F. C. 39 and 40. Rare.                                2 pieces
3736 AUGSBURG (City.) (Pine cone.) Klippes. Extra fine.  3 pieces
3737 —— Measure tokens; 3 sizes and 3 pieces.
3738 —— Rare tokens and coins with descriptions. 5 do.
3739 —— Coins.                                11 do.
3740 BADEN and Bamberg medalet and coins. Fine. 7 do.
3741 BAUMBERG, in Bavaria; monastery and porcelain factory in Bauenstein. Rare and pretty tokens.  2 pieces
3742 BATENBURG and Beckum Coins              4 do.
3743 BERG (Duchy), and City of Bocholt.      5 pieces
3744 BERLIN (City). Prize medal; fine wreath, locomotive, and Germania seated. Proof. Size 28
3745 —— Reformation medal and various tokens. 5 pieces

3746 BIELEFIELD. Turnerfest medal and lager-bier token; "Gute fur eine bier." Very fine. 2 pieces
3747 BRANDENBURG and Bretzenheim. (Siege piece.) 4 do.
3748 BREMEN Coins and tokens. Very fine. 20 do.
3749 BRUNSWICK and Barony of Bronkhorst Coins and tokens. Fine and rare lot. 20 pieces
3750 CAMING, Cassel, and Coburg Coins and tokens. "Ein schoppen bier." Fine and rare. 4 pieces
3751 COESFELD, Constanz, and Cologne Medal. (View of the cathedral finished and unfinished.) 25 pieces
3752 CORVEY. Old and rare coins. 13 do.
3753 DANTZIE and Diepholz ("1 fliller.") Fine, rare. 3 do.
3754 DORTMUND and Dresden coins and tokens. 9 do.
3755 DULMEN; coin of the city, 1622. Ex. fine and rare.
3756 ECKERNFORDE (City.) Medalets commemorating an event on the 5th April, 1849; a series from size 15 to 22. ZER STORUNG D. DAN LINIENSCHIEFFES CHRISTIAN VIII. UND FRORERUNG DER FREGATE GEFION. No duplicate. Fine bronze. 5 pieces
3757 EBBERFELD. Famine tokens, 1816 and 1847; 1 BROD, KORN VEREIN. 2 pieces
3758 —— Same. do. 2 do.
3759 —— do. do. 2 do.
3760 —— do. do. 3 do.
3761 EINBECK. [It was in this city that the Duke of Brunswick gave Dr. Luther a cask of beer.] Beautiful little coins of the city, 16th century. 12 pieces
3762 EICHSTEDT and Erfurt, (known by wheel.) 6 pieces
3763 EMDEN, Friedrichstal, and E. Fresia; coins and tokens.
3764 FRANKFURT Klippe, EINE ASS, two sprigs of olive crossed. Ex. rare. Size 16. 2 pieces
3765 —— Jews' hellers and pfennings and tokens of the city, said to be rare. Very fine. 13 pieces
3766 —— Coins of Duke Primas, known by his arms as Bishop of Mentz (wheel), and Medal of John of Austria, with view of State-house. 4 pieces
3767 —— City coins. 31 pieces

## Copper Coins of German Cities, etc. 231

3769 FRIEDBERG. Fine medal, with view of battle, and on reverse Frederick the Great on horseback; heavy silver-plate. Rare.  Size 25

3770 FREISING and Fraukenhausen.  5 pieces

3771 FULDA. (City.) Beer token and coin, and coins of the Count of Fugger.  6 pieces

3772 FURSTENBERG and Fürth. Tokens.  2 do.

3773 GEISLINGEN coins, and Guissen medal of Turner festival, 1862. All extra fine.  4 pieces

3774 GOSLAR, Gottingen, and Gotha. (Cities.) Coins and tokens.  23 pieces

3775 HALBERSTADT, Halle, and Hamm. Coins, tokens and shells. Many fine and rare.  22 pieces

3776 HANAU. Battle of 1813, and coins.  3 pieces

3777 HANOVER. Semi-centennial of Waterloo, 18th June, 1865; splendid proof medal in bronze.  Size 22

3778 —— Medals and tokens.  6 pieces

3779 HALLBERG and Haag, in Bavaria. Beautiful and rare tokens. (Baron Halberg founded a colony, etc.)  7 pcs

3780 HALTERN and Hameln. Very rare.  2 do.

3781 HAMBURG. Medal of Solomon Heine, founder of the Jewish Hospital, 1841; bust, and view of the hospital; fine bronze proof. Rare.  Size 30

3782 —— Medal; made from the copper roof of the cathedral, burnt 1842; and one in tin, with the bust of a Jewish doctor, Arn Heise.  2 pieces

3783 —— Tokens, dog marks, etc.  5 do.

3784 HEIDELBERG, beer token; Harburg token, Hildburghausen and Hervord coins.  7 pieces

3785 HILDESHEIM. Siege klippe, 1629; famine tokens, 1658, and coins. Extremely rare lot.  14 pieces

3786 HOLLAND. Reformation medals, third centennial, in 1817. Proof. Rare.  Size 19

3787 ILMENA (City); type, hen; and Ilsenberg, in the Hartz Mountains; miners' tokens. A fine and rare lot.  5 pcs

3788 ISMY and Iserlohn (cities). Beer tokens and coins. Fine.  3 pieces

3789 JEVER (Count), and Julich (Duchy), coins.  8 pieces

3790 JULICH. Siege klippe, 1543; thick piece of square copper, one inch diameter; shield with lion, branching tail. Ex. fine and rare.

3791 KARLSRUHE and Kuchen. Extra fine tokens and coins. 5 pieces

3792 LAUENBERG and Lend, in Bavaria; (cow lying down). rare.

3793 LEIPSIC. Jubilee of the 50th year after the French invasion, in 1813, and other tokens, medals, and coins; copper, brass, and tin. Fine lot. 7 pieces

3794 LIMBURG and Lindau, (linden tree), beautiful coins and tokens. 6 pieces

3795 LOHRA, Lübeck, and Lowenstein. 12 do.

3796 LUNEBURG and Luttich. 6 do.

3797 MANSFELD, (city). Early coins, rare. Marsberg City, coins, and one of the City of Minden. 13 pieces

3798 MAYENCE (Metz). Wheel; many varieties, both of the city and bishopric, including a bridge toll token. Rare. 16 pieces

3799 —— Siege coins of 5, 2, and 1 Sol., in different qualities of bronze; some very thick—with slight qualification, an uncirculated lot. "1798. Lau 2." Very rare. 8 pieces

3800 MONTFORT and Mülhausen; coins and tokens. 5 do.

3801 MUNICH. Turnerfest and saengerfest tokens, 1844–'64. Very fine. 4 pieces

3802 —— Pattern coins and medals in the antique Greek style—*gems*, and medal in tin with copper plug of Louis I., King, friend of Lola Montez. R. R. 8 pcs

3803 MUNSTER (of the city and Bishopric). *Domcapit·l* piece, broad coin. "Sogenanntes Bursarien-Zeichen," 1608. SAVLE. SAVLE QVID ME PERSEQVE; Saul on horseback, his hand uplifted; rev. within a garnished circle, * S * 1 * 1 * 1 *; date above; below, a counter stamp, E. V. B. Extra fine and rare. See Well., 7663 (marked R. R.) Size 22.

## Copper Coins of German Cities, etc.

3804 MUNSTER. Similar, same date; bust of St. Paul, etc., * 1 * 1 * 1. One * 1 * 1 * 1 * 1 with counterstamp. One * V * 1 * and stamp and other varieties not in .Wellenheim. Among the most interesting and rare in the copper collection; dates 1608and 1661.   7 piecse

3805 ——— Set of " Poor tokens" for church districts; KIRSPEL SANCTI MARTINI; rev. FUR. DIE ARMEN, 1699, etc. No two alike. Very fine and rare. Size 16
6 pieces

3806 ——— Other "Bursaurien" coins (a famous Episcopal chapter) similar to No. 3803.   6 pieces

3807 ——— Episcopal and city coins.   47 pieces

3808 NEUHENSEL medal, Newburg Monastery token, and coins of Nordheim, with coins and meraux of Nuremberg "the ancient." Fine lot.   13 pieces

3809 OFEN. Offenbach, Oldenburg; tokens of these cities and coins of Osnaburg.   10 pieces

3810 OSNABURG. Ex. fine coins, and very rare of Osterode in the Hartz.   17 pieces

3811 PADERBORN, Bishopric and city.   24 pieces

3812 ——— Siege coins. Very rare.   3 pieces

3813 PASSAROWITZ. Tin medal, 21 July, 1718. War with the Turk. Proof with copper plug.   Size 28

3814 PARCHIN AND PESTH (hospital token). Fine and rare.
3 pieces

3815 PFORZHEIM AND POMERANIA token and coins.   6 pieces

3816 PRAGUE AND 3 PRUSSIAN Jetons.   4 pieces

3817 RAGUSA (Italy) Ravensburg, on Lake Constance, (one-sided. Rare.   5 pieces

3818 REGENSBURG (City) Rare old coins and klippes, and 3 obsidional tokens. Valuable lot.   21 pieces

3819 RHEDA (Principality), and City of Rheine.   5 pieces

3820 RIDBERG (Count of), and City of Riga.   6 pieces

3821 ROSTOCK AND RUDOLSTADT, cities.   17 pieces

3822 ROMANIA. Proof set, 1867, 10. 5-2 and 1 BANI. 4 pieces.

3823 ——— Duplicate set. All bright proof.   4 pieces

3824 SAALFELD DUCHY. Principality of Salm, and Bishopric of Salzburg.   9 pieces

## Copper Coins of German Cities, etc.

3825 SALZTHALUM; token for a load of turf; Salzbergu and Schlensingen cities coins. 7 pieces

3826 SCHONAN, Sehmalkalden, Schweinfurth, and Schwaarsburg coins. 32 pieces

3827 SCHWEINFURTH Reformation medal, 31 Oct., 1717, view of the city; rev. angel flying with the Bible. Very fine and rare. Size 22

3828 SCHLESWIG-HOLSTEIN coins and medals, with loops, (1864.) Last Danish war, F. Jos: and William. Proof. 7 pieces

3829 SERVIA. Beautiful pattern coins, with Russian inscriptions. 10 Para, 5 Para, and 1 para. Obrenowitoch III. 1868. Very rare. Bright. 4 pieces

Cost 10 francs each.

3830 SOLM (Principality.) Soest city, and Speyer, Bishopric. 10 pieces

3831 STETTIN, STEVENSWORTH AND STRALSUND. (Cities). Rare. 6 pieces

3832 STRALSUND medalets, 1716 and 1717. Bust of Charles XII. of Sweden. "Tempus Revelat Omnia." Lion upright, holding sword and palm; uncirculated and bright. Very beautiful and rare. Size of Goereks Dalers. 2 pieces

3833 STOLBERG. Coins and token and beautiful token or coin of St. Liborius of Paderborn. Rare lot. 10 pieces

3834 TESCHEN. Masonic medal of Jos. II. and Fred. II. Busts of the two facing; rev. pillars of Jachin and Boaz. Extremely fine, tin. Size 30

3835 TREVES. Medal of John Hugo, Arch., 1676–1711, bust; rev. shields of cannons. Rare. Size 30

3836 —— Medalet of Francis Louis, Arch., bust; rev. hand from above guiding lion. Fine and rare. Size 14

3837 TEUTONIC ORDER. Teekenburg and Friedrichafen. 8 pieces

3838 ULM CITY; coins and tokens. Fine and rare lot. 12 pcs

3838* —— Medal, Gymnasium. Bridge over the Danube completed. Copper and tin. Very fine. Size 20 2 pieces

*Sundries.* 235

3839 VIENNA. Coins of the city. 5 *heads of barley?* Rare.
4 pieces
3840 WALDECK AND WARBURG. 26 piece
3841 WALTERHAUSEN AND WARENDORF, near Munster, (cities.)
Coins and tokens. Ex. fine. 4 pieces
3842 WEISINBURG, WERL, AND WESEL. The first city, the scene of the first battle of the late war; on the last. three weasels running. 3 pieces
3843 WESTPHALIA (under Jerome). 10 pieces
3844 WIED and Wiedenbruck. Winlass-wheel. 3 do.
3845 WISMAR (City). 9 do.
3846 WITTENBERG. Plague token. [See description of silver coins of this city, same type]. Rare. Size 20
3847 —— Dr. Martin Luther Medal. Bust, "born 10 Nov., 1483; died 15 Feb., 1546"; rev. Luther's monument. Bronze, fine proof. Size 24
3848 WURZBURG and Wurtemberg. 22 pieces
3849 ZEULENRODA. "Harmony" token. Rare.

## SUNDRIES.

3850 Two old Seals and a Roman dice of patinated copper.
3 pieces
3851 WOODEN Medal, bronze do., cast, and two Japanese Tempo. 4 pieces
3852 MEDALS in bronze and tin, about size 38. Argentine Republic and Montevideo. Very fine. 2 pieces
3853 MEDALS of Frederick the Great, Ferdinand VII., and copies of Jewish coins 4 pieces
3854 OLD Buttons, Coins, shell Medal, etc. 25 do.
3855 Box pearl Counters. Chinese.
3856 Box with jeweller's scale and 12 weights, made in 1675, at Hamburg, 5 x 2½ inches.
3857 —— With 33 weights, made in 1636, in Cologne; thicker than last. Same size.
3858 GOLD-TESTING ROD, 16 bars, from 16 to 1 carat fine, used by jewellers on touchstone. Valuable.

3859 SILVER TEASPOON, from the table service of the Emperor Napoleon I., with a letter relating thereto from the Grand Chamberlain of Napoleon III.'s household; has the Emperor's arms, etc. Very rare.

## NUMISMATIC BOOKS, CATALOGUES, AND PAPER MONEY.

3860 SIMON's Essay on Irish Coins, with appendix. Dublin, 1749. Small folio, calf.
3861 SNELLING's View of the Silver Coins and Coinage of England from the Conquest, etc. London, 1762 Folio, as it is.
3862 MADDEN's Jewish Coinage, with 254 wood-cuts and a plate of alphabets. London, 1864. Oct., half-calf.
3863 HUMPHREY's Coinage of the British Empire, illustrated by plates worked in gold, silver, and copper. London, 1868. Oct., cloth.
3864 WELLENHEIM's Catalogue in three volumes; the first being the antique portion of the collection in French, the other volumes in German. Very fine copy and very rare. Vienna, 1847, Octv., half morocco.
3865 SNOWDEN's Description of the Coins in the United States Mint Cabinet. Philadelphia. Oct., cloth.
3866 —— Description of the Washington Medals and other coins etc., of interest, in the Museum of the Mint. Philadelphia, 1861. Quarto, cloth.
3867 PRIME's Coins, Medals, and Seals, ancient and modern, illustrated and described. New York, 1864. Small quarto, cloth. Scarce.
3868 COIN CATALOGUES. A bundle containing 46 pieces.
3869 —— With illustrations and prices. Some rare. 8 pcs
3870 PAPER MONEY; Kossuth, Confederate, and Cuban Bonds, French Assignats, etc., etc. A bundle containing 130 pieces.
3871 IRON fire-proof Cabinet Safe.
<sub>This convenient and handsome Cabinet was made for the late Dr. Chilton. It has besides closets, sixty-six drawers, made to accommodate coins, medals, and other objects requiring more depth. It is 5 8-12 feet high, 4 broad, and 2 deep, with white marble top and double doors, velvet lined.</sub>

www.ingramcontent.com/pod-product-compliance
Lightning Source LLC
Chambersburg PA
CBHW031739230426
43669CB00007B/407